Documentary Research in the Social Sciences

Documentary Research *in the* Social Sciences

Malcolm Tight

$SAGE

Los Angeles | London | New Delhi
Singapore | Washington DC | Melbourne

$SAGE

Los Angeles | London | New Delhi
Singapore | Washington DC | Melbourne

SAGE Publications Ltd
1 Oliver's Yard
55 City Road
London EC1Y 1SP

SAGE Publications Inc.
2455 Teller Road
Thousand Oaks, California 91320

SAGE Publications India Pvt Ltd
B 1/I 1 Mohan Cooperative Industrial Area
Mathura Road
New Delhi 110 044

SAGE Publications Asia-Pacific Pte Ltd
3 Church Street
#10-04 Samsung Hub
Singapore 049483

Editor: Jai Seaman
Editorial Assistant: Charlotte Bush
Production Editor: Sushant Nailwal
Copyeditor: Sharon Cawood
Proofreader: Derek Markham
Index: Author
Marketing Manager: Susheel Gokarakonda
Cover Design: Shaun Mercier
Typeset by: C&M Digitals (P) Ltd, Chennai, India
Printed in the UK

© Malcolm Tight 2019

First published 2019

Apart from any fair dealing for the purposes of research or private study, or criticism or review, as permitted under the Copyright, Designs and Patents Act, 1988, this publication may be reproduced, stored or transmitted in any form, or by any means, only with the prior permission in writing of the publishers, or in the case of reprographic reproduction, in accordance with the terms of licences issued by the Copyright Licensing Agency. Enquiries concerning reproduction outside those terms should be sent to the publishers.

Library of Congress Control Number: 2018957573

British Library Cataloguing in Publication data

A catalogue record for this book is available from the British Library

978-1-5264-2664-2
978-1-5264-2665-9 (pbk)

At SAGE we take sustainability seriously. Most of our products are printed in the UK using responsibly sourced papers and boards. When we print overseas we ensure sustainable papers are used as measured by the PREPS grading system. We undertake an annual audit to monitor our sustainability.

CONTENTS

List of Boxes xi
About the Author xiii

Part 1 Starting Documentary Research 1

1 Introduction 3

   What this Book is for 4
   What the Book Contains 5
   How to Use this Book 6

2 Documents and Documentary Research 7

   Introduction 8
   What is a Document? 8
   Varieties of Document 10
   The Possibilities and Advantages of Documentary Research 13
   Documents in, or as the Focus of, Research 15
   The Purpose and Usage of Documents 18
   Conclusion 19
   Key Readings 19

3 Finding and Reading Documents 21

   Introduction 22
   Accessing Documents 22
      Using Online Search Engines 24

	Ethical Issues	24
	Sampling and Selection	27
	Issues to Consider when Researching Documents	29
	How to Read Documents	32
	Keeping Records	34
	Conclusion	35
	Key Readings	35
4	**Documentary Research in the Disciplines**	**37**
	Introduction	38
	Documentary Research in the Social Sciences	38
	Anthropology	40
	Business/Management	42
	Economics	43
	Education	44
	Geography	46
	Information Science	47
	Law	48
	Media Studies	48
	Political Science	49
	Psychology	51
	Social Work	52
	Sociology	54
	Documentary Research outside the Social Sciences	55
	Conclusion	56
	Key Readings	56

Part 2 Genres of Documentary Research — 59

5	**Designing Documentary Research**	**61**
	Introduction	62
	Documentary Research Designs	62
	Literature Reviews	62
	Systematic Reviews and Meta-Analyses	63
	Secondary Data Analysis	64
	Archival and Historical Research	64
	Policy Research	65
	The Five Genres in Combination	65
	Documentary Research and Other Research Designs	66
	Documentary Research as a Research Design	66
	The Qualitative/Quantitative Debate	67
	Documentary Research in Combination with Other Research Designs	68

	Conclusion	71
	Key Readings	71
6	Literature Reviews	73
	Introduction	74
	The Nature of Literature Reviews	74
	The Functions of Literature Reviews	76
	Types of Literature Review	78
	Conclusion	82
	Key Readings	83
7	Systematic Reviews and Meta-Analyses	85
	Introduction	86
	Systematic Reviews	87
	Meta-Analyses	91
	Conclusion	94
	Key Readings	94
8	Secondary Data Research	95
	Introduction	96
	Secondary Data and Secondary Data Analysis	97
	Advantages and Disadvantages of Secondary Data Research	98
	Types of Secondary Data Analysis	100
	Examples of Secondary Data Analysis	102
	Where to Get Secondary Data	105
	Conclusion	108
	Key Readings	108
9	Archival and Historical Research	109
	Introduction	110
	The Nature of Archival and Historical Research	110
	Types of Data and Sources	111
	Examples of Archival and Historical Research	115
	Conclusion	119
	Key Readings	119
10	Policy Research	121
	Introduction	122
	The Nature of Policy and Policy Research	122
	Types of Policy Research	125
	Examples of Policy Research	126
	Conclusion	130
	Key Readings	131

Part 3 Techniques for Documentary Analysis 133

11 Analysing Documents 135

    Introduction 136
    Analysis of Written Texts 136
    Analysis of Audio-Visual Texts 139
    Conclusion 142
    Key Readings 143

12 Quantitative Approaches 145

    Introduction 146
    Simple Quantitative Analysis 146
    Quantitative Content Analysis 148
    Other Forms of Quantitative Documentary Analysis 153
    Conclusion 154
    Key Readings 155

13 Qualitative Approaches 157

    Introduction 158
    Thematic Analysis 158
    Qualitative Content Analysis 160
    Discourse Analysis 163
    Conversation Analysis 167
    Narrative Analysis 169
    Conclusion 172
    Key Readings 173

14 Mixed Methods Approaches 175

    Introduction 176
    Triangulation and Mixed Methods 176
    Why and How to Combine Quantitative and Qualitative Approaches in Documentary Research 177
    Examples of Mixed Method Documentary Research 178
    Conclusion 180
    Key Readings 180

Part 4 Where Next? 181

15 Sharing and Disseminating Your Research 183

    Introduction 184
    Evaluating Your Research 184
    Seminars and Conference Presentations 185
    Writing Up for Publication 186

Planning Further Research	188
Conclusion	189
Key Readings	189
16 Conclusions	191
References	193
Index	215

LIST OF BOXES

2.1	Some Examples of Documentary Research	11
2.2	Some Examples of Documentary Research Being Used in Conjunction with Other Methods	15
3.1	Ethical Guidelines on Researching Online Documents	26
3.2	Some Examples of Sampling and Selection Approaches in Documentary Research	28
3.3	Issues to Consider when Researching Documents	30
5.1	Examples of Documentary Research Being Used in Conjunction with Other Research Designs	69
6.1	Purposes or Functions of a Literature Review	76
6.2	Processes Involved in Undertaking a Literature Review	80
6.3	Examples of Literature Reviews	81
7.1	Stages in a Systematic Review	89
7.2	Examples of Systematic Reviews	90
7.3	Examples of Meta-Analyses	92
8.1	Examples of Secondary Data Analysis	102

8.2	An Example of a National Data Service – the UK Data Service	105
8.3	Examples of Data Sets from ESRC-funded Projects Available Through the UK Data Service	106
9.1	Examples of Archival and Historical Research	116
10.1	Examples of Policy Research Based Solely on Documentary Analysis	126
10.2	Examples of Policy Research Using Documents and Other Methods	128
11.1	Examples of Audio-Visual Text Analysis	141
12.1	Examples of Quantitative Content Analysis	149
13.1	Examples of Thematic Analysis of Documents	159
13.2	Examples of Qualitative Content Analysis	162
13.3	Examples of Discourse Analysis in Documentary Research	166
13.4	Examples of Conversation Analysis in Documentary Research	169
13.5	Examples of Narrative Analysis in Documentary Research	171
14.1	Examples of Mixed Method Documentary Analysis	179

ABOUT THE AUTHOR

Malcolm Tight is Professor of Higher Education at Lancaster University, UK, where he has worked since 2004, having previously worked at the University of Warwick, Birkbeck College London and the Open University. His research interests are in mapping and analysing higher education research globally. He edits two academic journals and two book series.

PART 1

STARTING DOCUMENTARY RESEARCH

Part 1 contains four chapters, which together provide an overview of documentary research in the social sciences and beyond:

Chapter 1 provides an introduction to the book, explaining its purpose, content and different ways of making use of it.

Chapter 2 considers the nature of documents, how they vary, the possibilities and advantages of documentary research, and how documents can be used in research, either as the focus of study or in combination with some other method or methods.

Chapter 3 discusses the processes involved in finding and reading documents, including the use of search engines, ethical issues, sampling strategies, how to assess the veracity and usefulness of a document, and find what you want in it, and recording your research.

Chapter 4 examines the uses of documentary research in different disciplines, both within the social sciences (anthropology, business/management, economics, education, geography, information science, law, media studies, political science, psychology, social work, sociology) and beyond (notably in health care/medicine and history).

1
INTRODUCTION

CONTENTS

What this Book is for	4
What the Book Contains	5
How to Use this Book	6

This introductory chapter discusses what this book is for, what it contains and how you might use it.

What this Book is for

Documentary research is, arguably, one of the most overlooked aspects – yet in many ways one of the most critical aspects – of social research. Thousands of books have been written on social research, but only a relative handful has focused on documentary research. Yet all social research involves documents, even if only to provide a brief literature review to contextualise a study; while, in writing up social research, other documents are produced.

Indeed, some forms of social research (such as archival and historical research, policy research, secondary data analysis, systematic reviews and meta-analyses – as well as literature reviews – each of which are discussed in detail in Part 2 of this book) rely heavily or exclusively on documents. Yet even these have only generated small, niche literatures.

Why documentary research appears to have been so overlooked is, therefore, worthy of some speculative discussion. Is it, for example, that reading, analysing and interpreting documents is taken to be such a basic skill that anyone with a reasonable level of education will already be competent enough to handle it? Or is it that the collection and analysis of new empirical data – through surveys, experiments, interviews and/or observation – is felt to be so much more important, and perhaps also more engaging or exciting?

Or maybe it is because documentary research is not a single, homogeneous entity, but includes, as has already been indicated, a range of approaches demanding separate and specialist treatment? This, however, is true of many social research methods or methodologies, so cannot be the main reason. Or perhaps, finally, it is simply that documentary research is so obvious as a generic social research technique that it is effectively invisible?

Each and all of these speculations may hold some truth, but each of them reflects views which must be questioned. Reading, analysing and interpreting documents is far from being a straightforward exercise, so some guidance may be useful and appreciated. Collecting fresh data for analysis is undeniably important – especially for certain kinds of social research or certain topics – but there is much more data that already exists, is relevant and is readily accessible (especially now that so much of it is available online), and often freely so, particularly to bona fide researchers.

While there are specific or specialised forms of documentary research, there is also a great deal of common ground between them, and generic approaches to documentary research and analysis are far more common; indeed – as already argued – endemic. So they deserve both some considered attention and care in application.

This book, therefore, sets out to provide an introductory, comprehensive, single-volume and up-to-date guide to documentary research. While its broad audience includes all of those studying or researching in the social sciences, it should also be of relevance to other disciplines – for example, in the humanities and sciences – that make extensive use of documentary research.

The underlying aim of the book is to provide the support which is largely lacking in the social research methods literature for those interested in and undertaking documentary research. While this is undeniably a broad and disparate group, and more specialist support will be needed for many, the general guidance given here should be, at the very least, a useful starting point.

What the Book Contains

The book synthesises current thinking on documentary research in the social sciences, and provides practical guidance on how to carry out and engage with documentary research. The available literature on documentary research is examined, analysed, quoted and extensively referenced. Numerous and varied illustrative examples, carefully selected from the range of disciplines and from different nations (bearing in mind the limitations posed by a focus on English-language sources), are presented to show how documentary research has been and can be used.

As you will already have noticed if you have scanned the contents pages or flicked through the book, it is organised in four parts:

Part 1, *Starting Documentary Research*, contains three chapters in addition to this introductory chapter. These examine the nature and variety of documents, the processes involved in accessing and reading documents, and the place of documentary research in different disciplines in the social sciences and beyond.

Part 2, *Genres of Documentary Research*, provides a general discussion of documentary research designs, and then focuses on five specialist forms or genres of documentary research: literature reviews, systematic reviews and meta-analyses, secondary data analysis, archival and historical research, and policy research. These genres, though specialised, are each highly relevant to all those engaged in social research.

Part 3, *Techniques for Documentary Analysis*, examines the different ways in which documents may be analysed, including both standard forms of quantitative and qualitative analysis – and mixed methods which combine these – and more specialist techniques such as content analysis and conversation analysis. Attention is given to both simpler and more complex forms of analysis.

Part 4, *Where Next?*, discusses what to do when you have completed a documentary analysis – sharing, publishing and disseminating your findings – and engages in some speculation about how documentary research may develop further in the future.

How to Use this Book

It would be unusual to read through a book of this nature literally from start to finish, though that is, of course, an option, and the book has been structured so that it is in a kind of logical order. A more common strategy would be to focus on whatever elements are of particular interest at a given time, using the contents pages and/or index to navigate quickly to the specific pages that are likely to be of most immediate relevance for you.

Having done this, you should find that, in addition to a succinct overview of the topic or topics, the pages of interest also include relevant examples that show how documentary research has been applied, and plentiful references to published sources to allow you to explore the topic in more detail. At the end of each chapter, an annotated guide to selected key readings is provided.

The book has been written in what you will hopefully find to be an accessible and readable style. Academic jargon has been avoided as much as possible, though, where specialist terms are in widespread use, these have been explained. Extensive use has also been made of cross-referencing, so that readers can navigate smoothly between sections and chapters.

2

DOCUMENTS AND DOCUMENTARY RESEARCH

CONTENTS

Introduction	8
What is a Document?	8
Varieties of Document	10
The Possibilities and Advantages of Documentary Research	13
Documents in, or as the Focus of, Research	15
The Purpose and Usage of Documents	18
Conclusion	19

Introduction

This chapter considers what documents are, how they vary in nature, and the possibilities and advantages associated with undertaking documentary research. It then discusses the use of documentary research as the main approach or as part (i.e. alongside other approaches or techniques) of a research project, and the purpose and usage of documents.

Understanding something of the nature and variety of documents is key to being able to appreciate and undertake documentary research, as well as – given the ubiquitous nature of the documentary approach – research in general. Hopefully, such an understanding may encourage you to make more, and more varied, usage of documents in your research.

What is a Document?

The answer to this question may appear, on first thought, to be obvious, but a little more consideration reveals that it is not so. Indeed, a good deal of effort has been devoted to trying to provide a convincing answer to this question, but without yet achieving universal accord. Thus, as matters stand, the definition of a document is not fixed and/ or generally agreed; alternative sources offer their own definitions, and these both vary and change or develop over time (Buckland 1997). Or, in other words, what constitutes or characterises a document is contested.

This should not be a particular cause for concern, however, as this is a common state of affairs throughout the social sciences and beyond, where progress in our understanding occurs through debate and disagreement. Indeed, it might be said that anything worthy of serious consideration in the social sciences is a matter of contestation and debate.

This may be readily illustrated by the following four definitions of a document or documents, which have been ordered by ascending date to show some of the development that has taken place in our understanding over the last three decades. More and different definitions could, of course, have been employed, but these four usefully illustrate something of the variation and change apparent:

> [A] document in its most general sense is a written text. (Scott 1990, p. 12)
>
> Documents are texts that can be published or unpublished, written, oral and virtual and may reside in either the public, private or virtual domains. (Fitzgerald 2007, p. 281)
>
> A document is simply any written, printed, photographed, painted or recorded material that can be used to provide information or evidence. (Dolowitz, Buckler and Sweeney 2008, p. 39)
>
> A document may be defined briefly as a record of an event or process. (McCulloch 2011, p. 249)

Thus, Scott offers a relatively early and common-sense definition: documents are written texts – books, papers, scripts, diaries, committee minutes, etc. – things which have or can have (when they are printed) a physical form. Both Fitzgerald and Dolowitz et al.

add to or extend this definition, with Fitzgerald adding oral and virtual documents, and Dolowitz et al. extending the definition further to include photographs, paintings and recorded material. Writing at the beginning of the current decade, McCulloch reverts to a simpler but inclusive definition, portraying documents as records of something, without specifying, or limiting, the nature of the record.

We may identify both background and foreground modifications lying behind these changes in definition. In the background, affecting everything not just in academic life but globally, there have been many, and some quite profound, changes in the nearly 30 years since Scott was writing. Probably the most obvious of these is the impact of the internet, with the growing number of online sources available (including sources that were originally only available as written texts) forcing a broadening of the definition of a document away from the physical, written text.

Meanwhile, in the foreground, practices and fashions in research methodology have also evolved, with a growing interest in the visual and aural seeking to complement the focus on the written. Nevertheless, most of the interest in documentary research remains on the written text, whether online or in physical form. Most social researchers remain fairly conventional in their outlook and in the research techniques they employ.

Other authors, in seeking to define what a document is, have sought to distinguish it from other terms. After all, a common strategy in defining something is to state what it is not as well as what it is. Thus, Lincoln (1980) makes an interesting – but now perhaps rather outdated – distinction between documents and records:

> we shall define a record as a written statement prepared by an individual or an agency for the purpose of attesting to an event or providing an accounting, and a document as any written (or filmed) material other than a record and which was not prepared specifically in response to some request from or some task set by the investigator. (p. 4, emphasis in original)

By contrast, the authors previously quoted would all include such records as documents; indeed, McCulloch (2011) clearly sees the terms as pseudonyms.

Lincoln's (1980) definition is also of interest, however, for what it says – in the second part of the quotation – about what documents are not. In excluding material that was specifically prepared in response to a request or task set by the investigator (i.e. the researcher), she is drawing a line between documents and, for example, interview transcripts and survey responses. That this is a blurred line is, though, apparent, because it would allow – as most researchers would probably now accept – interview and survey data collected by someone else to be considered as documents by another researcher.

Does this mean, though, that almost anything can be considered as a document? If documents are not just written or printed texts, but may be oral or virtual, or filmed or painted, what then cannot (at least potentially) be considered as a document? The addition of the qualifier 'at least potentially' suggests that it depends very much on the researcher and their perspective. If they are treating the material – written, oral, virtual, visual – as a source for their research, and they have not recently generated the material themselves, then it may be considered as a document.

Rather than prescribe my own definition, and possibly add further to the potential confusion, or adopt one of the available definitions, I will proceed bearing all of these definitions and points in mind. In doing so, I will aim simultaneously to both keep the range of interest broad and acknowledge where the primary focus lies.

Varieties of Document

As the discussion in the previous section will have indicated, documents as a class may be very varied; but just how varied? We may, again, usefully compare what different documentary researchers have written at different times. Here are two sample categorisations or indicative lists:

> Documentary sources of information, of all kinds, figure centrally in the research of sociologists. Official statistics on crime, income distribution, health and illness, censuses of population, newspaper reports, diaries, reference books, government publications, and similar sources are the basis of much social research by academics and their students. Yet these materials have rarely been given the attention that they deserve in accounts of sociological research methods. (Scott 1990, p. ix)

> Documents that may be used for systematic evaluation as part of a study take a variety of forms. They include advertisements; agendas, attendance registers, and minutes of meetings; manuals; background papers; books and brochures; diaries and journals; event programs (i.e., printed outlines); letters and memoranda; maps and charts; newspapers (clippings/articles); press releases; program proposals, application forms, and summaries; radio and television program scripts; organisational or institutional reports; survey data; and various public records. Scrapbooks and photo albums can also furnish documentary material for research purposes. These types of documents are found in libraries, newspaper archives, historical society offices, and organisational or institutional files. (Bowen 2009, pp. 27–28)

The earlier of the two authors, Scott – in line with his definition quoted in the previous section – offers a broad, but by no means comprehensive, categorisation of different kinds of written texts that may be used as the basis for documentary research. Tellingly, he also argues (as I did in Chapter 1) that these sources have been relatively neglected; and, though he makes his case from the perspective of sociology, it might be extended to apply to all social research.

Bowen (2009), more recently, goes somewhat beyond Scott's (1990) purview – though much of his description relates to written texts – to add items such as scrapbooks and photo albums. He also usefully indicates where these kinds of items are likely to be found. We might, in the light of some of the later definitions quoted in the previous section, go even further. Documents may be texts or data sets, printed or hand-written, quantitative and/or qualitative, physical or online, personal or official, closed or open, visual or representational.

This is not to say, to pick up on the argument in the previous section, that everything is a document, or may be treated as a document, but rather – to turn it around slightly – that everything we can comprehend may be documented in some way. The key distinction between documentary and other forms of research is that documents already exist – even, perhaps, if we have previously created them ourselves – before we research them.

In experimental, interview-based, observational, survey and other forms of research, the first part of the research process involves the collection, creation or co-creation of new empirical data, which is then analysed. In documentary research, the data already exists. While it will still need to be accessed and/or collected, this should not take anything like the time involved in new empirical research. Documentary research does not set out to create new data, but to undertake analyses of existing data, whether that data has previously been analysed or not.

We can better illustrate the variety included within documentary research if we consider some examples. Box 2.1 summarises ten recent examples of published documentary research across a range of disciplines and from a variety of countries.

The selection of examples in Box 2.1 could not be said to be representative, but is, rather, meant to be illustrative. Many alternative examples could have been used instead. The selection of these examples (and this is the case throughout the book) should not be taken to imply that they are necessarily the highest quality research – though they may well be, having been published in refereed international journals – but rather that they are useful and interesting.

BOX 2.1

Some Examples of Documentary Research

1. Awang, Jindal-Snape and Barber (2013) analysed the Malaysian government's strategies for promoting 'positive behaviour' among the young by carrying out a content analysis of 91 official circulars issued to schools between 1969 and 2011. The circulars were read and analysed by the researchers to identify all mentions and examples of positive and negative behaviour, and of the strategies proposed for encouraging positive behaviour.
2. Boon et al. (2009), concerned about the role of pharmacists in North America, carried out a systematic search in selected health databases for articles relating to pharmacy, natural health products and dietary supplements. An in-depth, qualitative content analysis of 259 articles was carried out. Articles were coded in terms of the roles, responsibilities and behaviours of pharmacists.
3. Clark, Parker and Davey (2014), interested in the role of nurse practitioners in caring for the aged in Australia, carried out a documentary analysis of 32 project proposals awarded funding by the government department concerned. A content analysis was carried out

(Continued)

(Continued)

   to identify the key features and characteristics of the models of aged care that were successfully proposed.
4. Davis (2012) considers the use of leadership and change theory in changing practice in early years settings by undertaking an analysis of the scripts produced by 10 professionals writing about this for an MA course in the UK. In her analysis, she noted the cultural and pedagogic changes proposed and the theories used to justify them.
5. EzzelArab (2009) reports on a documentary and contextual analysis of 'al-La iha al-Wataniyya' ('The National Programme'), 'a proposal adopted in April 1879 by Egypt's economic and political elites as an expression of resistance to the fiscal program of European control' (p. 301). He examines both the Arabic and French versions of the document in terms of its signatories and contents.
6. Grazioli and Jarvenpaa (2003) focus on consumer and business deception on the internet, examining documentary evidence published between 1995 and 2000 relating to 201 cases of internet deception. They searched newspapers, journals and legal documents included in certain databases, as well as the internet sites of monitoring agencies, to identify the tactics adopted and what might be done to respond to them.
7. Himmelsbach et al. (2015) examine documentary data to reconstruct flood events on the Upper Rhine River and its tributaries in Europe since AD 1480. They employ critical source analysis to derive data from over 4,000 references – 'flood marks, drawings, flood maps, newspapers, gauge data and contemporaneous administrative reports and chronicles' (p. 4151) – relating to around 2,800 flood events.
8. Lampe et al. (2017) report on a systematic literature review carried out to assess the reliability of observational data on aggression. Two search engines (PsycINFO and PubMED) were used to identify relevant articles published between 1994 and 2014. Identifying 37 articles for analysis, they found that the inter-rater reliability of observing aggression was fair to excellent; though they noted that most observations took place in laboratory settings, with only a limited number in naturalistic settings.
9. Viswambharan and Priya (2016) carried out a documentary analysis of a documentary (i.e. a film) on the post-Godhra communal riots in India in 2002 to explore disaster mental health. They use constructionist grounded theory to examine the documentary as a whole and the different categories of survivors' suffering identified.
10. Williams (2015) analyses documentary data from company reports, news articles, industry analyst reports and industry magazines to explore how the Coca Cola Company successfully re-entered the Indian and Chinese markets following the liberalisation of their economies. Relevant documents over the period 1975–2012 were identified using keyword searches, and then triangulated across sources to create a narrative of events.

The range of disciplines covered includes business, climatology, education, health care, history, pharmacy and politics; in other words, it extends throughout and well beyond the social sciences that are the main focus of this book (though, in all cases, the researchers are, in essence, using elements of social science research methodology:

Chapter 4 contains a fuller discussion of documentary research in the disciplines). The countries discussed include not only (in articles published in the English language) the obvious English-speaking ones – the USA, the UK and Australia – but also developing countries such as China, Egypt, India and Malaysia.

The examples given also vary significantly in other ways. Thus, in terms of scale, while Himmelsbach et al. (2015) based their analysis on over 4,000 references, both Viswambharan and Priya (2016) and EzzelArab (2009) analyse a single document, in the former case a film documentary and in the latter case two different versions of a text. While most of the analyses were based on written texts – such as government circulars, articles, project proposals, historical chronicles and student assignments – others made use of a range of other kinds of 'documents'. These included drawings, film, flood marks and maps, and a variety of internet sources. Clearly, then, documents may not only be very varied, but also very useful for a wide range of research interests and projects.

The Possibilities and Advantages of Documentary Research

The discussion so far in this chapter should already have suggested some of the possibilities and advantages of documentary research. In a relatively early account, Lincoln – maintaining a firm distinction between documents and records which, as we have already suggested, many would disagree with – identifies six major advantages:

> First, documents and records are a stable, rich and rewarding resource ... Second, records (as opposed to documents, although occasionally the same will hold true for those writings also) constitute a legally unassailable base from which to defend oneself against allegations, interpretations and libel ... Third, both documents and records represent a 'natural' source of information – a delight to the naturalistic inquirer. Fourth, they are available on a low-cost or no cost basis, requiring often only the investigator's time and energy ... Fifth, documents and records both are non-reactive ... Sixth, whether or not the inquirer finally decides to interact with his [sic] subjects, content analysis and other forms of documentary and record analysis enable *supplementary* and *contextual* data to be gathered. (1980, pp. 10–12, emphasis in original)

However, Lincoln either overlooks or underplays two other advantages which – at least nowadays – might be seen as being of even greater significance: the accessibility and scale of documents. As documentary research does not create new data but analyses existing data, it offers considerable opportunities for social researchers in terms of both the accessibility and the scale of the research they can undertake within given time and resource constraints.

After all, most social researchers are operating under considerable constraints, particularly those who are expected to complete a project within a given, relatively short timescale. This is the case for many students completing dissertation projects at undergraduate or masters level, and even for research students undertaking PhDs, as well as for other researchers working inside or outside academe. The time and financial resources available will be limited, so analysing existing data where possible, rather than first collecting new data and then analysing that, offers considerable potential. Not only is the time taken in collecting new data saved, but existing data sets may be much larger, more representative and more detailed than an individual researcher, or a small team, could hope to collect in the time they have available.

Naturally enough, given the time at which she was writing, Lincoln also did not mention the online availability of documents. A huge and increasing amount of data – both quantitative and qualitative – is available for social research, much of it online and freely accessible, at least to bona fide researchers. It would be foolish not to at least explore the possibilities, whether as part of a research project or as the whole project, before committing to further data collection. Collecting new data poses much greater access and ethical challenges (ethical issues are discussed further in Chapter 3), and many of the potential targets for social research – i.e. the general public and various sub-groups of it – are now fatigued by and resistant to requests to complete yet another survey or be interviewed again.

One further advantage of documentary research is that there are kinds or topics of research which it is difficult or impossible to do in any other way. This is self-evidently the case with historical research that reaches further back than present-day lifetimes, as documents of various kinds will be the only sources of data available. More contemporaneously, it is similarly the case when the subject of the research concerns the internet and the material found on it, much of which is simply not available elsewhere or in other formats.

Documentary research may also be the only option when other forms of access are not possible. This was the case, for example, with the research carried out by Grazioli and Jarvenpaa (2003) on internet deception, outlined in Box 2.1. Since people engaged in deception would be difficult to contact and highly unlikely to be willing to cooperate with the research, they decided to search newspapers, legal documents and other sources for the data they required:

> Gathering real-world data on deviant behavior is usually difficult because perpetrators actively attempt to hide evidence that the behavior occurred ... Under these conditions, one viable methodology consists of identifying cases of Internet deception available in public records and performing content analysis on them. (p. 103)

Unless, therefore, you have a strong methodological or personal preference for engaging in other forms of research, you would be well advised to consider documentary research as an alternative or complementary approach. You can do documentary research without ever leaving the house or office, and you don't need to talk to anyone. You will likely complete your research much quicker this way than you would otherwise.

Indeed, I even considered using the expression 'social research for the anti-social' as the subtitle for this book – recognising that many who are involved in social research do not (like me) relish the close engagement with others necessitated in some forms of data collection – but did not want this to be taken in the wrong way.

Documents in, or as the Focus of, Research

If you do decide to carry out a piece of documentary research – or perhaps have this decided for you – then this book should, hopefully, be of considerable use. Even if you decide to take a different approach to your research, however, involving the collection of new empirical data, your research will almost certainly (as was pointed out in Chapter 1) involve an element of documentary research – for example, reading and analysing some of the relevant academic and/or policy literature. So this book should still be of some use.

Reviews of the academic and policy literatures are both classic genres of documentary research. Thus, literature reviews are considered in detail in Chapter 6; while their 'big brother', systematic reviews, form the subject of Chapter 7, along with meta-analyses; and policy research is the focus of Chapter 10. Each requires careful planning and reflection, and the approach taken should be made clear and justified when they are written up. Documentary research, even when it only forms part of a research project, demands just as much rigour and care as other forms of research.

Box 2.2 summarises ten recent examples of research that has made use of documentary analysis alongside other research methods. As with Box 2.1, it gives some idea of the diversity of mixed methodological approaches (see also Chapter 14) that are possible.

BOX 2.2

Some Examples of Documentary Research Being Used in Conjunction with Other Methods

1. Avby, Nilsen and Ellström (2017) explored knowledge use and learning among social workers engaged in everyday child investigation work in Sweden. They employed interviews, participant observation and reflective dialogues, as well as the documentary analysis of case files, to collect data. They characterise their overall research design as ethnography, and based their research in two children's services departments employing 40 social workers between them. The study focused on five cases and seven of the social workers.
2. Brunton and Mackintosh (2017) consider the purpose of university sport and its relation to national sport policy in the UK. Adopting an interpretivist approach, they carried out eight in-depth, semi-structured interviews with those with overall responsibility for sport at eight universities in the north of England. 'In addition, documentary analysis was carried out to consider the evidence of how universities link to government and national sports policy. The strategic plan of each university was analysed alongside key strategies for sport and higher

(Continued)

(Continued)

   education sport in England' (p. 382). Qualitative content analysis and thematic analysis were used.
3. Canonico et al. (2017) studied knowledge integration mechanisms in an interdisciplinary research project. They describe their research as a case study, focusing on a single university/industry research project in Italy. 'The authors used three data collection techniques: internal document analysis, observation/site visits and semi-structured interviews. Documentary analysis was used to understand the organizational structure and to identify knowledge integration issues. Observation and site visits at university research laboratories were used to increase understanding on particular issues. Staff interviewed included managers and academic researchers' (p. 604).
4. Del Río, Peñascoa and Mir-Artigues (2018) were interested in the drivers for, and barriers to, the deployment of concentrated solar power as an energy source in the European Union by 2030. They researched this by means of a 'thorough literature review and interviews with key stakeholders in the sector' (p. 1019). The literature review focused on material published in the most recent five-year period, 2011–15: 91 references are provided at the end of the article.
5. Foley et al. (2017) researched the impact of the reconfiguration of the emergency care system in Ireland. They adopted a comparative case study approach, examining the experience in three regions of the country. 'Documentary analysis of reconfiguration planning reports was used to identify planned public engagement activities. Semi-structured interviews with 74 purposively-sampled stakeholders explored their perspectives on reconfiguration, engagement activities and public responses to reconfiguration' (p. 800).
6. Giovannini (2016) discusses the new regional political voices developing in England, focusing on the example of Yorkshire First. She analyses the party's manifesto and other policy documents, and supplements this with the results of an online questionnaire survey sent to all of the party's members. This enables her to identify 'the emergence of a nascent grass-roots form of regionalism in Yorkshire that breaks away from past experiences and seeks to challenge the dominant narrative of regionalisation' (p. 598).
7. McGrattan and Williams (2017) examine the impact of devolution in the UK on national identification in Wales and Northern Ireland. They undertook an 'original qualitative research including data from documentary analysis, focus groups and structured interviews' (p. 465). In the Welsh case, the documentary evidence consists of 'selected quantitative data' in the form of responses to surveys on the desire for independence, while, in the Northern Irish case, it comes 'mainly from political party documents and the Northern Ireland Life and Times Surveys' (p. 471).
8. Rickinson et al. (2017) look at the relationship between evidence-informed practice and evidence-informed policy in education in Australia. Data collection involved: '(i) in-depth semi-structured interviews with 25 policy-makers who were involved in the development of the selected policies; (ii) documentary analysis of policy documents, background research reports and other relevant papers relating to the selected policies; (iii) unstructured observation (where possible) of meetings and events connected with the development of the selected policies; and (iv) feedback from 40 wider policy staff who took part in a verification workshop to discuss the project's emerging findings' (p. 173).

9. Teh, Hotte and Sumaila (2017) were concerned with whether fishery buybacks could achieve positive socio-economic results. They carried out four case studies of selected Australian, American, Canadian and Norwegian fisheries. They 'first conducted a desktop review of existing literature on the selected case studies. This information was then supplemented with in-depth telephone interviews conducted between December 2007 and February 2008 with nine experts who were either involved in the management, or had extensive knowledge and research experience about the respective fishery buybacks' (pp. 3–4).
10. Urbano and Keeton (2017) researched carbon dynamics in recovering secondary forests in northeastern USA. They 'employed a longitudinal study based on twelve years of empirical data (2001–2013) collected from 60 permanent monitoring plots within 16 reference stands at Marsh-Billings-Rockefeller National Historical Park in Woodstock, VT ... [and] 150 years of documentary data from park management records' (p. 21). The latter data was both qualitative and quantitative, and covered the 1880–2013 period.

Thus, the disciplines and/or topics represented include education, energy, fisheries, forestry, health care, politics, social work and sports. As with the examples given in Box 2.1, these go well beyond the social sciences. The documents being analysed include case files, internal institutional documents, manifestos, planning reports, policy documents, research reports, strategic plans and surveys. And the other methods being used range from interviews and focus groups to questionnaire surveys and participant and non-participant observation, and to longitudinal studies, reflective dialogues, site visits and workshops.

The question arises, of course, as to why you might or should use documents as well as other forms of data in research; does this not mean making more work for yourself? The answer is, in part, as has already been suggested, that this is what is expected: some discussion of the existing research and/or policy literature is a standard element of research projects in the social sciences and beyond. Otherwise, how would you be able to put your research in context, demonstrate what its contribution to the field of study is, and, possibly, avoid unnecessarily repeating research that had already been done?

The other, and perhaps more important, part of the answer to this question is that using more than one form of data and/or form of analysis adds value to a research project. It allows for what social science researchers call triangulation to take place (this is discussed in more detail in Chapter 14). For example, if you research a particular topic using documents and interviews, and the different sources of data suggest much the same conclusions, supporting each other, this makes your analysis and argument rather stronger and more convincing. Or, alternatively, if your sources and analyses suggest conflicting interpretations, this is also useful (if perhaps a little frustrating) as it alerts you to possible errors – in the data or in your analysis of it – or indicates that the issue you are researching is rather more complex or multifaceted than you previously thought.

The Purpose and Usage of Documents

> [W]e cannot treat records – however 'official' – as firm evidence of what they report ... We have to approach them for what they are and what they are used to accomplish. (Atkinson and Coffey 1997, p. 47)

Undertaking research into documents – or records, as Atkinson and Coffey term them – requires an appreciation and understanding of their purpose(s) and usage(s). No document should be treated as an objective *tabula rasa* or 'tablet of stone'; rather, they have all been created by highly subjective and interested individuals such as you and me. Documents need to be treated with care: 'if we are to get to grips with the nature of documents then we have to move away from a consideration of them as stable, static and pre-defined artefacts' (Prior 2003, p. 2).

Document analysis, then, is:

> a systematic procedure for reviewing or evaluating documents – both printed and electronic (computer-based and Internet-transmitted) material. Like other analytical methods in qualitative research, document analysis requires that data be examined and interpreted in order to elicit meaning, gain understanding, and develop empirical knowledge. Documents contain text (words) and images that have been recorded without a researcher's intervention. (Bowen 2009, p. 27)

While I would disagree with Bowen's emphasis on the use of qualitative research methods – documents may just as well be analysed quantitatively, or using a mixture of qualitative and quantitative methods (see Chapters 12, 13 and 14) – he is right to emphasise that documents, unlike other forms of research data, have normally been created without the researcher's involvement.

This means that we need to take particular care in their interpretation, just as we would, for example, in reading a party election manifesto that dropped through our letterbox, or an investment opportunity that arrived in our inbox. This would involve:

- considering who created the document, for what purposes and in what context
- reviewing how the document has been used and interpreted since its creation (what impact has it had?)
- examining the document in relation to similar and related documents (what is its relationship to other documents?)
- assessing what the document does and does not 'say' ('reading between the lines'), and how it says it.

These points are, of course, analogous to the processes that competent social researchers would go through in carrying out other forms of social research. They will be discussed further in the next chapter, Chapter 3, and returned to throughout the book.

Conclusion

This chapter has provided a brief introduction to documents and documentary research. It has argued that documentary research differs from other forms of research in that the objects of research (the data) exist already (in the form of documents). However, the processes involved in carrying out documentary research are analogous to, and should be just as rigorous as, those employed in other forms of social research.

Documents exist and are available in a huge variety, and social (and other) researchers should make much more use of them – on their own or in conjunction with other forms of research – than they currently do. As empirical research becomes more problematic, it behoves us as social researchers to fully exploit the data that already exists, and is often freely available.

KEY READINGS

Bowen, G (2009) Document Analysis as a Qualitative Research Method. *Qualitative Research Journal*, 9, 2, pp. 27–40.

A very accessible account, albeit focusing on qualitative analysis only.

McCulloch, G (2004) *Documentary Research in Education, History and the Social Sciences*. London, Routledge.

One of the few recent books on the topic, and still in print.

Prior, L (2003) *Using Documents in Social Research*. London, Sage.

Also still in print, and very readable.

Scott, J (1990) *A Matter of Record: Documentary source in social research*. Cambridge, Polity Press.

A classic in the field. While inevitably somewhat out of date, particularly with the massive expansion of online sources, this text still has much to offer.

3

FINDING AND READING DOCUMENTS

CONTENTS

Introduction	22
Accessing Documents	22
Ethical Issues	24
Sampling and Selection	27
Issues to Consider when Researching Documents	29
How to Read Documents	32
Keeping Records	34
Conclusion	35

Introduction

Having decided to use documents in – or perhaps as the basis for – your research, the issues concerned with how to find, and then how to read, the documents you want or need have to be considered. While the answers to these issues may, at first glance, seem simple or self-evident, this is often not the case, so some careful thought and planning may be called for.

At the very least, it is always a good idea to have an alternative or 'Plan B' up your sleeve in case there are problems with your original research intentions. For example, the documents you planned to analyse may not be available or, though available, turn out not to contain the information you need.

It is worth bearing in mind – both at this point and throughout the documentary research process – that documentary research is not fundamentally different from other forms of social research:

> the general principles involved in handling documents are no different from those involved in any other area of social research, but ... the specific features of documentary sources do require the consideration of their distinguishing features and the particular techniques needed to handle them. (Scott 1990, p. 1)

Just like other approaches to social research, therefore, documentary research requires due care and attention.

This chapter offers a guide to and through the issues involved in finding and reading documents. The main sections of the chapter focus on:

- accessing documents: where and how to get hold of them
- ethical issues: which are important even though documents already exist
- sampling and selection: how to choose which documents to study
- the issues to consider when researching documents
- how to read: getting what you need from documents
- keeping records: of what you have read and discovered.

The chapter closes with some conclusions and key readings.

Accessing Documents

Where and how you can access documents for research depends to a large degree on the nature of the documents themselves, but also to an extent on your own status. Are they academic documents, official documents, institutional documents or personal documents? Are they available only in physical form or online? Are they published or unpublished, public or private, contemporary or historical?

Academic documents – journal articles, books and monographs, reports and conference papers – are normally not difficult to access, especially if you are studying or working at a university or college. You may, however, have to pay for access if the university or college concerned does not possess a hard copy of the document you wish to read or have a subscription to it (allowing you free access) online.

There are, though, ways around such problems. Pre-publication versions of articles are often available freely online via a university, department or individual website. Or you may be able to get a copy of a document – whether published or unpublished – by contacting the author directly. Most authors, after all, are only too happy to encourage and enable others to read their work.

The availability of official documents – produced by government departments and other public authorities – will depend on their precise nature. Formal policy statements, for example, are normally readily available in democratic nations, though you may have to pay for them, especially if you want a hard copy (they will often be available freely online). Internal briefing documents, minutes of committees and the like may be much harder to access. Indeed, if they are deemed sensitive, they are often kept secret for periods of 30 years or more before being made available, perhaps even then only selectively, in archives.

With institutional documents, much depends on your connection to the institution concerned: whether you work there, know someone who does or have negotiated access with someone in authority. Promotional materials and legally required documents, such as annual reports, are likely to be readily accessible (often now through the institution's website), but much internal documentation will not be unless you have very good connections and are regarded as trustworthy. It may also be the case that the institution concerned, having allowed you access, will want to check and approve anything you write up from your research before it goes public.

Similar issues arise in the case of personal documents – such as diaries or letters – where individual or professional connections to the person or persons concerned are key. If the person concerned is dead, will their surviving relatives, or the institution to which they have bequeathed their papers, allow you access?

Here, much has changed in recent years, however, with the rise of social networking and the growing tendency for (particularly young) people to place a lot of information – often openly and freely accessible – about themselves, their relationships and their lives online. Though such information may be publicly available, it does raise particular ethical issues, which are considered in the next section.

As these changes illustrate, much also depends on whether the document(s) you are interested in gaining access to are contemporary or historical. All things considered, the former are likely to be easier to track down and are also more likely to be available online. Historical documents, by comparison, can be harder to access and may only be available in hard copy at a particular location; or they may have been lost or damaged, or perhaps no longer exist (or possibly never did exist).

Documentary research is necessarily constrained, therefore, by the documents that are available and accessible.

Using Online Search Engines

The task of finding relevant documents to analyse has been made immeasurably easier in recent decades by the development of the internet and of search engines for quickly finding material on or through it. There are scores of both general – for example, Ask, Google – and academic – for example, ERIC, Google Scholar, Scopus, World of Science – search engines available. Using these, it is possible to search for either a specific document (if you know the title) or documents by specific authors, or to perform more general searches for documents dealing with a particular topic (e.g. climate change, the 2016 General Election, human capital) using keywords.

If you are not searching for something specific, however, you will need to take care with the search terms or keywords that you use. Thus, using any of the three examples just given as a search term would likely yield thousands of hits, which could take you a good deal of time to work through before you found something of particular interest. So, it is important to make the search terms as specific as possible, or to use the and/or functions (also known as Boolean operators) or date restrictions to limit the number of results.

It is also helpful to use more than one search engine; they all have a different coverage, so, if you use only one, you may miss some key material. Academic search engines can also provide other useful information, such as how often a particular document has been cited, and by whom, which can help in narrowing down your focus or in deciding where to start. More highly cited documents are likely to have been particularly influential in thinking and research on the topic concerned.

It is important to highlight here one of the key issues – indeed, perhaps the key issue – with contemporary documentary analysis based on online searching; namely, the sheer volume of material (i.e. documents) that may be identified as being of relevance (see also the discussion of literature reviews, systematic analyses and meta-analyses in Chapters 6 and 7). In this situation, documentary researchers have to employ means of limiting – for example, by date, language, citations, combinations of keywords – at least initially, the numbers of documents they access.

Once you have identified an initial list of documents of interest, it is then a question of accessing and reading those documents. If some key documents are not (freely) available, you may have to consider alternatives. Remember that librarians can be very helpful in advising you on matters of access. The practical issues involved in reading documents are considered in a later section of this chapter.

Ethical Issues

It might be thought that, as documents already exist and have merely been accessed by the researcher, there are no (outstanding) ethical issues to consider in using them as research materials. Such ethical issues as there were – informed consent, anonymity, transparency, the right to withdraw, copyright, and so forth – will have been addressed and, one might presume, solved by those responsible for putting together the document. It is not always, however, as straightforward as that.

It is possible, for example, that the document's author(s) may not have acted in a rigorously ethical fashion. This issue is perhaps likely to be more pertinent for older documents, to which contemporary ethical standards will not have been applied (though, of course, those involved are less likely to still be alive). But it is also, as we shall discuss, highly pertinent for many contemporary, and often freely and easily available, documents.

Granted, there are many kinds of documents – for example, published books, articles and reports, official websites, national statistics – where ethical issues will not be a direct concern to those analysing them (after all, organisations and publishers employ lawyers to check, amongst other things, for any potential ethical problems prior to publication). This, indeed, is one of the attractions and advantages of doing documentary research. However, for other kinds of documents, and particularly personal documents, this may not be so, even when the documents in question are freely available, or where access has been granted.

Thus, Sixsmith and Murray (2001) discuss the example of emails:

We have discussed some of the key ethical considerations pertinent to qualitative documentary analysis of email content. In particular, ethical issues of accessing voices, consent, privacy, anonymity, interpretation, and ownership and authorship of material have been problematized. As can be seen, these ethical considerations are not simply related to data collection but are located throughout the research writing and publication process. (p. 430)

Similar kinds of issues or concerns may arise when other kinds of personal material – for example, diaries, letters, blogs, social media entries – are the focus for research. The authors may have placed their material in a publicly accessible forum, but the researcher still needs to carefully consider the ethical implications of using the material for research purposes. Will, for example, the author be identifiable, and, if so, will the presentation or publication of the research cast them in an unfavourable light, or possibly cause them distress? This is also the case with historical material, where the author may be long dead, but surviving relatives or descendants may be affected.

That your analysis of a document might place its author in an unfavourable light does not mean, though, that you should not carry out and publish the analysis; research, after all, has an important role in 'speaking truth to power'. What is important is your awareness of the issues involved, and the way in which you contextualise and present your analysis.

To give a fuller idea of the kinds of ethical issues that may be involved in researching documents, particularly those found online, Box 3.1 quotes from the *Ethical Guidelines for Educational Research* produced by the British Educational Research Association (BERA), a learned society. There are, of course, many learned societies and professional bodies across the world that produce their own ethical guidelines, and the reader would be well advised to consult those most directly relevant to them. The BERA guidelines are quoted here simply as an example.

---BOX 3.1---

Ethical Guidelines on Researching Online Documents

Where research draws on social media and online communities, it is important to remember that digital information is generated by individuals … [there] will be one or more human creators responsible for it, who could therefore be regarded as participants; whether and how these potential participants might be traceable should be considered…

In many cases the producers of publicly accessible data may not have considered the fact that it might be used for research purposes, and it should not be assumed that such data is available for researchers to use without consent … Seeking consent would not normally be expected for data that have been produced expressly for public use. There is no consensus, however, as to whether those in online communities perceive their data to be either public or private, even when copyrights are waived. Therefore, consent is an issue to be addressed with regard to each and any online data-source, with consideration given to the presumed intent of the creators of online content, the extent to which it identifies individuals or institutions, and the sensitivity of the data…

Consideration should be given to whether and how best to approach online communities (through members, gatekeepers or moderators, for example), or those involved in face-to-face public events and spaces, in order to inform them about the intended research.

When working with secondary or documentary data, the sensitivity of the data, who created it, the intended audience of its creators, its original purpose and its intended uses in the research are all important considerations. If secondary data concerning participants are to be reused, ownership of the datasets should be determined, and the owners consulted to ascertain whether they can give consent on behalf of the participants…

It is accepted that, sometimes, gaining consent from all concerned in public spaces (face-to-face or virtual, past or present) will not be feasible; however, attempts to make contact should be documented. In the event of a secondary source being untraceable, researchers should be able to evidence their attempts to gain consent. (BERA 2018, pp. 7, 10–12)

The BERA guidelines stress the importance of identifying the owners of documents that are to be researched, and gaining their consent where appropriate. They also urge researchers to consider how and whether the consent of those involved in online communities might be sought, or at least whether they might be informed of the research. The importance of sensitivity and of maintaining, where possible and desirable, the anonymity of those involved, underlies the guidelines.

As with other approaches to social research, therefore, the documentary researcher has a duty of care to their sources. The underlying principle of 'do no harm' – or perhaps 'do unto others as you would have them do unto you' – needs to be carefully borne in mind throughout the research process.

Sampling and Selection

Sampling and selection are obvious issues to consider if you are collecting original empirical data: typically, in the social sciences, through interviews, surveys or observation, though perhaps also through experimentation. It is important to be clear about the size and composition of your sample, and how you went about selecting it, so that those interested in the research can make judgements about its usefulness, representativeness and possible generalisability. But these issues are just as important if you are carrying out documentary research. Indeed, as should be apparent from the discussion in this chapter, most of the issues encountered in carrying out empirical research also apply to documentary research.

It is good practice, therefore, when you write up your research, to spell out how you chose the documents you analysed, and why you chose those documents rather than any others that might have been available or considered. This is so even when you are only analysing a single document – presumably because it is of such interest or significance – otherwise, why else would you be paying it so much attention? You should explain why it is of interest or significance, and thereby justify your choice.

When you are analysing a number of documents, clarity about their sampling and selection is equally important. For example, supposing you are carrying out a literature review (see also the extended discussion of this genre in Chapter 6), how did you go about identifying the books and articles you discuss?

The older approach (i.e. up until a few decades ago) would have involved identifying a few items to start with (from a reading list, a library catalogue, or from the advice of others), and then working backwards (through the references) and outwards (looking at books on the same library shelves and/or articles published in the same journals) to find other material. Each item would then be examined briefly to determine its relevance, and then either discarded or put aside for a closer reading later.

The modern approach would involve using one or more search engines (see the discussion in the previous section) and keywords to produce lists of possibly relevant material, then working through these to remove items that obviously aren't relevant, and then accessing the remaining books, reports or articles (online or in hard copy) to review them further. It would be strange, nowadays, not to use an approach along these lines, even if you had started your search in the more traditional fashion.

So, if you have carried out a literature review, you should be able to state:

- which search engines you used (and why)
- which keywords you used (and why)
- how many items you initially identified
- how you refined your search and excluded irrelevant or less relevant materials, and the number of items you ended up with
- any other restrictions you used in terms of language (e.g. English language only), date (e.g. only items published since 2000) or authors' background (e.g. restricting the review to those based in a particular country or countries), and why.

The point of all this is – as it would be for other forms of research – transparency and replicability. Those taking an interest in your research should then be better able to place it with respect to related research, and also take it further by adding to, updating or extending it. You are not expected to analyse all relevant documents on your topic; or, in the case of the literature review, to have identified and read all relevant publications. Clearly, in most cases, to do so would be impossible, so it is reasonable and practical to place limits on your research. You simply need to be open and honest about those limits, and to be able to justify them.

To illustrate these processes, Box 3.2 details two examples of sampling and selection strategies as applied to documentary research. One involved the use of a single, subject-specific database, while the other searched several, more generic databases. The first example took a random stratified approach, where relevant items were identified randomly until examples relating to all possible variable values had been identified. The second example took a more comprehensive approach, seeking to identify – through the use of keyword search terms and other strategies – all published studies that met the inclusion criteria.

BOX 3.2

Some Examples of Sampling and Selection Approaches in Documentary Research

1. To select the documents for analysis, a random stratified sample was drawn from the ICN [International Council of Nurses] database of nurse legislation. All legislation (n = 173 jurisdictions) was first coded according to the key dimensions of interest (geographic region of the world, GNI [gross national income] category, legal tradition, model of nurse regulation and administrative approach). Each variable of interest had a number of possible values, for example, legal tradition included civil, common and Islamic law. Accordingly, a series of Excel files, one for each of the variables of interest and sorted by the respective possible values, was created. These were then used to select, by use of the random function included as part of the Microsoft Excel 2010 package, legislation for inclusion in the analysis. Because every law was coded against all variables then, as soon as a law was selected to fulfil one of the variables of interest, this would have an impact on all other variables. Hence, the sequence of selection was determined on the basis of the least represented value in the variables of interest. Random selection continued until there was at least one example of each value for the variables of interest. (Benton et al. 2015, p. 209)
2. Coaching studies using a systematic observation method were searched using a 3-phase approach. Phase 1 involved searching the EBSCO HOST database. Specific databases searched were Academic Search Complete, Educational Research Complete, ERIC, PsycArticles, PsycBooks, PsycInfo and SPORTdiscus with FullText. Original search terms ... were systematic observation AND coaching AND behaviour. Closely related terms and those used in studies that were known to have used a systematic method, such as coach and athlete and learning were also included in searches to ensure all relevant articles that met the inclusion criteria were identified. Database searches stopped once a saturation point had been reached, which was when no new articles were found. Phase 2 expanded the search beyond the

databases to involve other studies that met the inclusion criterion: post 1997, empirical, peer-reviewed study, written in English, the participants of the study were coaches, and a category-based, systematic observation instrument to observe coaching behaviour directed towards players. This extended search was achieved by reading the reference lists of articles identified in phase 1, as well as emailing researchers who were known to conduct coaching research using a systematic observation method. Finally, colleagues directed the authors to any other studies that had not been identified through any other means. (Cope, Partington and Harvey 2017, pp. 2042–2043)

Each of these sampling and selection approaches meets the criteria identified by Fitzgerald (2007), namely that:

Documentary research allows for sufficient data to be collected for researchers to be able to:

- identify the significant features of a particular event, activities [sic] or case
- establish a plausible interpretation and explanation
- test for the credibility and validity of these interpretations
- construct an argument based on these interpretations
- relate the argument to policy trends, current practice or other relevant research
- create a convincing narrative for the reader
- provide an audit trail that offers other researchers opportunities to challenge the interpretation or construct alternative arguments. (p. 280)

In other words, as for other forms of social research, the sampling and selection approach adopted for documentary research should be both transparent and identify a sufficient quantity, range and variety of relevant sources to enable a convincing analysis to be carried out.

Issues to Consider when Researching Documents

Consideration of the authenticity of a document concerns its genuineness: whether it is actually what it purports to be. It may be thought that this is a relatively marginal consideration which arises only in extreme cases, but it constitutes a persistent and routine question in documentary research. (Scott 1990, p. 19)

Having accessed and selected the documents you wish to analyse, there are then a series of related issues which you need to bear in mind as you analyse them. Box 3.3 offers three perspectives on this from other authors.

================ BOX 3.3 ================

Issues to Consider when Researching Documents

Scott's Four Criteria

The four criteria of authenticity, credibility, representativeness and meaning should not be regarded as distinct stages in assessing the quality of documentary sources ... they are interdependent ... quality appraisal is a never-ending process. (Scott 1990, p. 35)

McCulloch and Richardson's Seven Issues

In developing a full understanding of the nature and potential use of published primary sources, it is important to clarify the following key issues:

1. Issues relating to the *text*...
2. Issues relating to the *author*...
3. Issues relating to the *context*...
4. Issues relating to the *audience* of the work...
5. Issues relating to the *influence* of the work...
6. The *processes* involved in its production...
7. The *interests* that underlay its development and the interactions that it involved between different groups and individuals. (McCulloch and Richardson 2000, pp. 91–92)

Fitzgerald's Eight Questions

Documentary research requires researchers to undertake a systematic interrogation and evaluation of the evidence ... This will involve asking a number of questions about the evidence, such as:

1. Who wrote the document? What is known about the personal and professional biography of the author?
2. When was the document written? What other events were occurring at that time?
3. What prompted the writing of this document? Were there social, political, economic or historical reasons that may have influenced the writer and the contents?
4. What audience was this written for? Does this document set a particular agenda?
5. What are the contents, the language and terms used and the key message(s)? What is the ideological position of the author?
6. What are the omissions? Was this deliberate? How do you know?
7. Are there any sources that can be used as a comparison?
8. Is this document reliable? (Fitzgerald 2007, p. 287)

The three perspectives are of different levels of complexity and take somewhat different foci. The oldest, Scott's, offers just four criteria; of authenticity, credibility, representativeness and meaning. McCulloch and Richardson proffer seven issues; relating to the text, author, content, audience, influence, production and underlying interests of the document. Fitzgerald poses eight questions, concerning the author, date, reason, audience, message, omissions, alternative sources and reliability of the document.

Clearly, there are both similarities and differences between the issues identified by these authors. Thus, both McCulloch and Richardson and Fitzgerald identify author and audience as key issues. Fitzgerald's identification of reliability could be seen as analogous to Scott's credibility; and the former's message and alternative sources could similarly be viewed as similar to the latter's meaning and representativeness. The relations between the other criteria, issues and questions identified are less clear, in part because the latter two perspectives are more detailed than Scott's, in part because their focus is different.

Other authors have brought up additional issues. Thus, Platt (1981a) offers the following:

> For the purposes of this discussion, which concentrates on questions of evidence and proof, the issues arising are defined as being: (i) how to establish the authenticity of a document; (ii) whether the relevant documents are available; (iii) problems of sampling; (iv) how to establish the extent to which a document can be taken to tell the truth about what it describes; (v) how to decide what inferences can be made from a document about matters other than the truth of its factual assertions. (p. 33)

Platt, like Scott, identifies authenticity as a key issue, but then brings in the issues of truth and inference. Truth could, of course, be seen as an alternative, blunter expression, more or less equivalent to credibility or reliability.

In a parallel article, Platt (1981b, p. 53) goes on to note that there are 'problems to do with the interpretation and presentation of documentary material, with special reference to questions of justification and proof'. For Platt, therefore, documentary researchers should operate in a quasi-legalistic fashion, interrogating their documents as witnesses for what they have to say about the particular topic or issue in question.

May (2001, p. 176) brings in a less hard-edged perspective in arguing that: 'Documents, read as the sedimentations of social practices, have the potential to inform and structure the decisions which people make on a daily and longer-term basis; they also constitute particular readings of social events'. The notion of a document as a 'reading' (as well as something to be read) seems to me to be a particularly powerful observation, offering a much more nuanced approach than seeking to establish its truth or otherwise. After all, in the social world that social scientists research, there are few, if any, absolutes; all may be viewed as a matter of interpretation, so what counts is how convincing given interpretations are.

May's notion of documents as 'sedimentations of social practices' adds to this, suggesting that the expression or meaning of a document builds up slowly over time, with additional nuances or forms of words added periodically. So, each document's 'reading' is a historical interpretation as much as a contemporary representation.

Abbott, Shaw and Elston (2004) provide a similar perspective, in their case drawn from the study of policy documents relating to the British National Health Service (NHS), but more broadly applicable as well:

> analysis may focus on one or more of three layers of meanings: those which are overt and explicit in the document; those which reflect the rhetoric of the policy environment and the government's intentions; and, those which reflect the ideology, usually implicit, underpinning policies at local and/or national level. (p. 259)

In other words, documents may be 'read', to use the more usual meaning of this word, and assessed at a number of different levels.

Finally, Prior (2003) adds a further slant in arguing that 'a study of the use of documents can be as telling as a study of content' (p. 14). This links clearly to McCulloch and Richardson's (2000) notion of the influence of a document. While it may seem particularly pertinent to research into policy documents (the subject of Chapter 10), such as those on which Abbott et al. (2004) focused – following the expression of policy through to its interpretation and application – it is also relevant to other kinds of document. For example, in the case of academic documents, their citation rates, and who has cited them in which contexts, may be of particular relevance.

Clearly, then, there are a whole range of interrelated issues to bear in mind when researching documents. To re-emphasise, they cannot simply be taken at face value. As well as gathering as much information as possible about the context for their production and usage – which the perspectives provided by McCulloch and Richardson (2000) and Fitzgerald (2007) chiefly focus upon – the researcher needs to carefully assess the credibility or reliability of each document. The interpretation of any document relies upon this and how it is read.

One obvious strategy to adopt, therefore – which is implied by the sources included in Box 3.3 – is to take a comparative approach, and not to examine any one document in isolation (even if that document is the focus of the research). Comparing similar documents – similar in that they were produced around the same time and place, by the same authors, or in that they focused on the same topic – should allow the reader to build up a clear picture of their relative strengths and weaknesses. It should certainly also address the issues of omissions and alternative sources identified by Fitzgerald (2007).

How to Read Documents

As has already been indicated, documentary research on almost any topic is likely to involve, at least potentially, the analysis of a large number of documents. This number can be limited – by placing restrictions on date of publication, language, country of origin, etc., and by only then analysing a sample of the documents identified – but is still likely to be considerable. After all, as a researcher, you will need and want to be able to argue that you have examined an adequate number of sources if your literature review, policy analysis, historical research or whatever is to be regarded as convincing.

This then raises practical and academic issues. How do you handle the documents you have for analysis in the limited time you have available? How can you read them with a reasonable amount of speed and efficiency, but without missing key points? And how do you ensure that your reading is sufficiently critical, as criticality is a key issue in research?

As with most things, practice, of course, helps a good deal. As you read more documents, your reading should become quicker. You will get more familiar with the ways in which the documents you are researching are organised, and should be able to get to the key points or aspects you are focusing on more efficiently. You will have read the different arguments made, and the references used, in other documents before. And, if you are focusing on particular authors, you will become increasingly familiar with the development of their argument over time.

Thankfully, there is also a lot of practical guidance available on reading techniques, though a lot of this is targeted at those revising their learning in preparation for examination. For example, the SQ3R reading method, 'a structured approach to reading that can be very helpful for learning or revision' (Hay et al. 2002, p. 29), suggests that you should read in five stages: survey, question, read, recall and review. While the last two of these betray the technique's orientation towards revision, the first three stages are of more generic use.

Start your reading by scanning the document, giving yourself a general overview of what it is and what it contains. In doing this, make use of the helpful features that many documents possess, such as abstracts, summaries, lists of contents, subtitles, signposting (i.e. short statements of what is coming next and why), conclusions and indexes. Be clear about what you want to get from the document, and what you are looking for in it. Don't, however, ignore the unexpected, which might significantly, but fruitfully, alter your research direction. Then scan through the text to find those aspects, details or answers of most relevance.

You will almost certainly not have the time to literally read the whole document – line by line, page by page, from start to finish – if you have a significant number of documents to study, so you will need to focus on what is important to you. You can always return to the document, repeatedly if need be, for further analysis if this later seems necessary (so keeping a copy of the document, if possible, or a record of it (see next section) is important, for this and other reasons).

If you deliberately approach documents in this kind of way, you should be able to analyse and get what you want from them with increasing efficiency. You might also find it helpful to set yourself deadlines or target times for dealing with specific documents or documents of a particular kind and length, but don't be too ruthless about this.

Criticality is also something that should become easier – indeed second nature, particularly if your research is academic– with practice. As Peelo (1994) notes, 'being critical is learning to assess the logic and rationale of arguments and the quality of the substantiating data … it is being able to ask how important the flaws are, and so to weigh the worth of evidence' (p. 59). Thomson (1996) offers a fuller account:

Critical reasoning is centrally concerned with giving reasons for one's beliefs and actions, analysing and evaluating one's own and other people's reasoning, devising and constructing better reasoning. Common to these activities are certain distinct skills, for example, recognising reasons and conclusions, recognising unstated assumptions, drawing conclusions, appraising evidence and evaluating statements, judging whether conclusions are warranted; and underlying all of these skills is the ability to use language with clarity and discrimination. (p. 2)

Criticality, therefore, involves questioning everything about a document, and then coming to your own assessment of its message and worth.

Qualitative and quantitative analysis software can also be helpful in reading documents, particularly if you are planning an in-depth analysis of a particular document or documents. The usage of such software is discussed further in Chapter 11.

Keeping Records

The importance of keeping records – of the documents you read and analyse, and of your opinions of them – cannot be stressed too highly, though it is easy to overlook if you just want to get on with your research. If you don't keep good records right from the start of your research, however, it is bound to knock you back and irritate you later, when it will take you more time to recover the details.

There are three kinds of records you need to keep, which are closely linked. First, you need to record the details of each document you study, so that you can reference it properly, and you (and others who are reading your work) will be able to access it again easily. If the document has been published, these details will include, if it is a book or report, the authors, title, date of publication, publisher and place of publication. If it is an article, they will include the authors, title, date of publication, journal title, volume, issue and page numbers. If the publication is online only, details of its online address need to be recorded, along with the date you accessed it.

If the document has not been published – perhaps because it is a personal document or an internal document produced within an organisation – you can keep a similar record. This also applies if the document is not a written text; the overriding need is to be able to give sufficient details of the document's source and authorship to enable others to identify it.

Bear in mind that different publication outlets (journals, book publishers) and disciplines will have different expectations regarding how these details are to be recorded in any outputs from your research; but, so long as you have recorded all of the relevant details, you will be able to provide these when the time comes.

Second, you need to keep a record of the contents of interest in each document. This may include a summary of the contents, verbatim extracts from it (remember to be clear about this, so as to avoid plagiarism issues, and to note the pages where the extracts come from), and the details of other documents referred to which may be of interest. Where possible, it will usually be simplest and most convenient to keep a copy of the actual document; a photocopy in your filing cabinet would have been the former technology, though now it is more likely to be a pdf file on your computer. If you have a copy, you will then be able to mark and annotate it as you wish.

Where it is not possible to have a copy of the document – if it is restricted to an archive, for example – you will need to make extensive notes. You may not realise the significance of something in the document on your first examination, and it may be difficult, time-consuming and expensive to return for a second reading.

Third, you need to record your own opinions of the document. If you have a copy, these can, of course, be written on the document itself; if not, they can be added to your notes. You may return to and update these on a number of occasions as your reading progresses, deepens and widens.

Lastly – and again obviously, but also, surprisingly, often overlooked – you need to keep your records safely. If they are on a computer, be sure to keep another copy on at least one separate data-storage device, and to back this up at least daily.

Conclusion

This chapter has offered lots of practical guidance on how to find and read documents. Assuming that you have some interest in the documents you are researching – otherwise, why would you be researching them? – the processes involved in accessing and reading them should be, at least partly, a pleasure. It should be evident from reading this chapter, however, that there is also an element of regularity, repetitiveness, perhaps even tedium, involved. It is crucial, therefore, that you approach documentary research – as you would any other kind of research – in a careful and disciplined fashion.

KEY READINGS

Fitzgerald, T (2007) Documents and Documentary Analysis: Reading between the lines. pp. 278–294 in Briggs, A, and Coleman, M (eds) *Research Methods in Educational Leadership and Management*. London, Sage, second edition.

A very readable introduction to many of the key issues.

May, T (2001) *Social Research: Issues, methods and process*. Buckingham, Open University Press, third edition.

Contains a very useful chapter on 'Documentary research: excavations and evidence'.

Sixsmith, J, and Murray, C (2001) Ethical Issues in the Documentary Data Analysis of Internet Posts and Archives. *Qualitative Health Research*, 11, 13, pp. 423–432.

An early discussion of the ethical issues involved in researching online materials.

4

DOCUMENTARY RESEARCH IN THE DISCIPLINES

CONTENTS

Introduction	38
Documentary Research in the Social Sciences	38
Documentary Research outside the Social Sciences	55
Conclusion	56

Introduction

Documentary research is used – to a greater or lesser extent – in all academic disciplines. While this may consist solely of a brief reference to some of the relevant academic or policy literature, it remains key to positioning the research undertaken. All research also produces documents – in the form of academic papers, books, reports, etc. – which may then themselves be the subject of further research (e.g. in bibliographic studies). Some disciplines have a particular focus on particular kinds of document: notably, history on archival and historical documents (see Chapter 9) and politics on policy documents (see Chapter 10).

This chapter will show how the usage of documents and the practice of documentary research varies from discipline to discipline. The main part of the chapter will focus on the use of documentary research methods in the social sciences (both generically and discipline by discipline), as this is the subject of this book. A shorter section will then review the usage of documentary research outside the social sciences, particularly in history and health care/medicine. Plentiful examples of recent published research will be referred to as illustrations.

Disciplines are not, of course, static entities, nor are they rigid and impervious. They are, rather, loose and overlapping collections of sub-disciplines and interests, which change and develop with time. The discussion in this chapter is necessarily organised, however, using a rather conventional categorisation of disciplines. Thus, the social sciences are seen as including disciplines such as economics, politics and sociology, as well as more vocational fields such as business, education and social work. Outside of the social sciences are the broad groupings of the arts and humanities, the sciences, engineering/technology and medicine/health.

The identity and location of all of these disciplines may be debated and challenged. For example, both geography and psychology may be viewed as sciences or social sciences, or perhaps both, but are here discussed under the social sciences.

Research may also be interdisciplinary, trans-disciplinary or multi-disciplinary in nature: that is, involve research expertise from more than one discipline or sub-discipline, and range across disciplinary borders. Some examples of documentary research of this kind will be discussed in the section which follows on the social sciences as a whole.

Documentary Research in the Social Sciences

The social sciences are a broad grouping of disciplines which share the characteristic of focusing on the social: that is, humans, their activities and behaviour. The discussion here will consider the 'conventional' disciplines of anthropology, economics, politics/political science and sociology, together with the 'vocational' disciplines of business/management, education, law, media studies and social work. Three other disciplines – geography, information science and psychology – which are sometimes viewed as social sciences and sometimes as sciences, or as combining elements of both, will also be discussed in this section.

Of course, not all research – or all researchers – can be neatly allocated to one or another discipline. Some research falls – and some researchers range – across the somewhat arbitrary and changing boundaries that we may identify, and is cross-disciplinary, inter-disciplinary or trans-disciplinary in nature. It may involve researchers trained in different disciplines working together, or may arise from a researcher exploring or moving outside of their usual territory. Or it may simply be that the research topic demands more than the conventional mono-disciplinary or sub-disciplinary approach.

A few examples will be discussed to illustrate these points, and also to indicate the way in which the discussion has been organised in the remainder of the chapter. It should be noted that, both here and throughout the chapter, while some of the examples concern research where documentary analysis has been the main or only approach used, in others (and these – naturally enough, given the universality of documentary research – greatly outnumber the former in practice) documentary analysis has been used in conjunction with, or in support of, other forms of research.

For example, the focus of Hudler and Richter (2002) is on the quality of life, an interest which could be said to impinge on all of the social sciences, as well as on many other disciplines beyond. Their particular interest is in comparing and assessing the quality of 'such cross-national and cross-sectional surveys as the World Values Survey, the International Social Survey Programme, the Eurobarometer and the New Democracies Barometer, as well as national longitudinal studies' (p. 217). These, then, are the documents they set out to analyse, with their article serving as an introduction to their project.

In a second example, Kosciejew's (2015) interest is in the documentation of apartheid in South Africa. As with Hudler and Richter's study, this might have been included within a range of disciplines, such as history, politics and sociology. Kosciejew makes an interesting distinction between document and information, arguing that:

> information is an important effect of documentation. It is in this way that documentation studies distinguishes between concepts of and practices with 'information' and 'document': that is, documentation studies helps illuminate how information is created, stabilized, and materialized such that it can emerge and, in turn, how it can then be controlled, deployed, enforced, entrenched, managed, and used in many different ways, in various settings, and for diverse purposes. Documentation, in other words, helps transform information into tangible entities that can be employed to shape, guide, and discipline its particular contextual setting. (pp. 96–97)

He then illustrates how, under the apartheid system, documentation impacted on all areas and aspects of life:

> Apartheid's documentation helped partition the country institutionally, politically, economically, spatially, and socially. These documents determined one's life trajectory: from their education to employment opportunities to political, economic, and social participation. These documents further managed daily life: from walking down a street to entering a building to using a bathroom. Even the pleasurable side of life, from enjoying a drink to shopping to having sexual intercourse,

was governed by these documents. Apartheid's documentation can best be presented as a taxonomy of four main categories: legal and political, personal, spatial, and social. (p. 102)

Lest this be thought to be rather an extreme example, we should note the general role of documents in proving residency, employment and social security rights in all societies.

A third and final example in this sub-section may, by comparison, seem much more banal. McKenzie and Davies (2010) analyse nine published wedding planning guides. They conclude:

> An analysis of wedding planning guides provides insight into the ways that wedding planners instruct novice brides to do document work and into the broader characteristics of planners as a genre. Insights in these areas can help to show how documentary planning tools give shape to and sustain the practices of larger communities of practice and broader organizational systems, and how the role of the novice bride is constituted within those communities and systems. (p. 802)

These three examples – focusing on the quality of life, apartheid and wedding planning – illustrate both the breadth of interests and topics accommodated within the social sciences, and the variety of documents and documentary analyses. The subject of the research may be very specific (wedding planning guides) or much more general (quality of life). It may involve the analysis of official, and now historical, documents (apartheid), or popular guides. The materials analysed may be national or international in orientation.

Anthropology

Anthropology is concerned with the study of humans, and human groups, both in the past and at the present time, and is particularly associated with the use of the ethnographic method (where the researcher embeds themselves into and lives with the group of interest for a period of time). Anthropologists use and research documents in a variety of ways, both conventionally and in increasingly novel formats (Kluckhorn 1945).

Anthropologists with an interest in past human behaviour, like historians, are particularly reliant on documents in their research. For example, Vieira and Brito (2017), in their examination of the historical exploitation of the manatee (a large sea mammal) in Brazil, revealed the varied range of documentary sources that they were able to draw upon:

> We have collected information from documentary sources that referred to manatees. These derived mainly from the early modern era, and included travel books, letters from Portuguese and Spanish missionaries and explorers, chronicles, scientific treatises, illustrated broadsheets, leaflets and images in naturalists' records, sailors' reports, folklore sources, poetry and literature. (p. 513)

Similarly, Berdan (2009), reviewing developments in the use of different kinds of documents and analyses for researching Mesoamerican ethnohistory, notes the increased availability of high quality reproductions of pictorial codices and translations of native-language texts. Added to these, a new genre of documentation was being increasingly exploited:

> This genre initially embraced Nahuatl [a native Mexican language] documents written in Roman script and then expanded to similar Mixtec and Mayan sources. These were for the most part civil and notarial records documenting daily life matters in colonial times – wills, litigations, taxes and tribute, censuses, town council minutes, even personal letters. (p. 212)

More contemporaneously, Lopes-Fernandes et al. (2016) were interested in the place of wolves in Portuguese literature: 'From a literary corpus compilation, 262 excerpts from 68 works that made reference to wolves were classified by grid analysis into 12 categories, encompassing the diversity of meanings attributed to these animals' (p. 5). Lew-Levy et al. (2017) provide a meta-ethnography (meta-analysis) of 58 publications focusing on how hunter-gatherer children learn subsistence skills.

Other anthropologists make use of documents alongside other forms of data and analysis. For example, Harkin (2010) discusses ethnohistory, which he describes as part of a rapprochement between history and anthropology. Ethnohistory, which uses a combination of ethnography and documentary material, 'arose out of the study of American Indian communities in the era of the Indian Claims Commission', and came into its own in the 1980s (p. 113). In a similar way, though she does not call it ethnohistory, Wellfelt (2009) reports on an analysis of collected material culture, unpublished field notes and photographs relating to Alor (an island in Indonesia) produced by an earlier anthropologist, which she has supplemented with information from contemporary informants.

The uses, indeed identification, of documents by anthropologists may be more innovative in nature. Thus, Enfield (2006) considers, in the particular context of Laos – a country renowned for its linguistic diversity – the role of languages as historical documents or archives. In a highly contemporary study, Cabot (2012) focuses on the 'pink card', the identity document issued to asylum seekers in Greece, and how state functionaries and asylum seekers engage with it. In other words, the document itself is the focus of the documentary analysis (c.f. the earlier discussion of documents in apartheid South Africa). He concludes: 'Through the material lives of this particular document, I have highlighted the complex series of movements through which governance unfolds and how diverse actors and objects reinforce, undermine, and reconfigure regulatory power' (p. 23).

Also focusing on the document as central to the analysis, Carta (2015) assesses documentary films as a source of data on Sardinia (i.e. the documentary film is treated as a document). He concludes that 'observational documentary and ethnographic films made in the last three decades express anthropologically thick descriptions, and that these descriptions represent a postmodern form of social documentation that achieves an accurate description of the world' (p. 227).

Collins et al. (2013) were interested in what they term public anthropology, where the focus is on social activism and collaboration. Their use of multimedia documents, produced and distributed through social media, also leads them to call their work networked anthropology, noting that: 'Networked anthropology ... works with an idea of a self-consciously created "public" that is an ongoing process of engagement rather than a closed set of practices, something that we strive to not just consciously create, but one that shapes our work' (p. 367).

Lemov (2009) reflects on a large-scale and long-term anthropological project, which collected a huge diversity of materials over the period from 1947 to 1961 in Micronesia, involving what she describes as an attempt to assemble 'a database of dreams'; in other words, the varieties of human subjectivity that were observable on the small islands that exist in this vast stretch of the Pacific Ocean.

Clearly, anthropology, like most disciplines, is a 'broad church', and its adherents make use of a huge diversity of documents and forms of documentary analysis in both conventional and highly creative ways, on their own or combined with other methods.

Business/Management

The field of business and management, with its focus on organisations, their operations and entrepreneurial activity, might seem, at first sight, to be much more practically orientated and very different from anthropology. While there is much to be said for this point of view, the field also employs documentary analysis in very varied ways.

The most common data collection and analysis strategy, however – as is the case in other disciplines – is to combine documents with another method. Often, the other method employed is the interview. Thus, Barbic, Hidalgo and Cagliano (2016) investigated the dynamics of multi-partner research and development alliances using interviews and documents. Three rounds of interviews were carried out in a longitudinal case study, complemented by documentary analysis of both internal materials and publicly available data.

O'Brien (2010) used the same techniques to study the development of tourism policy in Ireland. Interviews with eight 'key players' in the industry were complemented by:

> very extensive documentary analysis, which incorporated all official and archival state documents relating to tourism development in Ireland since the foundation of the state, all organisational records that were available through libraries, databases or directly from organisation's archives, annual reports, policy reports and papers from both public and private sector tourism organisations and legislative documents. (p. 568)

In Van Bommel's (2014) examination of the use of integrated reporting in the Netherlands, the balance was rather different, with 64 interviews completed alongside the documentary analysis.

Other business/management researchers make a virtue of the diversity of the documents they have identified, consulted and analysed alongside their interview data. For example, Ciasullo and Troisi (2013), in their study of sustainability in small and medium-sized enterprises, used interviews, documentary analysis, internal process data and archival material, involving the 'perusal of company web site documents (content analysis) and printed documentary sources such as corporate socio-sustainability reports, brochures, educational and promotional materials' (p. 48). Similarly, Galan, Sanchez and Zuniga-Vicente (2005), researching the strategic and organisational evolution of large firms, use documentary sources (annual reports, company histories, business directories, etc.) and interviews.

Documentary analysis may, of course, be employed alongside methods other than the interview. Thus, Bishop (2008), in a study of small businesses in the training market, made use of 'non-participant workplace observation' in addition to interviews and documentary analysis (of training plans, operating procedures, marketing materials, etc.). Henjewele, Sun and Fewings (2012), researching the factors affecting value for money in UK PFI (private finance initiative) projects, collected data in two stages, with a documentary review of project reports and publications followed up by a questionnaire survey to client representatives of PFI projects.

In other examples of research into business and management, documentary analysis is used on its own. For example, Hart's (2010) examination of corporate social responsibility (CSR) is based on:

> a review of the relevant literature in both workplace equality and safety ... identifying any similarities or differences in themes and arguments emerging from both areas of interest ... Documentary analysis of government statistical information, union newsletters, and CSR media coverage generated further information. (p. 587)

Michelini and Fiorentino (2012) were concerned with the use of business models for creating shared value. They derive their data from ten existing case studies (taken from research reports, white papers, industry publications, etc), and collect documentary materials from 'both internal (e.g. presentations, reports, etc) and external (e.g. web sites, press releases, publications, etc)' (pp. 566–567) sources for analysis.

Finally, in a study of gendered entrepreneurial regimes, Smith (2013, p. 180) 'made a thorough, wide ranging search of the internet using keywords such as "Essex-Boy", "Essex-Girl" and "Essex-Man", selecting documents via convenience sampling because they were readily available'. This enabled him to identify a more limited set of documents – a memoire, a novel, a biography, an advertising report and several newspaper articles – for thorough analysis.

Economics

Economics is nowadays sometimes viewed as a branch of business/management studies, but has a long history as a separate discipline. Unlike most of the other social sciences – at least outside of the USA, where qualitative studies are less developed – it has a clear focus on quantitative methods for research and analysis. This does not, however, limit its use of documentary research, as many documents – both historical and contemporary – are either wholly quantitative in nature or include significant quantitative components.

An example of a wholly quantitative documentary study is that by Fernández-Kranz, Lacuesta and Rodríguez-Planas (2013). They studied Spanish social security records – specifically 'data from the 2006 wave of the Continuous Sample of Working Histories, which is a 4 percent nonstratified random sample of the population registered with the Social Security Administration in 2006' (p. 176) – to explore how motherhood affects earnings.

A second such example, going back rather further in time, is that by McDonald (2010). He used data from the Domesday Book – on 333 'lay' estates in Wiltshire in the UK in 1086 – to carry out a data envelopment analysis (a complex form of multivariate analysis) of agricultural efficiency at that time. A final example, taking a longitudinal approach, is that of Abdullah (2016). Using data on the price of wheat in Egypt from 696 to 1517, he develops an Islamic monetary theory of value and equation of exchange.

Clearly, in economics, the documents used for research purposes are chiefly data sets, of various kinds and in various forms.

Education

Education, like business/management, is a broad field of study that is also concerned with the development of teachers at all levels; hence, a focus on educational practice and its improvement is evident in most research.

A fair amount of educational research is wholly, or chiefly, concerned with documentary analysis (see McCulloch 2004, 2011; McCulloch and Richardson 2000). Some of these studies are literature reviews or bibliometric analyses (discussed further in Chapters 6 and 7). Thus, Macfarlane, Zhang and Pun (2014) present a literature review of research and writing on academic integrity, examining 115 articles from the western and Chinese literatures. Schwippert (2002) provides a bibliometric analysis of the output of a single journal, the *International Review of Education*, over the period 1955 to 2000. Pirrie (2001) critiques the rise of evidence-based practice in educational research through a consideration of a systematic review of interprofessional education. And Donet, Pallares and Burillo (2017) offer a bibliometric analysis of articles on key competences indexed in the ERIC database for the period 1990 to 2013.

Many documentary analyses in the education field examine aspects of policy (policy research in general is the focus of Chapter 10). For example, Prøitz (2015) analyses Norwegian budget documents over a 14-year period for what they say about learning outcomes policy, noting how politicians have embraced this concept but conceptualised it differently over time. Power and Gewirtz (2001) provide an analysis of policy documents and funding applications regarding educational action zones in England, criticising the policy for its inadequate conceptualisation of social justice.

Jones and Symeonidou (2017) present a comparative study, based on primary documentary sources (i.e. legislation, statutory and non-statutory guidance and reports), of

Bale (1999) considers the use of historical photographs of Africans as contributing to a 'visual' geography. He argues that 'The photographs ... can be read as the intersection of the double image of mimicry, presenting no "authentic" image of Africa, nor of colonialism, but a fragmentary glimpse of the interaction between the indigenous peoples and European observers' (p. 32).

Geographers may also, of course, carry out more conventional analyses of more conventional documents. Thus, Clark et al. (1997) carried out a discourse analysis of EU agricultural policy documents, over the period 1973–91, supplemented by interviews with senior EU officials, to track the evolution of agri-environmental policy. In a bibliometric study, Foster et al. (2007) analysed economic geography articles, published between 1982 and 2006, focusing on citation patterns and behaviour. They find some evidence that this sub-discipline is beginning to internationalise, and that it is having a great influence on other fields.

Finally, as an example of the use of documentary analysis in physical geography, Wheeler and Garcia-Herrera (2008) discuss the relevance of ships' logbooks for climatological research. They note that 'Although early theories concerning global air circulations by Halley and Hadley were based on information gathered by mariners and recorded in their logbooks, it has only been in the last two decades that interest has returned to this important, but long-overlooked, source of climatic information' (p. 1).

Information Science

Information science is a field that focuses on the use of information by humans, so may be considered to be a social science, though it may also be classified as a science. With this focus, the use and analysis of documents are central to the field.

Some of the studies using documentary research referred to under other sections in this chapter could also be said to be using an information science approach. Three studies will be discussed here to illustrate something of the range of strategies adopted.

Wallace and Stuchell (2011) examine the archive created by the National Commission on Terrorist Acts upon the United States (the 9/11 Commission), and some of the issues that it raises. They argue that 'the composition, accumulation, access to, and control of the archival record surrounding 9/11 was shaped as much by political concerns over blame and responsibility (and evading it) as it was by good faith efforts to get to the heart of the matter' (p. 125).

Less conventionally, Turner (2012a, 2012b) discusses 'oral documents' – that is, oral exchanges that have the characteristics of a document – exploring how they can be observed, identified and captured. Of course, once an oral exchange has been captured – for example, by recording and/or transcribing it – it assumes the form of a more conventional document (c.f. conversation analysis, discussed in Chapter 13).

Rowlands (1999) reports on a bibliometric study of patterns of communication in information policy, analysing a database of 771 articles published between 1972 and

1996. He concludes that 'the structure and dynamics of the information policy journal literature diverges in several respects from typical social science literatures. Information policy is characterised by very rapid growth, high immediacy, rapid reception and ageing processes and relatively low documentary scatter' (p. 59).

Law

Law as a field of practice is also closely concerned with documents – both as sources of evidence and records of judgments – but legal researchers rarely seem to conceive of themselves as documentary researchers. However, there are some examples where their research resembles practices in other social sciences.

Thus, Kort (1960), in an early study, employs quantitative content analysis (see Chapter 12) of published judicial opinions to identify where 'some combinations of a given set of circumstances require one decision, and other combinations require the opposite decision' (p. 11).

Houle (1994) reviews the work of the Documentation, Information and Research Branch of Canada's Immigration and Refugee Board (IRB), which was set up in 1988 to document conditions in refugee-producing countries. He concludes that 'Because it ensures an acceptable degree of impartiality of its research and the documents it produces, it may be a useful model for other tribunals adjudicating in fields where evidence is either difficult to gather, or is otherwise complex' (p. 7).

Carruthers and Halliday (2006) provide a third example. They use documentary analysis, along with interviews and observation, to examine the globalisation of bankruptcy law, with a particular focus on Asian insolvency regimes. They note that globalisation is negotiated locally, depending on the relative power of the actors involved, but that a 'global script' of bankruptcy law appears to be emerging.

Media Studies

Media studies, like information science, implies a close concern with a particular kind of document. Media are also, of course, often interrogated in research in other social science disciplines, as is illustrated in a number of the examples discussed in this chapter (e.g. Carta (2015) in anthropology; Gerstl-Pepin (2015) in education; Bale (1999) in geography; Hight and Coleborne (2006) in psychology; Rose and Flynn (2018) in social work; Herkenrath and Knoll (2011) in sociology).

Media analysts may focus on the role of media. Thus, Aaltonen and Kortti (2015) argue for the role of television and documentary films in understanding history:

> current audio-visual history presentations, with their reenactments and other means of producing history, have the potential to provide new ways in sensing and understanding history,

sometimes better than ordinary literary forms. Instead of disdaining history documentary films, academic historians should learn to read them along with visual history culture in general. Television documentaries have a significant role in history culture, and vice versa. (pp. 121–122)

Chu (2009) examined teachers' beliefs about the use of media in school in Hong Kong. She focused on their applications for funding to set up school television stations, carrying out an analysis of the associated documentation: 'these proposals and evaluation reports provide a rich set of data for uncovering the otherwise rarely articulated beliefs of teachers and schools towards the nature of media and school media' (p. 4).

Media researchers, like other social scientists, may also focus on particular examples. Devlin (2015, p. 167) notes that 'Previous research has shown that media representations of young people consistently portray them as in one way or another "problematic", but little such research has focused specifically on the medium of radio'. He presents:

a detailed case study of a radio documentary series broadcast in Ireland called *The Teenage Years*. It explores the editorial, rhetorical and narrative devices used to construct and sustain a mainstream clinical–psychological discourse of adolescence, one which effectively 'pathologizes' the teenage years. It also 'homogenizes' them, privileging age as an explanatory factor in shaping identity and development and thereby systematically ignoring other aspects of social inequality and stratification. (Devlin 2015, p. 167)

Greer and McLaughlin (2013) employ a 'qualitative thematic press analysis' (p. 247) to study the Jimmy Savile child sex abuse scandal, and Takeshita (2017) provides a counter-narrative analysis of the representation of childbirth in a documentary and a TV series.

All of the studies so far referred to have carried out documentary analyses of documents (i.e. media), but media studies may also involve other methods alongside documentary analysis. Ciaglia's (2016) focus was on public service broadcasting in South Africa. He carried out 'a content analysis of South African civil society organisations' online archives, a documentary analysis of South African media legislation, and three semi-structured interviews with South Africa's civil society representatives' (p. 95), concluding that 'under certain circumstances, the state and market can successfully coexist and fruitfully cooperate by emptying the public broadcaster of its true and distinctive value compared to other broadcasters: its publicness' (p. 95). Pidduck (2012) uses interviews, observations and documentary analysis to research the role of the Democratic Voice of Burma, a Burmese exile media organisation based in Oslo, in Burma's 2010 elections.

Political Science

Political science is concerned with the study of politics, and often linked to international studies or relations. Like many other social scientists, political researchers make use of documents in a variety of ways. Often, this is done in conjunction with other forms of research. For example, Leston-Bandeira (2016) studied parliamentary public engagement in the UK, using interviews with parliamentary officials and documentary analysis of reports produced by relevant parliamentary committees.

Many other analyses rely solely on documents. Where these are historical, the documents will often be found in archives (Frisch et al. 2012; see also Chapter 9). Thus, Balmer (2010) looks at UK chemical weapon policy in the 1960s, making use of recently declassified documents in the UK National Archives. Heavens (2016), to give a second example of this kind of research, also uses the UK National Archives, together with personal archives stored at the Scott Polar Research Institute, to examine the role of a significant individual, Brian Roberts, in the 1959 Antarctic Treaty.

Zhang and Du (2016) studied the Shanghai Municipal Council's (SMC's) opium policies, 1906–17, based on documentary analysis of its records. They found that:

> Over almost a decade, the SMC shifted emphasis from political regulation of a social, recreational practice to maximising financial benefit. In the process, SMC made full use of the opportunities it gained from a period of ambivalent Chinese and British power relations and local community rule. (p. 136)

Studies of more recent policy developments may make use of a greater variety of available documentation. Thus, Kaehne and Taylor (2016) were able to investigate a public consultation by way of an analysis of the submissions made, which were publicly available. They developed a coding matrix to analyse this data:

> The matrix allowed the raters to collect evidence on: Who participated in the consultation? What was the nature and content of the submissions? To operationalise these questions, a set of indicators were developed collecting evidence about the origin of submission (such as the type of organisation; Welsh or UK/England based), the size of individual submissions, the compliance/non-compliance of respondents with consultation brief. (p. 86)

Rassool (2010) offers a critique of South African political biography. He traces:

> The evolution of documentary approaches to South African resistance history, produced almost entirely by American and American-trained scholars ... The methods and concerns of this approach continue to form the basis of a great deal of research on South African political history. In this approach, the conception of politics and resistance has remained characterised by a focus on organised bodies, led by great men whose leadership has largely been taken as given. These histories of political organisations have been told through the lives, speeches and opinions of leaders. Political documents and the documentary collection, in the form of statements, speeches or minutes of meetings, viewed transparently as storehouses of facts of a story of resistance, have remained the essence of their methodology. (p. 29)

He argues for a move away from chronological narrative towards biographical contestation.

Focusing on the present day, and on contemporary technologies, Sullivan (2013) explores the use of electronic data to study elite political behaviour in Taiwan. He notes that:

> the primary resources and methods needed are already in place. A variety of political texts created by political actors at all levels of office (and indeed, in opposition) are readily accessible online. With a small degree of processing, these electronic texts can easily be rendered in machine-readable format for analysis by means of computer-assisted content analysis software. (p. 186)

Clearly, as in other disciplines and fields, the documents available to political scientists for analysis will continue to multiply, with an increasing bias towards online documentation.

Psychology

Psychology may be viewed as a science or a social science. While its emphasis on quantification and experimentation may identify it more as the former, a growing minority of psychological researchers make use of other techniques, including qualitative research and documentary analysis, and this is of long standing (e.g. Allport 1942). Some of this research is, as in other disciplines, quite innovative in methodological terms. Thus, Bridger (2014) used a 'situationist qualitative methodology' involving mobile methods and documentary strategies (diaries, cameras and maps) to explore urban environments.

As in other disciplines, documentary methods are often applied by psychologists alongside other data collection techniques, notably interviews of various kinds. For example, Milla, Faturochman and Ancok (2013) examined leader–follower interactions and radicalisation in the case of the Bali bombers:

> Data were obtained through interviews, observation and close readings of documents including previously unavailable primary sources such as personal letters, in addition to published materials written by or about the Bali bombers. Previously unanalyzed writings by Ali Ghufron including letters to his wife, brother and brother-in-law, three handwritten wills, the unpublished manuscript of a biography, two manuscripts of public statements, and the manuscript of a book entitled *Wisdom from Dreams* are especially significant. We also rely on video and audio recordings of interviews with authorities and of sermons Imron and others delivered while in custody. (pp. 92–93)

Haas and Levasseur (2013) studied the issues of collective forgetfulness and rumour, in the specific context of flooding in Abbeville in France, using a combination of initial documentary research followed up by focus group interviews:

> Our study was based on a qualitative design and conducted in a diachronic manner. Initial research focused on documents concerning one of the two main themes of the rumour: the history of floods or more precisely the question of the 'memory of water' as the link between the inhabitants and the river. This first stage allowed us to identify the 'objective' facts of the town's history: Abbeville was a coastal town and for centuries had made its name from water, which constituted its main economic and social activity. The documents also inform us that the town had long suffered from terrible floods. (p. 65)

This research might equally well have been labelled as geography or sociology, but is included here as psychology because of the disciplinary allegiance of the authors/researchers.

Psychologists have also focused on audio-visual documents for the light they shed on issues of concern to them. Hight and Coleborne (2006) argued that 'the praxis and research of health psychology might benefit from strategic and interdisciplinary readings of media texts ... insights from current documentary theory are important because they show us how documentary texts are structured and how medical documentary deploys techniques from medicine itself in order to effect certain persuasive discursive shifts in our wider culture' (p. 233). They demonstrate this through an analysis of the BBC documentary series *Superhuman*.

Social Work

Social work researchers, like educational researchers, are strongly focused on using research to improve practice. They also have a multitude of documents available and suitable for analysis, and a varying interest in the methodologies that they might use to analyse them.

For example, Gilbert et al. (2013) employ qualitative content analysis (see also Chapter 13) in examining documents from 25 English local authorities to explore elder financial abuse:

> In total, 21 sets of adult safeguarding/adult protection policy, procedural and practice guidance documents, each comprising multiple parts, from 13 London Boroughs and documentation from three Home Counties were reviewed for explicit reference to elder financial abuse. (pp. 156–157)

Reyneke (2017) also reports on a content analysis, but in this case of the texts produced by 89 social work students who had taken part in an adventure-based experiential activity as part of their diversity training at a South African university.

Other social work researchers simply identify their approach as documentary analysis in a generic sense. Thus, Morrison, Bickerstaff and Taylor (2009) examined data on 252 referrals to a learning disability social work team over a ten-year period. This involved handling a considerable amount of data:

Three documentary sources were used in the study: (i) hard-bound referral books gave a complete record of all referrals including date of birth, age, gender, ethnic origin, date of referral and referral source; (ii) case numbers and reasons for closures were taken from the electronic client database SOSCARE which is used in most Health and Social Care Trusts in Northern Ireland; and (iii) social work files provided all other data, largely taken from eligibility assessment details, referral letters and first assessment forms. (p. 169)

Waldschmidt (2009) provides a review of European disability policy documentation over the period 1958–2005. He finds that: 'from the late 1970s up to the middle of the 1990s EU disability policy has centred around labour market integration. During the last decade, however, the equal rights approach has got more and more dominant' (p. 8).

Smith (2010) takes a careful and critical approach to the analysis of documents, considering how documentary sources construct and reify a particular version of the past. Reviewing recent reports on historical abuse in children's homes, he argues that:

Victim accounts demand the same methodological scepticism as any other form of knowledge. A genuinely 'thick' and rigorous account of what residential child care was like requires that other voices, those of other children raised in care and of staff who worked in such settings be afforded the same status as those of the 'victim'. It also demands that these accounts are subject to rigorous hermeneutic and reflexive interrogation and interpretation by those with a grounded understanding of practice in this area. The interests of genuine victims of abuse, of those encouraged, for whatever reason, to believe they were abused and of residential workers accused of abuse are not well served by a situation where ideology and preconception too often supplant rigorous inquiry. (p. 317)

This example usefully re-emphasises the importance of not treating documents, whether written or otherwise, as 'facts' (see also Chapter 3), perhaps because of mistaken assumptions regarding the truthfulness of their authors.

Taking a more innovative approach, Rose and Flynn (2018) focus on the use of documents in disseminating social work research findings, taking as an example the work of a non-profit organisation in Australia that works with children who have parents in prison:

Transcripts of social work interviews with the children were modified into screenplays to be animated by communication design students. The animated documentary has advantages over the expository documentary mode, including protecting the identity of the subject and creating an affective video that constitutes a dual-process model of entertainment providing for a more socially connected pleasure. (p. 25)

The resulting videos – a different and more accessible and affecting form of document than a transcript – could be used in a number of ways.

Sociology

Sociology, with its focus on the social, might be argued to be central to the social sciences. This is evident in its widespread and varied use of different forms of documentary analysis in research, which is also of long standing (e.g. Angell 1945).

Many sociology researchers – in one sense all of them, as research articles are expected to include at least a brief literature review – combine documentary analysis with other methodologies. An interesting example is provided by Hubbard and Colosi (2015), who studied attitudes towards lap dancing clubs using a mixture of documentary analysis, surveys and interviews:

> In the first instance, we completed a discourse analysis of the formal objections made to the SEVs [sexual entertainment venues] licensed in each location up to 1 April 2012 (i.e. in the first year that licences could be applied for). These objections were often few in number – and several clubs were not objected to at all – but the fact they had been solicited through well-advertised processes allowing interested parties to express opinions about the appropriateness of specific venues meant they were revealing of concerns that might have been more widely shared. (p. 785)

As in other disciplines, some researchers have focused on particular documentary sources or approaches. For example, Herkenrath and Knoll (2011) examine how the coverage of protest events varies between the national and international press. They find some interesting patterns of bias:

> Using the example of some 1800 protest events in Argentina, Mexico and Paraguay in the year 2006, the present study shows that there are remarkable differences between national and international (English-language) newspapers when it comes to frequency of reporting. On the one hand, a mere 5.3 percent of all protest events that are reported nationally also attract the attention of the international press. On the other hand, the percentage of international reporting depends considerably and to a statistically significant extent on the country in which the protest takes place. (p. 163)

Savage (2008) uses Mass Observation data (see Harrisson and Madge 1939/1986) to study post-war class identity in Britain, comparing responses from 1948 and 1990. He finds that:

> there were significant changes in the way that class was narrated in these two periods. There is not simple decline [sic] of class identities, but rather a subtle reworking of the means by which class is articulated. In the earlier period Mass Observers are ambivalent about class in ways which indicate the power of class as a form of ascriptive inscription. By 1990, Mass-Observers do not see class identities as the ascribed product of their birth and upbringing, but rather they elaborate a reflexive and individualised account of their mobility between class positions in ways which emphasise the continued importance of class identities. (p. 46)

He concludes by highlighting 'the value of the re-use of qualitative data as a means of examining patterns and processes of historical change' (p. 46).

Payne, Williams and Chamberlain (2004) provide a bibliometric analysis of the output of four 'mainstream' British sociology journals, focusing on methodological preferences. They conclude (somewhat in contrast to Savage) that more attention needs to be given to the application and development of quantitative methods.

Other sociologists have contributed to the further development of documentary research methods. Thus, Crawshaw and Fowler (2008) offer a methodology for the incorporation of creative fiction into mobilities research. Hirschauer (2006), focusing on the silent dimension of the social, considers ethnographic description as a documentary process. Guggenheim's (2015) interest is in visual sociology, and he argues for different ways to think about and analyse media. Sim's (2015) focus is on feminists researching the everyday, and the use of documentary photography to assist in doing so.

In sociology, as in the social sciences more generally, considerable creativity and innovativeness has been demonstrated by researchers using documentary methods.

Documentary Research Outside the Social Sciences

Documentary research is, of course, widely used outside the social sciences as well as within them. While the focus of this book is on the social sciences, it makes sense to be aware of these broader uses. Two broad areas in which documentary research is particularly prevalent outside the social sciences are health care and history, both of which, of course, have social concerns and strong links to the social sciences.

Within health care, the areas in which the use of documentary methods has been explored include complementary and alternative medicine (e.g. Dew 2005, 2006), nursing (e.g. Benton et al. 2015, Hargreaves 2008, Momeni, Jirwe and Emami 2008, Spitzer and Perrenoud 2007, Sweeney 2005), psychiatry (Hak 1998) and public health (e.g. Bernitz 2008). The documents analysed have included environmental impact statements for proposed transport infrastructure (Riley et al. 2018), grant proposals (Drabble et al. 2014), the portrayal of medicine on television (e.g. Johnson and Johnson 1993), a national archive of patient experience narratives (Locock et al. 2014), the reports produced by 'global health actors' (Robert and Ridde 2013) and national policy statements (e.g. Shaw, Elston and Abbott 2004, Thomas and Gilson 2004). The particular techniques employed have included the use of patient diaries (e.g. Milligan, Bingley and Gattrell 2005), systematic reviews of the literature (Mpinga et al. 2011), and the creation of 'life trajectories' (Robert, Séguin and O'Connor 2010).

Within the broad field or discipline of history, social history may be considered as being a social science, or at least as overlapping the humanities and social sciences. Much documentary research has, of course, been based on archives of various kinds and specialists (e.g. Gottschalk 1945, Kamberi 1999, Kynaston 2008, Lekgoathi 2009,

McCullough 2008, Sanders and Woodward 2014, Simien and McGuire 2014; Chapter 9 discusses archival and historical research as applied to the social sciences).

Historical researchers have discussed the use and value of different types of document, including diaries (e.g. McKay 2005), letters (Neufeld 2011), maps (e.g. Laxton 1999), museum artefacts (Smiraglia 2005) and printed questionnaires (Fox 2010; in this case dating back to the seventeenth and eighteenth centuries). The particular techniques employed have been as diverse as ethnomethodology (Whittle and Wilson 2015), mapping (Winder 2010) and multi-level modelling (Clubine-Ito 2004), and the topics researched have been as varied as Norwegian witchcraft trials (Knutsen 2003), the heights of transported convicts (Nicholas and Steckel 1991) and the admission of women to guilds (Smith 2005).

Documentary research is employed, as we have repeatedly emphasised, to a greater or lesser extent in all disciplines and fields. It is applied in areas as diverse as, for example, nanotechnology (e.g. Boholm 2014), linguistics (e.g. Bakari, Bellot and Neji 2017), biodiversity (e.g. Cevasco, Moreno and Hearn 2015), philosophy (e.g. Hengstermann 2017) and physics (e.g. Kiselev 2008). It is arguably one of the most extensively used research methods; indeed, perhaps the most extensively used.

Conclusion

This exploration of documentary research in the disciplines – both in the social sciences and beyond – confirms this form of research as being both ubiquitous and highly diverse. While most researchers making use of documentary forms of research do so in fairly standard ways (e.g. employing content analysis and related strategies; see also Chapters 12 and 13), others display considerable creativity, both in terms of the documents they research and how they choose to analyse them.

KEY READINGS

Listed here are a range of readings which display something of the breadth and variety of documentary research across the social sciences:

Aaltonen, J, and Kortti, J (2015) From Evidence to Re-enactment: History, television and documentary film. *Journal of Media Practice*, 16, 2, pp. 108–125.
Bale, J (1999) Foreign Bodies: Representing the African and the European in an early twentieth century 'contact zone'. *Geography*, 84, 1, pp. 25–33.
Barbic, F, Hidalgo, A, and Cagliano, R (2016) Governance Dynamics in Multi-Partner R&D Alliances. *Baltic Journal of Management*, 11, 4, pp. 405–429.
Bridger, A (2014) Visualizing Manchester: Exploring new ways to study urban environments with reference to situationist theory, the dérive and qualitative research. *Qualitative Research in Psychology*, 11, 1, pp. 78–97.

Ciaglia, A (2016) Democratising Public Service Broadcasting: the South African Broadcasting Corporation – between politicization and commercialization. *African Journalism Studies*, 37, 2, pp. 95–115.

Enfield, N (2006) Languages as Historical Documents: The endangered archive in Laos. *South East Asia Research*, 14, 3, pp. 471–488.

Hordosy, R (2014) Who Knows What School Leavers and Graduates are Doing? Comparing information systems within Europe. *Comparative Education*, 50, 4, pp. 448–473.

Kosciejew, M (2015) Disciplinary Documentation in Apartheid South Africa: A conceptual framework of documents, associated practices and their effects. *Journal of Documentation*, 71, 1, pp. 96–115.

Savage, M (2008) Changing Social Class Identities in Post-war Britain: Perspectives from mass-observation. *Historical Social Research*, 33, 3, pp. 46–67.

Sullivan, J (2013) Electronic Resources in the Study of Elite Political Behaviour in Taiwan. *The China Quarterly*, 213, pp. 172–188.

Wallace, D, and Stuchell, L (2011) Understanding the 9/11 Commission Archive: Control, access and the politics of manipulation. *Archival Science*, 11, pp. 125–168.

PART 2

GENRES OF DOCUMENTARY RESEARCH

Part 2 contains six chapters, which identify and focus on five key documentary research designs or genres.

Chapter 5 discusses the range of different documentary research designs, how they relate to and can be combined with other research designs, and their relation to qualitative and quantitative approaches to research. Five key documentary research designs or genres – literature reviews; systematic reviews and meta-analyses; secondary data analysis; archival and historical research; and policy research – are identified, which form the foci for the next five chapters.

Chapter 6 considers what is involved in carrying out literature reviews – their nature, functions and types – with illustrative examples.

Chapter 7 examines systematic reviews and meta-analyses, noting their differences and their relation to literature reviews, with illustrative examples.

Chapter 8 focuses on secondary data analysis, its advantages and disadvantages, and discusses where to get secondary data, with illustrative examples.

Chapter 9 examines archival and historical research, reviewing the types and sources of data used, with illustrative examples.

Chapter 10 focuses on policy research, considering the relations between policy and research, and types of policy research, with illustrative examples.

5
DESIGNING DOCUMENTARY RESEARCH

CONTENTS

Introduction	62
Documentary Research Designs	62
Documentary Research and other Research Designs	66
Documentary Research in Combination with Other Research Designs	68
Conclusion	71

Introduction

This chapter identifies and discusses the main kinds of documentary research that are practised in the social sciences and beyond. It identifies five main genres or designs of documentary research – literature reviews, systematic reviews and meta-analyses, secondary data analysis, archival and historical research, and policy research – which are then explored in detail in the following five chapters (Chapters 6 to 10 respectively).

The relations between documentary research and other research designs – surveys, interviews and observation; quantitative, qualitative and mixed methods – are then considered. The use of documentary research in combination with other research designs is discussed, with illustrative examples, before some conclusions are drawn.

Documentary Research Designs

There are, of course, various ways in which different types of documentary research may be identified and characterised. Somewhat confusingly, but probably inevitably, different authorities also sometimes use different terms for what are essentially the same things, so some care and clarity are needed.

This book identifies five main types of documentary research or genres: literature reviews, systematic reviews and meta-analyses, secondary data analysis, archival and historical research, and policy research. In this section, these five genres will be introduced and explained; they will then each be discussed in more detail in Chapters 6 to 10.

It has to be acknowledged immediately that these five genres overlap significantly with each other. Thus, both systematic reviews and meta-analyses can be thought of as alternative forms of literature review, but they are sufficiently distinct to merit separate treatment. More fundamentally, secondary data research can be viewed as being virtually synonymous with documentary research. However, each of these genres has its own literature (or sub-literature), advocates and practitioners, so it makes sense to consider them in turn while noting their close relationships.

Literature Reviews

Literature reviews are a form of documentary research where the focus is on written academic texts (i.e. the literature). These are identified, collected together and analysed to present a synthesis or account (the review) of the status of research in a particular field, or on a particular topic, or using a particular method. The existing research is summarised, either for its own sake (literature reviews may be invaluable for researchers coming new to a particular field), or in order to identify a new research project and locate it within the existing literature.

Literature reviews are, therefore, endemic to academic research in the social sciences and beyond. All researchers need to be competent in undertaking and writing up literature reviews – at different lengths and to different degrees of detail – in order to meet the expectations for journal articles, books and reports.

In a literature review, the focus will likely be on key publications by the key authors (both past and present) who have researched the area or topic of interest. Examples of other publications may be used to illustrate the range and variety of research locations, interests and findings.

The scope or size of a literature review may vary greatly, depending on the time available, the author's familiarity with the literature, and the space available to write up or report on the review. For example, in a typical academic article, there may be fewer than a thousand words available in which to summarise the key literature, whereas, in a dissertation or thesis, several thousand words, or a whole chapter, may be given over to this.

While literature reviews will most often be carried out as part of a larger research project, they may also be the sole object of the research project and designed to stand on their own. As literature reviews become longer, more extensive and more ambitious, they shade into systematic reviews, which are discussed in the next section.

Literature reviews are explored in more detail in Chapter 6.

Systematic Reviews and Meta-Analyses

The key difference between literature reviews (discussed in the previous section) and systematic reviews is that the latter are more thorough and comprehensive. Meta-analyses differ from systematic reviews in that their focus is on summarising the quantitative results of all the relevant studies identified, whereas systematic reviews focus on the qualitative findings.

In a systematic review, the aim is to identify everything that has been published on a particular area or topic of research. Of course, it is difficult to locate literally 'everything', so some limitations will normally be applied, such as language and date restrictions, as well as accessibility or availability. But the intent is to be as thorough as possible, so that the researcher can not only identify and analyse the research that has been done, but also what has not been done and might, therefore, be prioritised for the future.

In a meta-analysis, the aim is to identify everything that has been published on a particular area or topic of research that reports quantitative results (e.g. on the impact of an innovation). The results from all of the analyses identified are then weighted and pooled to give an overall or summary result.

For both systematic reviews and meta-analyses (and also, though to a lesser extent, literature reviews), the advent of academic databases and search engines has been extremely helpful, even revelatory. Indeed, it is difficult to imagine being able to do a systematic review or meta-analysis nowadays, when so much more is being researched and published year on year, without access to these facilities.

Systematic reviews and meta-analyses are examined in more detail in Chapter 7.

Secondary Data Analysis

Secondary data is data that you have not collected yourself (data which you have collected yourself is called primary data), but which has been collected by someone else. This definition is very close, however, to some definitions of documentary research (see Chapter 2), so a little more explanation is called for.

With secondary data, the focus is chiefly on large (or larger) data sets – mostly, but not always or wholly, quantitative in nature – which have been painstakingly collected, often at national or international level. These data sets may result from one-off projects or be regularly collected each year or every so many years (as, for example, with census data, typically collected once a decade).

The key advantage of secondary data, rather obviously, is that you don't have to collect it yourself. Not only does this save a great deal of time, cost and trouble, but, for most social researchers, working on their own or in a small team, it would simply be unfeasible to collect such a substantial data set. If it relates to a topic of interest to you, and you can get access to it, its analysis is, therefore, likely to be very useful; either instead of collecting more data yourself, or as a supplement, comparator or context to this.

Because you have not collected it yourself, it is important to be aware of the context in which secondary data was collected, and to understand any problems or deficiencies it might have. Those responsible for the collection and storage of large data sets, particularly in western democracies, typically want their data to be used, however, and will be aware of and publicise any issues in the guidance material provided.

Secondary data analysis is explored in more detail in Chapter 8.

Archival and Historical Research

Archival research and historical research are closely related designs or genres. Archival research is – as the term indicates – research carried out in an archive, a place (physical and/or virtual) where documents on a particular topic or topics, or from a particular source, are deliberately collected for the purposes of safeguarding them, keeping them together and allowing them to be researched. Archives are essentially, therefore, historical, so archival research is a (prominent) branch of historical research.

But not all historical research involves the use of archives. Historians make use of written texts from a wide variety of sources (such as diaries, company reports and newspapers), which may not be collected in designated archives, and of non-written documents (such as oral history, paintings, maps and the landscape itself) as well. Indeed, as keen researchers exploring something which by definition no longer exists (at least not in the form that it once was), they make use of whatever sources they can get their hands on.

While history is not usually thought of as a social science – the focus of this book – one prominent branch of it, social history, is. All of the social sciences also have a historical component and are home to researchers who make this their focus. Our understanding of the present, and our hopes and predictions for the future, rest largely on our understanding of the past, so historical research should not be neglected.

Archival and historical research are explored in more detail in Chapter 9.

Policy Research

Policy research is also essentially self-explanatory; it comprises research focusing on policy. Like historical research, policy research is relevant to all of the social sciences (and beyond). Policies enacted at international, national, local or institutional levels impact on the topics of interest to researchers in, for example, economics, geography or sociology, and particularly strongly on those researching in professional fields such as education, nursing or social work.

Policy research lends itself to documentary research because most policies are enshrined in documents, in addition to which there are many further documents drafting, implementing, modifying, evaluating and critiquing any policy of interest. Much interest lies in comparing the different policies advanced by different interests, or in different organisations or countries, to tackle the same issues; and in exploring how the intentions of the policy-makers are carried out, interpreted or implemented in practice.

Unlike literature reviews, systematic reviews and meta-analyses, secondary data analysis, or archival and historical research, policy research lends itself particularly well to mixed methods research designs (though these are also possible in the other genres identified, as when systematic reviews and meta-analyses of the same sources are carried out in tandem). Thus, where the policy being researched is contemporary or recent, the policy-makers and implementers, plus of course those affected by the policy, may all also be the subject of research, typically using interviews, surveys or some other research design alongside documentary analysis.

Policy research is explored in more detail in Chapter 10.

The Five Genres in Combination

Of course, it is possible to combine these five designs or genres with each other. Most research will, as we have noted, contain some kind of literature review, even where this is not the main focus of the research. The secondary data being analysed may be historical in nature, or it may relate to the implementation of a policy. The policy being researched may also be historical, so a wide variety of combined research designs can be envisaged.

Similarly, as indicated in the discussion of policy research, these genres may also be combined with other research designs or methods. For example, as Bowen (2009) notes:

> Documents can serve a variety of purposes as part of a research undertaking ... First ... documents can provide data on the context within which research participants operate ...

Second, information contained in documents can suggest some questions that need to be asked and situations that need to be observed as part of the research ... Third, documents provide supplementary research data ... Fourth, documents provide a means of tracking change and development ... Fifth, documents can be analysed as a way to verify findings or corroborate evidence from other sources. (pp. 29–30)

The relation of documentary research to other research designs is considered further in the next section.

Documentary Research and Other Research Designs

Documentary Research as a Research Design

The attention given to documentary research in the social research methods literature varies widely. Some texts ignore or barely mention it – clearly not considering it to be a major research method or design – while others give it considerable space. We will look at how it is treated in six popular texts (note that most of these texts have appeared in more than one edition, so the latest version may present documentary research in a somewhat different light). Of course, there are many other social research methods texts which we might also examine, but this small sample should serve to illustrate something of the range of alternative perspectives that are taken on documentary research.

To start at the minimalist end, Punch (2005) gives documentary research just four pages; or, to be more precise, two pages on documentary data and two pages on documentary analysis. Ironically, he begins his treatment by stating that:

> Documents, both historical and contemporary, are a rich source of data for social research. A distinguishing feature of our society may well be the vast array of 'documentary evidence' which is routinely compiled and retained, yet much of this is neglected by researchers, perhaps because the collection of other sorts of social data (experiments, surveys, interviews, observations) has become more fashionable. (p. 184)

This is a fashion, then, that Punch appears to follow and cater for, as those other methods dominate his text.

Burns (2000) could be said to take an even more minimalist approach, partly because he divides his text into two main parts, dealing with quantitative and qualitative methods. The word 'document' does not even appear in the index, though there is a short (10-page) chapter in the section on qualitative methods focusing on historical research.

Blaxter, Hughes and Tight (2010, p. 64) give documents much more recognition, identifying them as one of four 'research techniques' – that is, means for collecting data – alongside interviews, observations and questionnaires. Documentary research might not be accorded a chapter of its own, but it is regularly considered throughout the book.

May (2001) identifies documentary research as one of six 'methods of social research', alongside official statistics, social surveys, interviewing, participant observation and comparative research. It is discussed in a substantive (25-page) chapter, subtitled 'Excavations and evidence'. He notes:

> There are a wide variety of documentary sources at our disposal for social research. Documents, read as the sedimentations of social practices, have the potential to inform and structure the decisions which people make on a daily and longer-term basis; they also constitute particular readings of social events. They tell us about the aspirations and intentions of the periods to which they refer and describe places and social relationships at a time when we may not have been born, or were simply not present. Nevertheless, despite their importance for research purposes and in permitting a range of research designs, relative to other methods we have come across, the volume of writings devoted to this topic is not so great. (p. 176)

His last comment, of course, provides support for the underlying purpose of this book.

Bryman (2004) takes a similar overall approach to Burns, in dividing his book between quantitative and qualitative research, but documentary methods feature strongly in both parts. Thus, in the quantitative part there are two chapters on content analysis (19 pages) and secondary analysis and official statistics (18 pages), while in the qualitative part there is a chapter on 'documents as sources of data' (18 pages).

Finally, Cohen, Manion and Morrison (2011) take a different strategy again, but it is one in which documents and their analysis receive repeated attention. Thus, in a section on 'styles of educational research', historical and documentary research is given a brief chapter (8 pages: McCulloch 2011), as are 'meta-analysis, research syntheses and systematic reviews' (9 pages). In the following section on 'strategies and instruments for data collection and researching', there are chapters on accounts (12 pages) and visual media (7 pages); while, in the 'data analysis' section, we find chapters on coding and content analysis (15 pages), discourses (14 pages) and analysing visual media (10 pages).

Clearly, then, there is no one standard, definitive, agreed or even widely accepted way in which social research is understood and categorised. That should neither be surprising nor a particular cause for concern; social research is characterised by dispute, debate and contestation, and this is unlikely to change any time soon.

My aim in this book is to help to make documentary research a more widely accepted and recognised, understood and applied part of the social research landscape. It seems most sensible to view documentary research as a research design, comprising the five genres identified in this chapter. As such, documentary research represents a way of pursuing a particular research project or projects. Within this research design, as within others, particular methods and theoretical frameworks may then be adopted in order to progress the research.

The Qualitative/Quantitative Debate

As you may well be aware, much energy and paper during the last several decades have been expended on arguing the relative merits of qualitative and quantitative forms of research, and a great deal of this has not – at least in my view – been particularly productive. Indeed, it might be said that the qualitative/quantitative debate in the social sciences has been one of the greatest wastes of time and energy in academic history.

Often – as is commonly the practice, of course, in political debates – opponents in the debate have employed stereotypical or misleading representations of each other's assumptions and practices so as to be better able to critique and knock them down. Indeed, it is not uncommon to hear or read the view expressed that qualitative and quantitative research are based on fundamentally different views of the world and how it can, or should, be studied. If so, it would be very difficult – and, some would argue, completely out of the question – to employ both qualitative and quantitative methods in the same research study.

Thus, quantitative researchers may align themselves with the scientific method, portraying themselves as searchers for the objective truth about the world (social or physical) and how it works; and dismiss qualitative research as subjective, small-scale, lacking in rigour, and non-generalisable. Qualitative researchers, for their part, may highlight the supposed richness and depth of their data and analysis, while accusing quantitative research of superficiality, arguing that not everything – and certainly not the social world – can be reduced to mere numbers.

Often, of course, these preferences are linked to the skill sets or methodological biases of the researchers concerned (e.g. some people feel at home with large data sets and multivariate analyses, while others are much more comfortable talking to or observing other people in natural settings). They may also reflect their underlying world view of knowledge and how it can be accessed or developed (i.e. their ontologies and epistemologies).

Nowadays, however, more pragmatically orientated researchers (of which, as you may have surmised, I consider myself to be one) have distanced themselves from these debates, arguing that mixed methods research, making use of both qualitative and quantitative methods as appropriate, has much more to offer (e.g. Bryman 2004, Scott 2007, Tashakkori and Teddlie 1998; see also Chapter 14). Indeed, I would go further, in arguing that all researchers (or, at least, all social researchers) should be able to use, and interpret, both qualitative and quantitative methods, at least to some level of understanding.

The same argument may be applied to documentary research, which, though it is sometimes claimed by qualitative researchers (typically when a small-scale and detailed focus is being employed), may make use of quantitative techniques as well as, or instead of, qualitative methods. Indeed, combining qualitative and quantitative methods in documentary research is only likely to add to the explanatory power of the research undertaken.

Documentary Research in Combination with Other Research Designs

As we have already argued (see Chapter 2, especially Box 2.2), documentary research is commonly used together with other research methods or designs. Indeed, with literature reviews recognised as one of the five key genres of documentary research, such combined research designs could be said to be endemic throughout the social sciences.

Box 5.1 gives three extended examples of such usage, from business/management, political science and educational research. The first two examples show documentary analysis being employed together with interviews, which is probably the commonest combination, while the third example is of documentary research being used alongside a survey plus a more limited number of interviews.

BOX 5.1

Examples of Documentary Research Being Used in Conjunction with Other Research Designs

1. First, we use several documentary sources such as press reports, company histories, teaching cases, business directories and annual reports in order to obtain a historical overview of the Zeltia and Cortefiel groups. With all this information, and the information existing on the Internet, we learnt about the history of both firms from their foundation, and more specifically from 1991 to 2001 (management team, members of staff, number of employees, performance and so on). However, apart from company information sources such as annual reports, the public information sources did not provide us with enough data on the processes of strategic and structural change. For this reason, the data obtained from these documentary sources were supplemented by individual interviews specifically designed for this research. Informants in both cases (Zeltia and Cortefiel groups) included each general manager, several divisional managers and lower-level managers. Specifically, we conducted seven semi-structured interviews with this group of managers in each company. (Galan, Sanchez and Zuniga-Vicente 2005, pp. 282–283)

2. Our study adopts a qualitative research methods approach, exploring an in-depth analysis of the meanings attributed and pursued in the development of the public engagement activity in the UK parliament. We utilise evidence from a series of elite in-depth semi-structured interviews developed with parliamentary officials, clerks and members of parliament (MPs), between October 2010 and January 2013 in the UK Parliament ... Overall, the project included 58 interviews, of which 15 were the UK Parliament [sic] ... Our interviewees were selected through a purposive sampling strategy, according to their role in the management and implementation of Parliament's public engagement ... The interviews complemented extensive documentary analysis of key documents informing on the management of the institution and particularly on the strategies developed to implement public engagement. This includes the annual reports of the House of Commons Commission from 1999/2000 to 2013/2014, as well as reports from key relevant select committees such as the Administration Committee, the Finance and Services Committee and the Modernisation Committee. The documentary analysis was used to map the expansion of public engagement and its

(Continued)

(Continued)

>
> respective key priorities, as well as to triangulate the interviews. Our research focuses therefore on the narrative presented by the institution and its officials. (Leston-Bandeira 2016, pp. 500–501)
>
> 3. We ... offer an analysis of how policy moves from inception through to implementation. Specifically we consider the trajectory of the Leadership Standards for Social Justice in Scotland, as set out in the Standards for Leadership and Management, launched in 2013. Our enquiry had three phases: (i) an analysis of the policy documents that led to the creation of the Standards; (ii) an online survey of 63 head teachers of nursery, primary and secondary schools in Scotland; (iii) follow-up telephone interviews with five of these head teachers. (Ward et al. 2016, p. 47)

Galan, Sanchez and Zuniga-Vicente (2005) studied strategy and change in two case study businesses (Zeltia and Cortefiel) in Spain. They used available documents (both hard copy and online) to compile a history of the two companies, supplementing these with interviews with managers to provide more detailed information on the processes involved in change.

Leston-Bandeira (2016) examined the UK parliament's commitment to, and involvement in, public engagement. They analysed key parliamentary documents to map the expansion of public engagement over time, using selected interviews with those working in parliament to provide perspectives on the meaning and purpose of increasing public engagement. Taken together, the documents and the interviews are seen as producing 'the narrative presented by the institution and its officials' (p. 501), effectively triangulating each other (triangulation is the process whereby two or more forms of data collection and analysis are used to confirm and complement each other, and is discussed in more detail in Chapter 14).

The third example, Ward et al. (2016), looks at the movement from policy to implementation, focusing on the leadership standards for social justice in Scottish education. They used a three-phase research design, with analysis of the policy documents underlying the leadership standards followed up by an online survey of head teachers and telephone interviews with five of those respondents.

Many other examples of documentary research being used in combination with other research designs could, of course, have been given. Thus, to offer just three more examples, Weller and Malheiros da Silva (2011) use what they call the documentary method (a particular form of documentary research) in combination with participatory research in ethnographic studies of young people; Wright and Sharpley (2018) combine the use of a representational or artistic photograph with interviews to explore tourist responses to disaster; and Baker and Hüttner (2017) combine 'documentary analyses of institutional websites, classroom observations and linguistic landscaping' (p. 505) with surveys and interviews with lecturers and students in a study of the roles and conceptualisations of language in English-medium multilingual universities in Europe and Asia.

Documentary analysis, then, is an extremely flexible research design, which may either be used on its own (in a wide variety of ways) or in combination with almost any other research design. It has a huge amount to offer social research, social researchers and others.

Conclusion

Documentary research may, and should, be viewed as a major research design within the social sciences and beyond. It may be practised using quantitative, qualitative or mixed methods, on its own or in combination with other research designs. Within documentary research, five main sub-designs or genres may be recognised: literature reviews, systematic reviews and meta-analyses, secondary data analysis, archival and historical research, and policy research. Each of these genres will now be considered in more detail in the succeeding chapters.

KEY READINGS

Listed here are three social research methods texts which give substantive attention to documentary research alongside other approaches to research:

Bryman, A (2015) *Social Research Methods*. Oxford, Oxford University Press, fifth edition.
Cohen, L, Manion, L, and Morrison, K (2017) *Research Methods in Education*. London, Routledge, eighth edition.
Seale, C (ed.) (2018b) *Researching Society and Culture*. London, Sage, fourth edition.

6
LITERATURE REVIEWS

CONTENTS

Introduction	74
The Nature of Literature Reviews	74
The Functions of Literature Reviews	76
Types of Literature Review	78
Conclusion	82

Introduction

The literature review is, arguably, the commonest and most significant, yet most overlooked, genre of documentary research. Any piece of academic writing in the social sciences – whether it be a book, report, book chapter, article, conference paper or whatever – is likely to contain a literature review. It may be a fairly minimal literature review, because of the limited space available; perhaps just a few paragraphs and a handful of references in the introductory section of a short paper. Similarly, it may not be labelled as a literature review – doing so is, after all, rather formulaic and boring – but it will almost certainly be there in any meaningful piece of academic writing.

At the other extreme, the whole piece of writing – whether at book or article length – may be a literature review and identified as such. A great deal of academic writing has been published, and the amount is increasing year on year, so there is a great deal of literature out there to review – and to keep up to date with – on a huge range of subjects. Literature reviews are an underrated, but extremely valuable, genre of academic writing (particularly for those new to the field reviewed, and who want to get a quick grasp of its scope and major debates).

There are, of course, a variety of positions between these two extremes, including where the literature review forms a discrete chapter in a book or thesis, or a major, named section in a journal article. Some journals require that each article includes a section entitled 'Literature review', while others are more flexible, just as some universities specify that masters or doctoral theses should contain a literature review chapter.

Given its ubiquity, it is important, then, to understand the varied functions of the literature review, how to go about producing one and how existing literature reviews may be assessed and used. Addressing these issues is the major purpose of this chapter.

The Nature of Literature Reviews

In one of the relatively few texts to have been written specifically on literature reviews, Jesson, Matheson and Lacey (2011, p. 10) offer a simple definition: 'A literature review is a written appraisal of what is already known – existing knowledge on a topic – with no prescribed methodology'. This appears reasonable enough, as far as it goes, but their final qualification, 'with no prescribed methodology', reads a little strangely, as the methodology may, in practice, be highly prescribed. Jesson et al. also usefully acknowledge that 'the literature review can be a research method in its own right' (2011, p. 9), which is the perspective adopted in this chapter.

Another definition of a literature review is offered by Hart (1998), in another of the limited number of texts focusing on literature reviews:

> The selection of available documents (both published and unpublished) on the topic, which contain information, ideas, data and evidence written from a particular standpoint to fulfil certain aims or express certain ideas on the nature of the topic and how it is to be investigated, and the effective evaluation of these documents in relation to the research being proposed. (p. 13)

This suggests a slightly different approach, recognising that the literature chosen for review, and the way in which it is presented and discussed, might be slanted towards a 'particular standpoint'. This is not to say that literature reviews are necessarily deliberately 'biased', though some subjectivity is, of course, inevitable. Authors may choose (consciously or subconsciously) to emphasise the literature that supports their point of view, perhaps while briefly dismissing that which does not.

The key point, however, is that – unlike systematic reviews (which are discussed in the next chapter) – literature reviews do not attempt to cover everything that has been published or written. This implies that those reading and using them, as well as those compiling them, need to have some awareness of what has been left out, and why, as well as what has been included.

Hart also indicates that the literature review may be a precursor to, or vehicle for, identifying the proposed research project, methodology and questions, so it is doubly important. In other words, it is through the literature review that a research gap is identified – on which there appears to be no, or only limited, literature – which the proposed research then sets out to fill. Indeed, in an academic article or doctoral thesis, the literature review might lead directly to the identification of the research question(s) or hypotheses.

That may sound rather neat or formulaic, however, so it is important to qualify matters. For, while a typical academic article, book or thesis will have a fairly standard organisation – moving from introduction to literature review, methodology, findings, discussion and conclusions (even if they are not explicitly labelled as such) – it has to be recognised that this is an artefact, and that the actual research probably did not take place in the smooth and linear fashion this implies.

So, while the literature review may help to identify research questions and the outline of a research project, it does not end at that point. What is found through the research may lead to further interrogation of the literature, with the review being updated during the life of the project, and the research questions revised to reflect what has actually been addressed or answered in the conclusions.

Torgerson (2003) picks up Hart's (1998) point about the focus or subjectivity of a literature review, but puts her view rather more strongly. She argues that literature reviews, which she terms traditional narrative reviews, are often biased:

> The research literature included in traditional narrative reviews tends to be a 'biased' sample of the full range of the literature on the subject. It is usually undertaken through the perspective of the reviewer who gathers and interprets the literature in a given field. The reasons for including some studies and excluding others are often not made explicit ... If the search strategy and inclusion criteria have not been made explicit it will not be possible for the review to be replicated by a third party. (p. 5)

While her argument about bias is probably expressed rather too strongly ('selected' might be a better term to use than 'biased'), her second point about the desirability of discussing search strategy and inclusion criteria is much stronger.

For, just as you would expect researchers to discuss their sample frame, strategy and size if they were carrying out an interview or questionnaire-based study, so it is good practice for them to set out, albeit perhaps more briefly, how they went about the literature review. This might include details of which search engines or strategies were used, the date and language limitations applied, and the reasons for focusing on particular areas of the literature rather than others. That would then make the literature review replicable, at least potentially, and would also allow it to be updated or extended.

Fink (2005, p. 3) also emphasises this point about replication or reproducibility, stating that: 'A research literature review is a systematic, explicit and reproducible method for identifying, evaluating and synthesising the existing body of completed and recorded work produced by researchers, scholars and practitioners' (though, with the use of the terms 'systematic' and 'synthesising', this does read more like a definition of a systematic, rather than a literature, review). Like other aspects of research, the ability for others to be able to follow and check what you have done is crucial in their evaluation of its worth.

Goddard and Carey (2017, pp. 173–174) take a somewhat contrary approach, in pointing out what a literature review is not:

> Your reading of secondary sources is typically built into something called a *literature review*, which confusingly is neither about literary texts nor a review in any ordinary sense of the word. Instead, the word 'literature' is used in its widest sense, to refer to things that are written. And the review is not concerned with evaluation in the sense of TripAdvisor or music journalism, where a reviewer discusses the whole experience or artefact and aims to cover all the different aspects ... The rationale for discussing what you have read is that you will pick out only the ideas or approaches or evidence from the material that [have] relevance for your study.

Literature reviews can, then, 'cherry pick' only those sources which are favourable to the argument being put forward in the article, book or thesis in which they are contained. In order to assess their usefulness, therefore, it is critical to know how they were put together.

The Functions of Literature Reviews

Accepting that the term 'literature review' has a particular meaning in academic circles, what can we say further about its functions or purposes? Two formulations are shown in Box 6.1. Hart (1998) identifies up to 11 purposes for a literature review, though he implies that there may be others as well, while Branley, Seale and Zacharias (2018) set out five key functions.

BOX 6.1

Purposes or Functions of a Literature Review

The review serves at least the following purposes in research:

1. distinguishing what has been done from what needs to be done
2. discovering important variables relevant to the topic

important. The expectation in social research, after all, is that everything you read will be critically assessed for its strengths and weaknesses and its relation to other research.

What Jesson and colleagues (2011) called a traditional review is similar to what Torgerson (2003) termed the traditional narrative review (not least, of course, in each using the term 'traditional', in both cases in a positive sense). Similarly, a conceptual review seems analogous to Hart's ninth purpose of a literature review, focusing on the theories that have been applied to the topic. However, Jesson et al., perhaps because their focus is on the topic reviewed, do not separately identify the methodological review (Hart's tenth purpose).

Another typology of literature reviews, but one somewhat unusually based on empirical research, is offered by Bruce (1994). She asked 41 students on a higher research degree course at an Australian university to reflect upon, and then write down, their perceptions of what a literature review was. Analysing their writing phenomenographically (a method which seeks to identify the range of perceptions or conceptions of a particular phenomenon held by the group researched), she identified six conceptions of a literature review:

- *as a list* ... the literature review is seen/understood as a listing/collection of items representing the literature of the subject...
- *as a search* ... the literature review is seen/understood as the process of identifying relevant information/literature...
- *as a survey* ... the literature review is seen/understood as an investigation of past and present writing or research in one or more areas of interest...
- *as a vehicle for learning* ... the literature review is seen/understood as having an impact on the researcher...
- *as a research facilitator* ... the literature review is seen/understood as relating specifically to the research being, or about to be, undertaken...
- *as a report* ... the literature review is seen/understood as a written discussion of the literature drawing on investigations previously undertaken. (pp. 221-223)

The earlier conceptions are seen as less well developed, and the later ones as more developed and encompassing the earlier ones. The idea of a literature review as a list – not an attractive or engaging possibility for the reader – is certainly one that teachers would wish to encourage students to move away from. By contrast, the notion of the literature review as a research facilitator is very close to the idea of the literature review naturally leading to the identification of the research question(s).

Bruce's (1994) typology is rather different from that of Jesson et al. (2011), but is perhaps rather more practical, suggesting some of the processes that need to be gone through to produce an acceptable literature review. Box 6.2 offers a more comprehensive account of the processes involved in producing a literature review (see also Galvan and Galvan 2017 and Pan 2017 for alternative practical guides).

Box 6.2 is not meant to be interpreted as a series of stages which you will go through sequentially one by one. The actual experience of doing a literature review – as of doing research in general – will inevitably be messier, with some doubling back and reconsideration called for. Nevertheless, there will also be quite a lot of routine behaviours involved, reading items one by one and extracting what you need from them.

BOX 6.2

Processes Involved in Undertaking a Literature Review

Note that these processes might not be undertaken in the order that they are listed, and some may be undertaken simultaneously. You will probably need to return to some of them on more than one occasion, as the scope and focus of your literature review is modified in the light of your experience of carrying it, and the broader research project (if there is one), out.

- Define your topic: you need somewhere to start from, so be as clear as you can about your focus.
- Seek advice from those more experienced or knowledgeable than you: this might include your supervisor(s), manager, colleagues and friends, as well as the subject librarian and conference participants. What do they think are the key publications on your topic?
- Identify previous literature reviews of relevance: if you can do this, they may offer a useful short cut. Don't, however, rely too much on them; at the very least, they will need updating. They may also have missed publications which turn out to be key for your research, and may have misinterpreted or dismissed others.
- Limit the range of material you are going to assess; for instance, in terms of language and/or date and/or place and/or type of publication. It is common to limit the search to items in your native language and published within the most recent period (e.g. the last 10 or 20 years). You might also choose to limit yourself to material from your own country. Bear in mind, though, the constraints this may place on your review, and check out what you are missing as a consequence.
- Identify possibly relevant material. This is arguably the key process and can be time-consuming or relatively straightforward. The straightforward approach is to use an online search engine (such as ERIC, Google Scholar, World of Science or Scopus), preferably more than one, and to search using keywords. You may need to refine your keywords to get a manageable number of hits, perhaps by date. The more time-consuming, old-fashioned approach is to work with hard copies of material in a good academic library; you'll still need to make use of the library catalogue though.
- Get copies of possibly relevant material. You might prefer to work with hard copies, in which case quite a bit of printing and regular library visits will be involved. Or you might be happy to manage it all online, in which case you can put pdf copies of potentially relevant materials in designated files (remember to back them up regularly).
- Assess the relevance of the material. This can be a painstaking and lengthy process, but one which you should become more proficient at with experience. Study the abstract or introduction, and scan through the rest of the publication, to assess its relevance to your topic. Then either ditch it (though you might still want to keep a copy and/or a note of the details, in case you change your mind) or save it.

- Identify other possibly relevant material from the references used; even the most comprehensive search engines do not cover everything (particularly older material), so it is possible you will find some especially relevant material here (perhaps unpublished or published in an obscure outlet, or just old).
- Read the material identified as being of relevance. This is also time-consuming, though you should again speed up with practice (see also Chapter 3).
- Identify key sources, authors, theories and methods; these will likely be at the core of your literature review. You may get suggestions on what these are from your advisors, or may identify them from the review itself: they will likely be the ones that get referenced again and again.
- Draft the structure of your review: identify sub-headings (you can always change or add to these). There may also be space limitations you will need to bear in mind.
- Write the review: this is obviously another difficult part, particularly if you haven't done something like this before. One approach is to slot details into your overall structure as you read the material you have gathered. Summarise key ideas and findings, and your perspective on them (don't neglect this, or it will just be a list of what other people have written rather than your literature review); note particularly apposite quotations and don't forget to add the details to your references. You will likely have to go through a number of drafts before you get the literature review into the shape and size you want.

Box 6.3 summarises two contrasting examples of completed, and published, literature reviews to illustrate some of the possibilities. The first is a literary example from anthropology, where the authors were interested in the place of wolves in Portuguese literature. They accessed a random sample of relevant items from an established database, and then categorised them in terms of a pre-established grid. The second example made use of a range of keywords in searching several online databases. Certain kinds of material identified were then excluded from the study, with the remainder analysed in terms of theme and methodology.

BOX 6.3

Examples of Literature Reviews

1. For this study we used excerpts of a random sample of Portuguese literary works registered in a database. The works were read by us and several collaborators, and were selected if the text could be assigned to an identified geographic place. The novels, stories, chronicles, diaries, and poetry cover a time frame from Romanticism to the present. Animal stories such as fables or fairy tales were excluded. As with other animals, references to wolves were registered every time their common names appeared in the text. Those references constitute our sample, and

(Continued)

(Continued)

were extracted from the broader literary corpus of around 4,000 excerpts of works published between 1875 and 2010. Each excerpt's content was classified in terms of one or several categories from a grid analysis set up for this study. We have selected some extracts and translated them into English to illustrate the main ideas presented. (Lopes-Fernandes et al. 2016, pp. 7–8)

2. Keyword searches were made in library catalogues and the following online article databases: Academic Search Premier, CSA Internet Database Service, Educational Administration Abstracts, ERIC, International ERIC, ProQuest and Scopus. The literature in Chinese was searched separately using the China National Knowledge Infrastructure. The two main foci were 'academic integrity' and 'higher education'. Hence, the searching of databases incorporated words and phrases such as 'higher education' or 'university' or 'faculty' plus 'integrity' or 'ethics' or 'misconduct'. Synonyms and alternate terms like 'university' (private and public), 'college', as well as 'tutors', 'faculty', 'academic staff', and 'professors' were highlighted. These terms were used to narrow the scope of the search. Articles were excluded if they were in the format of a newspaper article or reflection ... What is sometimes termed 'grey literature', such as working papers and reports produced outside conventional publication channels, were omitted. It was also important to distinguish, and exclude, articles that related to the moral education or academic dishonesty of students ... either in university or secondary schools. Other articles were excluded where they related primarily to ethics in the context of business or professional learning. Even so, the online databases still produced hundreds of results from which only a small proportion fully met requirements in terms of relevance and quality. Citation searches of key articles were performed and reference lists were then searched for further relevant papers. The final selection of 115 articles was classified and grouped according to its main themes and research methodologies. Commonly occurring themes were identified and grouped by teaching, research and service activities. (Macfarlane, Zhang and Pun 2014, p. 341)

The second example also demonstrates that the borderline between a literature review and a systematic review is rather fuzzy; this example could be categorised as either, though its authors refer to it as a literature review.

Conclusion

This chapter has considered the documentary research genre of the literature review. It has argued that, even if you are 'only' doing a 'simple' literature review, there is a need to go about the work systematically and to spell out, in any report on the work, how you did it.

The next chapter examines the more comprehensive strategies – qualitative and quantitative respectively – of systematic reviews and meta-analyses.

KEY READINGS

Fink, A (2014) *Conducting Research Literature Reviews: From the internet to paper.* Thousand Oaks, CA; Sage, fourth edition.

A popular American text.

Galvan, J, and Galvan, M (2017) *Writing Literature Reviews: A guide for students of the social and behavioral sciences.* New York, Routledge, seventh edition.

Another popular and much revised American text.

Hart, C (2018) *Doing a Literature Review: Releasing the research imagination.* London, Sage, second edition.

A recent revision of a classic book.

Jesson, J, Matheson, L, and Lacey, F (2011) *Doing Your Literature Review: Traditional and systematic techniques.* London, Sage.

A very accessible and readable text.

7

SYSTEMATIC REVIEWS AND META-ANALYSES

CONTENTS

Introduction	86
Systematic Reviews	87
Meta-Analyses	91
Conclusion	94

Introduction

As the previous chapter indicated, there is a close relationship between the literature review and the systematic review. Indeed, sometimes the terms are used interchangeably, or are combined, as in systematic literature review. It is probably simplest to regard systematic reviews as being part of the literature review 'family', but as rather more ambitious – a literature review plus, if you like. There is, in other words, a difference in scope between literature reviews and systematic reviews, hence their separate treatment in this book.

Systematic reviews seek to identify and review everything – or, at least, everything that is available and accessible – that has been written and published on a particular topic. In other words, they aim to synthesise all of the research to date on the topic selected. Because of their comprehensive coverage, they are potentially even more valuable to the interested reader than literature reviews, even though the detail given on individual sources may not be so extensive.

Systematic reviews and meta-analyses are also closely related, and, again, the terms are sometimes used interchangeably. Thus, Oliver and Tripney (2017) identify three different approaches to systematic review: for testing hypotheses, for generating theory and for exploring theory. They, however, treat systematic reviews and meta-analyses as overlapping, under the umbrella heading of 'analyses of multiple studies'. They then make the following distinction in terms of the qualitative/quantitative research spectrum:

> Between these two extremes of syntheses that build theory from qualitative studies and syntheses that test theory with quantitative studies, are mixed methods syntheses that explore theories and assumptions. These reviews start with an existing framework or theory to direct the initial search for evidence and progress by amending the initial framework or theory in light of emerging evidence. (p. 467)

The first of these 'extremes' (i.e. building theory from qualitative studies) could be termed systematic reviews, and the second (testing theory with quantitative studies) meta-analyses, while the third might involve elements of both.

Other researchers recognise a wider range of research synthesis methods. Suri and Clarke (2009, p. 397), for example, offer the following sixfold categorisation, based partly on methodology and partly on other factors:

- *Statistical research syntheses* ... such as meta-analysis and best-evidence synthesis.
- *Systematic reviews* ... emphasises a priori protocols, comprehensive searches, transparency to reduce biases, and the involvement of stakeholders in the review process.
- *Qualitative research syntheses* ... various formally proposed individual methods for synthesising qualitative research.
- *Qualitative syntheses of qualitative and quantitative research*...
- *Critical impetus in reviewing research* ... discussions on a range of critical issues associated with the production and use of research syntheses...
- *Exemplary syntheses*: explicit critiques or taxonomies of published syntheses.

They go on to propose 'three general guiding principles for a quality research synthesis: informed subjectivity and reflexivity, purposefully informed selective inclusivity, and audience-appropriate transparency' (p. 408). In short, they emphasise the practical or pragmatic issues involved in carrying out a research synthesis, recognising that some selectivity may be necessary in what is reviewed, and that the end result should never be viewed as an 'objective' analysis.

Here we will make the simpler, twofold distinction between systematic reviews and meta-analyses in terms of their emphasis. Meta-analyses are similar to systematic reviews in intent, but focus on the quantitative results of research, aiming to pool them all together to better generalise the research findings. The underlying idea is that, while 20, 30 or 50 quantitative studies of a particular issue will each individually be of interest, a single, combined quantitative synthesis of all of their results will have much more power and generalisability.

While, therefore, a systematic review provides a mainly qualitative overview of a research field, meta-analyses aim to offer a quantitative summary of the findings on a particular topic.

Systematic Reviews

The methodology of systematic reviews was first developed and popularised in health care research, where their promise has been highly extolled:

> Systematic reviews have several advantages over other types of research that have led to them being regarded as particularly important tools for decision-makers. Systematic reviews take precedence over other types of research in many hierarchies of evidence, as it inherently makes sense for decisions to be based on the totality of evidence rather than a single study. Moreover, they can generally be conducted more quickly than new primary research and, as a result, may be attractive to policy-makers required to make a rapid response to a new policy issue. (Bunn et al. 2015, p. 1)

Bunn et al. go on to note, however, that their usage by policy-makers is not as much as might be expected.

Systematic reviews have only latterly been adopted in the social sciences more generally (Bearman et al. 2012), and then rather too slowly for some. They have not, however, always been welcomed, as, for example, in the case of education, where their usage has become bundled together with the ongoing debate on evidence-based practice (see, for example, Light and Pillemer 1982, Maclure 2005, Thomas and Pring 2004).

Unsurprisingly, systematic reviews have been defined in rather divergent ways. Here are two somewhat contrasting definitions:

> A systematic review differs from a traditional narrative review in that its methods are explicit and open to scrutiny. It seeks to identify *all* the available evidence with respect to a given

theme. Systematic reviews have the advantage of including all the studies in a field (sometimes positive and negative studies), so the reader can judge using the *totality* of evidence. (Torgerson 2003, p. 6)

We ... define a systematic review as a review with a clear stated purpose, a question, a defined search approach, stating inclusion and exclusion criteria, producing a qualitative appraisal of articles. (Jesson, Matheson and Lacey 2011, p. 12)

Thus, while Torgerson emphasises 'all' and 'totality', Jesson, Matheson and Lacey simply stress the systematic nature of the review. The difference between this approach and that of a literature review (or a traditional narrative review, as Torgerson calls it), particularly if the literature review is carried out in a systematic fashion while not seeking to encompass the totality of the literature on the particular topic, is unclear. Yet, as we have already argued, systematic reviews and literature reviews are on the same spectrum, and must, therefore, elide into each other at some point.

Torgerson's (2003) definition seems to me, however, to be clearer and hence preferable. I would, though, differ from her in arguing that, even in the more limited literature review, the methods used to select the literature and compile the review should be 'explicit and open to scrutiny'.

Torgerson goes further in identifying nine aims for a systematic review:

1. to address a specific (well focused, relevant) question;
2. to search for, locate and collate the results of the research in a systematic way;
3. to reduce bias at all stages of the review (publication, selection and other forms of bias);
4. to appraise the quality of the research in the light of the research question;
5. to synthesise the results of the review in an explicit way;
6. to make the knowledge base more accessible;
7. to identify gaps; to place new proposals in the context of existing knowledge;
8. to propose a future research agenda; to make recommendations;
9. to present all stages of the review in the final report to enable critical appraisal and replication.
(2003, pp. 7–8)

This adds a number of important features to what you might expect from a basic literature review, while also including some things that a competent literature review would also be expected to deliver.

Thus, the aims of reducing bias, in part by examining all relevant research, and then by carefully appraising quality, are of key importance. The end result of producing an accessible and transparent synthesis of the research field, clearly presented in a report, is also paramount.

However, the proposed use of the systematic review to identify knowledge gaps and propose a future research agenda is something that a literature review might also attempt, particularly perhaps in the context of an academic thesis or dissertation. Conversely, these might not be part of the aims of a systematic review, which could serve simply to synthesise the knowledge in a particular field or topic, leaving it to others to identify knowledge gaps and/or generate future research agendas.

Box 7.1 provides four alternative conceptualisations of the stages involved in carrying out a systematic review; or a 'research synthesis', as Cooper (2010) and Suri and Clarke (2009) refer to it. There are many similarities between these formulations, each of which involves six or seven stages or steps. They also share a lot in common with Box 6.2, which details the processes involved in undertaking a literature review, though that is much more detailed. All stress the importance of evaluating the quality of the material collected – which is, of course, key to all social research – and then integrating or synthesising the findings.

BOX 7.1

Stages in a Systematic Review

1. Research synthesis is divided into seven steps:

    - Step 1: Formulating the problem
    - Step 2: Searching the literature
    - Step 3: Gathering information from studies
    - Step 4: Evaluating the quality of studies
    - Step 5: Analysing and integrating the outcomes of studies
    - Step 6: Interpreting the evidence
    - Step 7: Presenting the results. (Cooper 2010, p. 12)

2. The seven main stages of a systematic review are well established in health care, social policy and educational research. The stages include: writing the protocol (including the inclusion and exclusion criteria); searching and screening; 'scoping' or 'mapping' the research; extracting data from the included studies and quality appraising them; synthesizing the studies in a narrative, and sometimes in a meta-analysis; writing and disseminating the report. (Torgerson 2003, p. 25)

3. We describe six essential stages of methodology that you should work through in undertaking a systematic review: 1. Define the research question. 2. Design the plan. 3. Search for literature. 4. Apply exclusion and inclusion criteria. 5. Apply quality assessment. 6. Synthesis. (Jesson, Matheson and Lacey 2011, p. 12)

4. Six phases of considerations relevant to any quality research synthesis:

    1. drawing from pertinent philosophical and theoretical discussions;
    2. identifying an appropriate purpose;
    3. searching for relevant evidence;
    4. evaluating, interpreting, and distilling evidence;
    5. constructing connected understandings; and
    6. communicating with an audience. (Suri and Clarke 2009, p. 414)

Box 7.2 reports on three examples of published systematic reviews. Each follows a similar format: databases and search engines are specified, the date limiters are given and the keywords used in the search are listed. The stages involved in getting from the initial list of publications identified down to a more focused set for analysis are identified.

One of the articles (Lampe et al. 2017) refers to a particular set of guidelines for carrying out systematic reviews and meta-analyses that has been developed in the medical field. These guidelines, the Preferred Reporting Items for Systematic Reviews and Meta-Analyses (PRISMA: see Moher et al. 2009), are widely employed in that field.

BOX 7.2

Examples of Systematic Reviews

1. On the basis of a search for resources indexed in the Educational Resources Information Centre (ERIC) database, we established a population composed of 2016 references published from 1990 to 2013.This database, sponsored by the United States Department of Education, is considered one of the most wide-ranging reference sources in the field of education. To date, it contains over one million records obtained from a variety of sources: books, academic papers, government documents, theses, teaching materials and journal articles. Secondly, we used the keyword 'key competence' and the option search 'peer reviewed' to select just a sample of journal articles. This decision was made for the following reasons: (a) we were dealing with resources considered by the scientific community as highly regarded rigorous studies; (b) due to their relatively uniform format, it was easy to analyse and compare resources, regardless of the journal in which they were published; (c) ERIC provides a considerable and up-to-date volume of bibliographic resources while also providing good advanced search and retrieve functions ... we had a sample of 616 articles. Allowing for a 5% margin of error and a 95% confidence interval, the minimum number of items required would be 323. Consequently, we concluded that our sample was more than adequately representative. (Donet, Pallares and Burrilo 2017, p. 147)

2. We systematically searched the literature in concordance with the statement of the Preferred Reporting Items for Systematic Reviews and Meta-Analyses (PRISMA) and other recommendations and guidelines. Multiple search engines were used. Using the assistance of a specialized librarian, a search syntax and strategies that were tailored to the engines [sic]. We focused on electronic databases in the fields of psychology (PsycINFO, by using EBSCO) and medicine (PubMED) to retrieve relevant English written and peer-reviewed papers (articles) being published between 1st of January 1994 and 1st of January 2014. Next to the search term 'observation', variations of the following search terms were used: assessment, diagnosis, screening and rating. To be included, the words impulsivity or aggression had to be in the abstract, title or key-words. This search strategy was refined and tested by crosschecking the results with a list of known relevant tools to ensure that we did not miss major publications on the observation of aggression or impulsivity. Within the search query for PsycINFO, a publication date limiter was included. In PubMED a limiter was used after the search was performed. Both search results were combined in one database and duplicates were removed ... studies were selected for further study if they met all of the following inclusion criteria: (1) the observed study

subjects were humans; (2) the observed behavior was impulsivity or aggression; (3) the observation was not restricted to behavior that took place during a test or assignment (e.g., a computer paradigm to provoke aggression); (4) the IRR [inter-rater reliability] for the observation of aggression or impulsivity was reported; and (5) the information retrieved from the observation was registered within 24h. (Lampe et al. 2017, pp. 13–14)

3. A systematic review of the French and English literature was undertaken, targeting the period of January 1, 1999 to December 31, 2008. The following databases were explored: Medline, Embase, BDSP, Wholis, Saphir, Rero and Web of Science. The investigated keywords were 'health and human rights' in English and 'santé et droits de l'homme' or 'santé et droits humains' in French. The research strategy focused on the Mesh descriptors associated with the keywords human rights, human rights abuses, health, health status disparities, delivery of health care, health policy, public health, health services accessibility, état de santé, santé publique, accès aux soins, inégalités de soins, droits fondamentaux ... A first selection identified 2,072 references. After excluding papers without an abstract, official recommendations, judicial comments or decisions, declarations, conferences [sic] proceedings, book reviews, press releases, and glossaries, a final list of 928 articles was available for analysis. Where there were differences of opinion regarding the status of the item (n = 22), these were allocated through discussion within the team and were finally included into the studied set. (Mpinga et al. 2011, p. 105)

Anyone reading the articles from which these extracts in Box 7.2 have been quoted, so long as they had access to the databases and search engines specified, should be able to replicate, extend and/or update the reviews produced. In this way, systematic reviews serve as a record of the state of research on a particular topic at a given time, a record which may be returned to again and again.

Meta-Analyses

As already indicated, while systematic reviews take a predominantly qualitative approach to the analysis and synthesis of multiple studies on a particular topic, in meta-analyses the approach is explicitly quantitative.

Jesson, Matheson and Lacey (2011) offer a useful definition: 'Meta-analysis is a statistical technique which has been developed to combine quantitative results obtained from independent studies that have been published' (p. 129). Cooper (2010), while noting that terms like systematic review, research synthesis and meta-analysis are often used interchangeably, concurs, restricting meta-analysis to 'the quantitative procedures used to statistically combine the results of studies' (p. 6).

The stages involved in a meta-analysis are similar to those involved in a systematic review (Box 7.1), as it is equally important to identify all of the studies on the topic concerned, and then assess their quality. The key difference is that a meta-analysis aims at a quantitative synthesis of the results of all of the studies identified, rather than a qualitative summary or categorisation:

> Meta-analysis permits summary of studies' results and is designed for scenarios in which the primary studies' raw data are not available. The meta-analytic process involves summarizing the results of each study using an effect size (ES), calculating an overall average across studies of the resulting ESs, and exploring study- and sample-related sources of possible heterogeneity in the ESs. The overall average ES provides a single best estimate of the overall effect of interest to the meta-analyst. (Beretvas 2010, p. 255)

The ability to carry out a meta-analysis without access to the raw data of the studies being analysed is particularly convenient, saving a great deal of time.

There are a number of ways, of varying degrees of complexity, in which meta-analyses may be carried out (see, for example, Cooper 2010), and software is, of course, available to do the number crunching. The basic method involves identifying the effect sizes (a measure of the difference between the experimental and control groups) reported by each study, and then combining these in an average effect size, with the studies weighted in accordance with their sample sizes.

Box 7.3 summarises three examples of published meta-analyses in the social sciences. The quotations given were actually taken from the article abstracts in each case, illustrating the formulaic way in which such studies are typically reported. In many ways, the details reported are similar to the systematic reviews highlighted in Box 7.2, with the exception that the focus of the meta-analyses is on the quantitative findings arrived at by combining the identified studies together.

BOX 7.3

Examples of Meta-Analyses

1. I identify educational interventions with an impact on student learning in Sub-Saharan Africa. After a systematic literature search, I conducted a meta-analysis synthesizing 56 articles containing 66 separate experiments and quasi-experiments and 83 treatment aims. I evaluated 12 types of education interventions such as the provision of school supplies, the use of teacher incentives, and school-based management programs. I examine each intervention type, present analytics on relative effectiveness, and explore why certain interventions seem to be more effective. A key finding is that programs that alter teacher pedagogy or classroom instructional techniques had an effect size approximately 0.30 standard deviations greater than all other types of programs combined. Limited evidence further suggests that pedagogical programs that employed adaptive instruction or teacher coaching were particularly effective. (Conn 2017, p. 863)
2. This meta-analysis examined the relationship between moral identity and moral behavior. It was based on 111 studies from a broad range of academic fields including business, developmental psychology and education, marketing, sociology, and sport sciences. Moral identity was found to be significantly associated with moral behavior (random effects model, $r = .22$, $p < .01$, 95% CI [.19, .25]). Effect sizes did not differ for behavioral outcomes (prosocial behavior, avoidance of antisocial behavior, ethical behavior). Studies that were entirely

based on self-reports yielded larger effect sizes. In contrast, the smallest effect was found for studies that were based on implicit measures or used priming techniques to elicit moral identity. Moreover, a marginally significant effect of culture indicated that studies conducted in collectivistic cultures yielded lower effect sizes than studies from individualistic cultures. Overall, the meta-analysis provides support for the notion that moral identity strengthens individuals' readiness to engage in prosocial and ethical behavior as well as to abstain from antisocial behavior. However, moral identity fares no better as a predictor of moral action than other psychological constructs. (Hertz and Krettenauer 2016, p. 129)

3. Four electronic databases (MEDLINE, EMBASE, PsycINFO and International Bibliography of the Social Sciences, IBSS) and grey literature were searched from inception to May 2015 for comparative epidemiological studies (cross-sectional and cohort studies) that reported the relation between exposure to smoking in movies and smoking initiation in adolescence (10–19 years). Reference lists of studies and previous reviews were also screened. Two authors screened papers and extracted data independently. Seventeen studies met our inclusion criteria. Random-effects meta-analysis of nine cross-sectional studies demonstrated higher exposure (typically highest versus lowest quantile) to smoking in movies was associated significantly with a doubling in risk of ever trying smoking [relative risk (RR)=1.93, 95% confidence interval (CI) =1.66–2.25]. In eight longitudinal studies (all deemed high quality), higher exposure to smoking in movies was associated significantly with a 46% increased risk of initiating smoking (RR=1.46; 95% CI=1.23–1.73). These pooled estimates were significantly different from each other (P = 0.02). Moderate levels of heterogeneity were seen in the meta-analyses. The cross-sectional association between young people reporting having seen smoking imagery in films and smoking status is greater than the prospective association. Both associations are substantial, but it is not clear whether or not they are causal. (Leonardi-Bee, Nderi & Britton 2016, p. 1750)

One other aspect that Box 7.3 illustrates is that meta-analyses don't have to be that large. It depends, naturally enough, on what your topic is, how closely it has been defined and how extensively it has been researched. There may simply not have been many prior studies of relevance. Thus, the third study identified in Box 7.3 is based on only 17 previous studies, while the first and the second examine 56 and 111 respectively. Meta-analyses should, therefore, be within the scope of most competent researchers, providing you have access to the necessary software.

Some researchers have, however, gone much further. For example, Hattie (2009) synthesises over 800 meta-analyses 'which encompassed 52,637 studies, and provided 146,142 effect sizes about the influence of some program, policy, or innovation on academic achievement in school' (p. 15). This was truly a major piece of research, which took up a substantial part of one man's academic career.

Others (e.g. Gomez et al. 2015) have combined the results of meta-analyses and systematic reviews:

A mixed methods study with embedded design was conducted which included two methodological components ... The first component was a synthesis of evidence from systematic reviews and meta-analyses conducted to document the effectiveness of urban environment interventions linked with the promotion of physical activity. The second component was a narrative documentation of some socio-political barriers and facilitators linked with physical activity in urban Latin-American contexts. (2015, p. 20)

The potential scope and flexibility of meta-analyses are, therefore, quite broad, though, as ever, the limitations and assumptions of the methodology have to be borne in mind.

Conclusion

This chapter has considered the linked documentary research genres of systematic reviews and meta-analyses, relating them also to the literature review genre considered in the previous chapter. The more thorough or comprehensive techniques of systematic review and meta-analysis are available to those with a little more time and the determination to get a global perspective on the research done on a particular topic, and what its implications are.

KEY READINGS

Cooper, H (2010) *Research Synthesis and Meta-Analysis: A step-by-step approach*. Thousand Oaks, CA, Sage, fourth edition.

A popular American guide to systematic reviews and meta-analyses.

Hattie, J (2009) *Visible Learning: A synthesis of over 800 meta-analyses relating to achievement*. London, Routledge.

A fascinating example of the power of meta-analysis as a tool for extracting overall conclusions from multiple existing studies.

Suri, H, and Clarke, D (2009) Advancements in Research Synthesis Methods: From a methodologically inclusive perspective. *Review of Educational Research*, 79, 1, pp. 395–430.

A thoughtful and thorough discussion of the state of meta-analyses, systematic reviews and related techniques.

Torgerson, C (2003) *Systematic Reviews*. London, Continuum.

A very accessible and readable guide to systematic reviews.

8

SECONDARY DATA RESEARCH

CONTENTS

Introduction	96
Secondary Data and Secondary Data Analysis	97
Advantages and Disadvantages of Secondary Data Research	98
Types of Secondary Data Analysis	100
Examples of Secondary Data Analysis	102
Where to Get Secondary Data	105
Conclusion	108

Introduction

Secondary data research, or secondary data analysis, is probably the most widely overlooked genre of documentary research. It might also be termed the core genre of documentary research.

In a sense, documentary research and secondary data research are much the same thing, almost synonymous, in that both involve research using materials (whether called documents or data) that the researcher has not directly collected or recently produced themselves. We will, however, treat secondary data research as a genre of documentary research, as it involves taking a particular perspective, and is distinct from, though overlapping with, the other genres identified in this book.

Throughout the social sciences, there is a widespread belief that researchers should collect (or create or co-create) their own empirical data as part of the research process, before going on to analyse it (perhaps while continuing to collect data). This can be seen in the status accorded to fieldwork, and in the way in which many disciplines, departments and institutions expect research students to engage in data collection as part of their research training. It is almost as if data collection and preparation are an essential rite of passage that all social researchers need to go through. There is, of course, much to be said for that – as social researchers we need to develop a practical familiarity with, and knowledge of, the tools of our trade – but we need to look beyond it as well, at other possibilities.

As an earlier author put it:

> Most social scientists, when contemplating the initiation of a research project, will automatically think in terms of collecting new data. Few will think of reanalysing existing data sets. Researchers like to think that their idea for a research project is original, and hence to assume that relevant data could not yet have been collected by anyone else. But original research can often be done with 'old' data. (Hakim 1982, p. 1; see also Dale, Arber and Procter 1988)

The potential of secondary data research is enormous. Thus, on the one hand, there are increasing amounts of high quality secondary data becoming available every year. National and local governments, international agencies, public and private institutions, research funders and researchers archive huge amounts of data (now increasingly online) for use by other researchers, and it is often freely available and readily accessible. Some of this data stems from one-off projects, but a lot of it is in the form of regular reports or surveys – perhaps annual, perhaps every few years (as in the case of national censuses, commonly held every ten years) – allowing for valuable longitudinal research studies to be carried out.

On the other hand, small-scale social science research – by individual researchers or small teams – is simply unable to generate large quantities of new, primary data; neither the time nor the resources are available. So, as with documentary research in general, if secondary data exists that is relevant to your research interests – and it is highly likely that it does – it makes sense to make use of it if possible. This secondary data analysis might become the focus of your research project, or it might be analysed alongside the limited amount of primary data you have collected. In the latter case, it could be used to provide the context for your research, or for comparison or triangulation (this is discussed in more detail in Chapter 14).

This chapter will successively examine:

- secondary data and secondary data analysis
- advantages and disadvantages of secondary data analysis
- types of secondary data analysis
- examples of secondary data analysis
- where to get secondary data.

Having studied this chapter, you should be well placed to engage in secondary data research and analysis yourself.

Secondary Data and Secondary Data Analysis

The answer to the question 'what is secondary data?' has already been partially addressed in the introduction. But, to be absolutely clear, primary data is data that you have collected yourself or with a team of colleagues. This is fresh, empirical data that did not exist before you collected it. Primary data should, therefore, relate directly to your research interests. Secondary data are data that have been collected by someone else (or, perhaps, by yourself some time ago, and probably for a different purpose). While they may relate closely to your research interests, they are unlikely to align precisely with them; if you had been doing the data collection, for example, you might have asked different or additional questions.

We may also recognise other levels of data, of decreasing interest for research purposes. Thus, tertiary data may be defined as data that have been collected by someone else and then analysed by someone else (who might, or might not, be the same person), and you only have access to the findings (this is the case, for example, with meta-analyses, discussed in Chapter 7). You, as the researcher, are then placed at an increased distance from the original data, and the usefulness of such tertiary data is likely to be confined to an interest in what other researchers have done and why, and in drawing together their findings.

Secondary data analysis, then, simply refers to the analysis of secondary data: 'Secondary analysis is a research strategy which makes use of pre-existing quantitative data or pre-existing qualitative research data for the purposes of investigating new questions or verifying previous studies' (Heaton 2004, p. 16). Heaton is right to stress that secondary data may be either quantitative or qualitative, because the assumption has often been that such data are primarily or only quantitative in nature (i.e. they are the result of large-scale, national or international surveys). Nowadays, however, increasing amounts of qualitative secondary data are also available:

> These data include material such as semi structured interviews, responses to open-ended questions in questionnaires, field notes and research diaries ... this focus on non-naturalistic

qualitative data distinguishes secondary analysis from documentary analysis, which involves working with naturalistic or 'found' materials, such as auto-biographies, personal diaries and photographs. However, some types of qualitative material, such as life stories and diaries, may be subject to either secondary analysis or documentary analysis, depending on to what extent the material was solicited and shaped by researchers' involvement in collecting the material. In revisiting the actual data, secondary analysis is also distinct from meta-analysis and systematic reviews of quantitative and qualitative research because these approaches usually involve going back over the published findings of previous studies and not revisiting and reworking the data. (Heaton 2008, pp. 34–35)

The distinctions being made here by Heaton – between naturalistic and non-naturalistic data, secondary analysis and documentary analysis, and secondary analysis and systematic review and meta-analysis – may seem a little arbitrary or forced. An alternative, and perhaps more honest, response is to recognise that all of these categories are both a little slippery and overlapping. Each of the other genres discussed in this part of the book – literature reviews, systematic reviews and meta-analyses, archival and historical research, and policy research – could be seen as secondary data research. Because they are distinct genres of documentary research, however, it makes sense to treat them separately.

Secondary data analysis may be seen as having come of age in recent decades, as more and more secondary data have become available, typically freely and increasingly online. Whereas, formerly, those researchers wishing to access and use secondary data had to – much like historical researchers continue to do now (see Chapter 9) – physically go to the archive, records office, institution or library where the data was stored, or arrange for a copy of the data to be sent to them through the post, nowadays most secondary data researchers will simply access their material online: 'Quantitative data sets, in particular, are now widely and readily available in electronic form from data archives' (Heaton 2004, p. 20).

This has made secondary data research even more practical, and ideally suited to those researchers who do not have the time or inclination to engage in extensive fieldwork and original data collection.

Advantages and Disadvantages of Secondary Data Research

As with all research designs, secondary data research has advantages and disadvantages, and any researcher using it should be aware of and carefully consider these.

Hakim (1982) identified a series of potential advantages of secondary data analysis related to the characteristics of the researcher and their research interests:

by specialising in secondary analysis the independent researcher can work alone while taking advantage of data collected by well-equipped teams ... researchers whose primary interest is in assessing the empirical evidence for theories can avoid the practical difficulties of ... new data collection ... Researchers interested in the development of social indicators ... will rely exclusively on ... large national datasets. For others, the lack of resources (time and/or money) for new empirical research can be overcome by secondary analysis. (p. 169)

Hakim went on to expand this list by arguing that secondary data research might be particularly appealing to graduate students, academics with large teaching loads, those unable to obtain research grants, and those in senior and administrative positions.

Heaton (2004, pp. 27–30) also identified a long list of potential benefits associated with what she calls 'data sharing' for both quantitative and qualitative research in the social sciences. In addition to those mentioned by Hakim, these included verifying or replicating existing studies, developing theoretical or methodological understanding, enabling comparative and longitudinal studies, improving research standards, promoting mixed methods research and generalisability, and avoiding over-burdening research informants.

Heaton's last point gets stronger with each passing year as, with more and more researchers – academic and commercial – seeking to research more and more topics, the public's resistance to being interviewed, surveyed or observed understandably gets greater and greater.

Taken together, Hakim's and Heaton's lists of advantages are undeniably impressive, giving great support for the further development of secondary data research. It would be over-optimistic, however, to think that all of these benefits would apply to all such research projects. Heaton (2004) also helpfully identifies a (rather shorter) series of potential problems with quantitative secondary data analysis in particular:

poor condition and documentation of data sets; efforts and costs of data sharing; loss of control over data; risk of criticism of the original work by peers; lack of credentials of some secondary users; incompatibility of computer hardware and software of data donors and data users; difficulties of accessing data; primary researchers' proprietary interests in the data; lack of incentives to donate data; existence of disincentives to donate data; risk to confidentiality; difficulties of obtaining informed consent. (p. 28)

It is interesting that quite a few of these relate to researchers' personalities, their willingness to cooperate and potential jealousies. The research field is not always as open and welcoming, or collaborative and supporting, as we might wish it to be.

Somewhat curiously, however, Heaton expresses greater concerns regarding the secondary analysis of qualitative data:

the re-use of qualitative data is generally perceived to be more problematic than that of quantitative data ... First, doubts have been expressed over whether secondary data analysis of qualitative data is as cost-effective as that of quantitative data ... Second, attention has been drawn to the difficulties of sharing data while respecting confidentiality agreements with research participants ... Finally, various epistemological concerns have been raised about the re-use of qualitative data. For example ... it is a matter of debate as to whether qualitative studies are amenable to verification through re-analysis in the same ways as studies based on quantitative methods. (Heaton 2004, pp. 28–30)

The cost-effectiveness reservation is that qualitative data analysis, relatively speaking, takes more time than quantitative data analysis, largely because the analytical software isn't so developed, or the analysis is done manually, and a greater degree of interpretation is called for. Yet, secondary qualitative data analysis still avoids the considerable amount of time involved in qualitative data collection (and, typically in the case of recorded interview data, the much greater amount of time involved in transcribing and then checking the data).

Problems regarding confidentiality agreements are also resolvable (but see the discussion of ethics in Chapter 3). Indeed, many research funding agencies now expect data to be collected so that this does not become an issue. The epistemological concerns reflect the kind of ongoing in-depth debates beloved of many qualitative researchers, and qualitative data may be re-examined for many reasons other than verification of the original research. In short, Heaton's particular concerns about the secondary analysis of qualitative data appear to be rather over-stated.

Dale, Arber and Procter (1988, pp. 20–27; drawing on Stewart 1984, pp. 23–30) take a rather different approach to Heaton, suggesting six questions which those planning secondary data analysis should ask themselves:

1. What was the purpose of the study?
2. What information has been collected?
3. What sampling frame was used, and what is the sampling unit?
4. Who was responsible for collecting the data? What is the quality of the data?
5. Is the survey nationally representative?
6. When was the data collected?

While the wording of one of these questions indicates that the authors were primarily interested in the secondary analysis of quantitative survey data, the questions are generic in nature. Indeed, they are precisely the sorts of questions which documentary researchers need to consider when researching any document (see the discussion in Chapter 3).

Clearly, then, there is a balance to be drawn in using and analysing secondary data, whether it is the focus of a research project or just a part of it. In most cases, however, the advantages are likely to significantly outweigh the disadvantages.

Types of Secondary Data Analysis

Heaton (2004, 2008) usefully distinguishes three main modes and five types of secondary data analysis. The first, and main, mode she terms formal data sharing:

Here researchers access datasets deposited in public or institutional archives and re-use them in secondary research. In this mode of secondary analysis, researchers are re-using data that were independently collected by others. These data are likely to have been well documented for archiving purposes and to have met the necessary ethical and legal requirements for being shared with other researchers, possibly subject to certain conditions being met. (2008, p. 35)

The other two modes are informal data sharing, where two or more researchers or research groups agree to share their data with each other in various ways, and where researchers re-use their own data for different purposes or to check their original findings. Neither of these two modes is likely to be as common or as useful, however, as the first mode.

The five types of secondary data analysis identified are:

supplementary analysis, a more in-depth analysis of an emergent issue or aspect of the data, that was not addressed or was only partially addressed in the primary study ... *supra analysis*, where the aims and focus of the secondary study transcend those of the original research ... *re-analysis*, where data are re-examined in order to confirm and validate findings of a primary study ... in *amplified analysis*, two or more existing qualitative datasets may be compared or combined for purposes of secondary analysis ... in *assorted analysis*, re-use of existing qualitative data is carried out alongside the collection and analysis of primary qualitative data for the same study. (Heaton 2008, p. 39)

Though Heaton sets her categorisation within qualitative research, the same distinctions could be made for quantitative or mixed methods research. While re-analysis and supplementary analysis both imply relatively small-scale projects – at least relative to the size of the original project – the other three types involve larger-scale projects, with the secondary data set examined alongside other data.

Re-analysis is a particularly interesting kind of research, but is rarely carried out in the social sciences, particularly in qualitative research. We may only speculate as to why this is so, but it probably has something to do with our trust in the original researchers, and a reluctance to, in effect, challenge their interpretations, plus the wish to do something new or different.

What Heaton terms amplified analysis is also appealing but little undertaken, yet well suited to small-scale research. It suggests a way of combining original data collection with secondary data analysis, with the researcher repeating the approach taken by a previous researcher on another sample, and then comparing the two studies for similarities and differences. This might also be termed comparative or multiple case study research (Tight 2017).

What Heaton's typology does not recognise, however – probably because of its focus on qualitative research – is that secondary data analysis may not follow other research. The data may simply have been collected, and then left un-analysed for later researchers to do what they wished with.

Examples of Secondary Data Analysis

Box 8.1 contains four examples of secondary data analysis. These relate to 139 grant applications for inpatient hospice building improvements in the UK (Rigby, Milligan and Payne 2014); 269 investigation reports into care practices from three Swedish municipalities (Rytterstrom, Arman and Unosson 2013); 429 newspaper articles, 208 industry magazine articles and seven market reports on the activities of the Coca-Cola company in China and India (Williams 2015); and 1767 cited economic geography articles (Foster et al. 2007).

Interestingly, these examples confirm, amongst other things, that there is little, if any, distinction between secondary data analysis and documentary analysis, as data and documents are essentially the same thing. Thus, whereas the other genres of documentary research considered in this book – literature reviews, systematic reviews and meta-analyses, archival and historical research, and policy research – have specialist foci and/or methods, secondary data analysis is a more generic approach.

It is also interesting that the fourth example given referred to 'a systematic review of the contents of 26 journals'. It is considered here as secondary data analysis, however, because it characterised itself as a citation analysis in its title and introduction.

While the third and fourth of the examples in Box 8.1 used major national or international archives, the first and second did not. Rather, they are examples of the creative use of existing, accessible documents to help answer particular research questions. All four articles are also based wholly on documentary analysis. The studies varied somewhat in scale, though all were fairly substantive pieces of research, and the searching and sifting processes undertaken by Williams (the third example), in particular, would have taken a considerable amount of time.

BOX 8.1

Examples of Secondary Data Analysis

1. Electronic copies were obtained of the 191 grant application forms which had been awarded funding under the 2006 DH [Department of Health] Capital grants scheme (unfunded applications were excluded). Since the focus of the analysis was on inpatient hospice building improvements, applications were selected for inclusion if they were wholly or partly for the benefit of hospice inpatients, and were excluded if they were solely for the benefit of hospice day patients. Having examined the grant applications, 139 were identified as suitable for inclusion. These applications came from 111 hospices (because 17 hospices had made multiple applications for different projects within their hospice) ... A content analysis of all 139 included application forms was undertaken, to identify 'key patterns, themes and categories' from the data. This involved a careful reading of the application forms and the extraction of the following data into prepared templates: (a) The types of improvements that were proposed (for example, replacement of flooring, installation of artwork, refurbishment

of bathrooms). (b) The reasons given by the applicants for making these improvements, including the use of evidence from service user consultations, academic papers, etc. The research team met regularly to identify and agree on emerging themes, and data was re-sorted and re-categorised as the research progressed. (Rigby, Milligan and Payne 2014, pp. 188–189)

2. An analysis was conducted of written investigation reports that reported suspected abuse, failure of care or care practices that violated a person's integrity, security or dignity, as defined by the Lex Sarah legislation [the name given in Sweden to the Social Service Act]. The analysis included all Lex Sarah reports (n = 269 cases) during 2007 in three municipalities in Sweden: one small rural district and two middle-sized city municipalities. The selected reports included all archived material from each investigation including a registration form with supplementary attachments. The registration form was produced and structured by the municipal authorities and comprised a number of sections where the staff reported on where, when and how the incident happened. The form also included notes on how the investigation was conducted, and recommended measures to ensure the violations are not repeated. The attachments included archived documents such as printouts of e-mail conversations, written accounts from personnel and management, fax messages, letters from relatives, and the decision of the Social Welfare Committee and the Lex Sarah investigator. How a Lex Sarah investigation is managed differs across Swedish municipalities, but the municipalities that formed the basis for this study used similar procedures and documentation for their Lex Sarah investigations. Critical hermeneutics ... was chosen as the interpretative methodology. This involves analysing both the texts as abstracted, official entities and the socio-historical context in which they are embedded. (Rytterstrom, Arman and Unosson 2013, p. 355)

3. This paper takes a public health perspective in critically interpreting documents that focus on the activities of the Coca-Cola Company in China and India ... Data for this study were taken from the following documentary sources: company annual and quarterly reports; market reports; news media articles; and food and beverage industry magazines and journals. Coca-Cola annual and quarterly reports (2003–2014) were downloaded from the company's website and analyzed in detail. Newspaper articles (including all English language publications) were found using Nexis database searches ... documents were identified using a structured but iterative search, and were assessed for relevance. The date range was fixed at 1975–2012 - to cover the company's activity during the liberalization of the Indian and Chinese markets. The following keywords were used to guide the search: 'China', 'Chinese', 'India', 'Indian', and 'Coca-Cola' or 'Coke'. Articles were deemed relevant if they had as their primary focus the Coca-Cola Company and its activities in China or India, or issues that pertained to China or India. A total of 429 newspaper articles were identified and reviewed. To supplement these articles, search engine searches of online news articles were conducted for articles published between 2012 and 2014. Additionally, 208 industry magazine articles were analyzed in depth ... Finally, market reports (n = 7) were primarily drawn from EuroMonitor Passport Global Market Information database ... documents were triangulated across sources in order to reconstruct a narrative of events and explore company activities. (Williams 2015, pp. 456–457)

(Continued)

(Continued)

4. Casting our net widely, to include most of the journal outlets indexed in the ISI's Web of Knowledge in which economic geographers frequently publish, we conducted a systematic review of the contents of 26 journals over the period since the early 1980s. This yielded an initial 'population' of 17119 separate journal articles. We then established some basic parameters by including only those articles that can, on this evidence, be said to have made some 'impact' – those with 10 or more citations. Subsequent analysis then focused on those articles, which are herein referred to as 'cited articles', that could be deemed to fall within our broad definition of economic geography. For the two specialist journals in the field, Economic Geography and the Journal of Economic Geography, this was a straightforward task, since all their papers can be considered, by definition, works of economic geography. For the remaining 24 journals, an item by item review of their contents was conducted, in order to capture all those papers within the broad ambit of 'economic geography'. These processes of sifting and selecting resulted in a database of 1767 (cited) economic geography articles, from which the following analysis is derived. (Foster et al. 2007, p. 297)

The methods used in the analysis of the data collected illustrate something of the range of approaches and concerns. Rigby, Milligan and Payne undertook a content analysis of their grant applications to identify key patterns, themes and categories, making use of prepared templates. Rytterstrom, Arman and Unosson employed critical hermeneutics, so as to place the official texts examined in their socio-historical context. Williams used the different data sources collected to triangulate each other, and to produce a narrative of events. Foster et al. performed a bibliometric analysis of the characteristics of the 1767 articles selected. Their study was unusual amongst the four examples chosen in being primarily quantitative in nature.

It would be relatively easy to add to these examples. The creative analysis of existing secondary documentation appears to be particularly common in the broad health care area, as in Froggatt's (2007) content analysis, using NVivo, of the feedback provided in 352 inspection reports of care homes in South Yorkshire in the UK; and in Halabi et al.'s (2012) examination of 24 curricula for HIV/AIDS education programmes in Ghana, gathered through snowball sampling. Similarly, Momeni, Jirwe and Emami (2008) analysed the educational plans and courses of 26 Swedish nursing schools, amounting to around 1300 pages, coding them using keywords; while Morrison, Bickerstaff and Taylor (2009) examined the administrative and social work records of the learning disability social work team in North Belfast between 1996 and 2005.

Paul and Hill (2013) focused on policies on self-harm in organisations working with young people in the UK; and, perhaps more innovatively, Milligan, Bingley and Gatrell (2005) used solicited diaries to explore health issues among older people in the north-west of England. They concluded that 'Through the gathering of chronologically ordered data about daily activities, diaries can act as both a record and reflection of the health experiences, activities and life-worlds inhabited by older people' (p. 1882).

Such research is, though, by no means confined to the health care disciplines. Thus, in education, Hordosy (2014) reports on an analysis of school leavers' and graduates' information systems in Europe, using web-based official documents, the information in which was then coded and cross-tabulated. In business, Michelini and Fiorentino (2012) studied the features of inclusive business and social business models, focusing on ten cases, with external and internal documents collected and coded for analysis. And, in a final example, Henninger and Scifleet (2016) carried out a qualitative content analysis of communications on social networking sites (SNS) during a national event 'to investigate potential contributions of SNS to social and cultural memory including their subsequent custodianship' (p. 277).

The scope for secondary data analysis is clearly, therefore, both massive and cross-disciplinary.

Where to Get Secondary Data

If you don't already know what sort of secondary data research you want to undertake, or where to look for relevant data to analyse, getting started may seem very difficult. Actually, however, the problem may be more one of how to cope with the surfeit of data, growing daily, that is out there and available to be analysed. Box 8.2 gives a brief outline of the plethora of material that may be accessed through just one data service, the UK Data Service. While this is just one national provider, and may not seem relevant if you are based in a different country, there are similar providers in many other countries, and, as will become apparent, the UK Data Service works with and links to many of them.

BOX 8.2

An Example of a National Data Service – the UK Data Service

The UK Data Service (ukdataservice.ac.uk) gathers together data on all topics online, with links to other data providers and archives throughout the UK and internationally.

For example, on its website you can find details of, and guides, as well as access, to:

- *UK surveys*: such as British Social Attitudes, conducted since 1983, with over 3,000 respondents annually; the Family Expenditure Survey, carried out since 1957; and the Labour Force Survey, carried out since 1973.

(Continued)

(Continued)

- *Cross-national surveys*: such as the European Quality of Life Survey, carried out in 2003 and 2007; and the Eurobarometer Surveys, carried out since 1974.
- *Longitudinal surveys*: such as the 1970 British Cohort Study, which has been following over 17,000 people born in one week in 1970; and the National Child Development Study, which has been following those born in one week in 1958.
- *Qualitative/mixed surveys*: such as Family Life and Work Experience before 1918, which completed 537 life-story interviews in the 1970s.

The UK Data Service also hosts data sets (qualitative and quantitative) produced by research projects funded by the Economic and Social Research Council (ESRC), and formerly held on the Economic and Social Data Service (ESDS) site at the University of Essex (see Box 8.3).

There are links with international data providers, such as Eurostat, the European Union statistical gateway, the Organisation for Economic Cooperation and Development and the United Nations.

And there are links with national statistics agencies and archives, such as Research Data Australia; the Indian Council of Social Science Research; the Israel Social Sciences Data Center; the South African Data Archive; and, within the United States, the National Opinion Research Center and the Social Science Data Archive.

As Box 8.2 makes clear, the UK Data Service provides data from, and links to, UK surveys, cross-national surveys (typically European in scope), longitudinal surveys and some – though most of the data it houses is quantitative – qualitative or mixed method surveys. It also provides links to international data providers, and to dozens of national data providers and archives across the globe. Indeed, if secondary data research is your interest, you could happily spend hours browsing the UK Data Service website and the many other sites it links to.

The UK Data Service hosts data collected for research projects funded by the Economic and Social Research Council (ESRC), for which a condition of funding now is the deposit of the data collected in re-useable form (unless there are compelling reasons why this shouldn't be done). Box 8.3 identifies 15 of these, giving details of their titles, the years in which data were collected and the methods used for doing so.

BOX 8.3

Examples of Data Sets from ESRC-funded Projects Available Through the UK Data Service

The titles of selected projects are given, together with the dates of data collection and the methods used:

Poverty and Social Exclusion in the UK (2010–2014), focus groups.

Directors, Boards and Corporate Governance (2009–2011), quantitative data set.

Impact Assessment in Complex Contexts of Rural Livelihood Transformation in Africa (2012–2013), longitudinal household income data and interviews.

The 2013/2014 Winter Floods and Policy Change (2014–2015), interviews and survey.

Sustainable Supply Chain Management (2012–2015), interviews with company directors and trade associations.

Retail Competition and Consumer Choice (2002–2004), survey.

Mapping Urban Energy Landscapes (2013–2016), interviews and observations.

Working Class Conservatives in Urban England (1958–1960), interviews.

Social History of Alcohol in East Africa (1997–1998), surveys, interviews, photographs, journals.

Learning to Perform: data from a UK conservatoire of music (2004–2007), interviews and surveys (longitudinal).

The Role of Schools in Supporting Children Affected by HIV in Zimbabwe (2012–2014), survey plus interviews and focus groups.

Research Capacity Building Network Skills Survey (2001–2002), survey and interviews.

Collection of Tweets mentioning the UK petitions (2011–2014), a study of online political behaviour.

Culture and Visual Imagery in a Town Built on Coal (1997), focus groups.

Household Survey on Agency and Governance in Maharashtra, India (2010–2013), structured questionnaire survey.

Box 8.3 should give some idea of the variety of research being carried out using ESRC funds – in terms of disciplines and subject areas, and in terms of data collection methods used. Some of the research projects were primarily qualitative, some primarily quantitative and some used a variety of data collection methods. While most focused on economic or social issues in the UK, there were also numbers of projects which involved undertaking research, often collaboratively, in other countries. Both data and guidance information are available for each project.

While the UK Data Service is a particularly good example, in terms of the breadth and variety of secondary data it holds and makes available for research purposes, similar sorts of data may be found in many countries, though not necessarily gathered together in one place. Here, for example, is an account of a research project using available national data sets in Spain:

We use data from the 2006 wave of the Continuous Sample of Working Histories (hereafter CSWH), which is a 4 percent nonstratified random sample of the population registered with the Social Security Administration in 2006. The CSWH provides information on:
(1) sociodemographic characteristics of the worker (such as sex, education, nationality, province of residence); (2) worker's job information (such as type of contract, part-time status,

occupation, the dates the employment spell started and ended, and monthly earnings); (3) employer's information (such as industry, public versus private sector, the number of workers in the firm, and the location). Although not reported in the CSWH, other variables such as experience and tenure can be easily calculated. In addition, information on the individual's education level, and the number and date of birth of children living in the household at the time of the interview, (including but not distinguishing own natural, adopted, step and foster children) are available in the 2006 Spanish Municipal Registry of Inhabitants, which is matched at the person level with the Social Security records. (Fernández-Kranz, Lacuesta and Rodríguez-Planas 2013, pp. 177–178)

In addition to such national, quantitative data sets, numerous others will be available at a local, institutional or even individual level, with quantitative or qualitative data or both. By searching on the internet, the accessible and available sets of secondary data of relevance and interest to you should be relatively easy to track down; after all, that is how I got hold of the information discussed in this section.

Conclusion

Secondary data, then, is both increasingly widespread and available, and may be analysed or re-analysed in a variety of ways, depending on the nature of the data available. There are many advantages to secondary data analysis, not least the time saved by not collecting the data yourself, and the ability to produce larger-scale analyses than would otherwise be possible. There are also, of course, some disadvantages, including that the secondary data available may not be precisely what you wanted.

Even if you don't choose to base the whole of your research project on available secondary data, however, it makes good sense to explore the possibilities, if only to use secondary data analysis alongside your main research strategy or design.

KEY READINGS

Dale, A, Arber, S, and Procter, M (1988) *Doing Secondary Analysis*. London, Unwin Hyman.

A somewhat dated but still useful introduction to the field.

Hakim, C (1982) *Secondary Analysis in Social Research: A guide to data sources and methods with examples*. London, George Allen & Unwin.

Another dated text (more contemporary accounts are few in number), but a valuable guide, particularly if you are interested in post-war UK quantitative sources of data.

Heaton, J (2004) *Reworking Qualitative Data*. London, Sage.

A more recent text, though focused on qualitative data sources and uses.

9

ARCHIVAL AND HISTORICAL RESEARCH

CONTENTS

Introduction	110
The Nature of Archival and Historical Research	110
Types of Data and Sources	111
Examples of Archival and Historical Research	115
Conclusion	119

Introduction

Archival and historical research may sound like much the same thing, and they undoubtedly overlap to a considerable degree, but the distinction is valuable and is being made here for two reasons. First, historians do not only use archives in carrying out their research, though archives – whether physical or virtual – are most often their major source for data. Second, researchers other than historians also use archives, which collect and preserve documents and data relating to all subjects and disciplines.

Historical research is not, therefore, solely the province of historians. In all fields, including all of the social sciences, it behoves researchers and practitioners to have some awareness of history, and in particular the history of their field. This will help in enabling them to not overlook relevant previous research and findings, or make the mistake of assuming that something is new, original or innovative (because they have just thought of it). There is much to be learnt from the past and from past research.

This chapter considers:

- the nature of archival and historical research
- the types of data and sources used in this research
- examples of archival and historical research in different disciplines.

It ends with some general conclusions and suggestions for further reading.

The Nature of Archival and Historical Research

Rather like documentary research in general (see the discussion in Chapter 1), historical researchers and academics have usually seen little need to discuss how they go about their work; they just do it and then write it up for publication. Nor have they felt the need to prepare their students for undertaking historical research other than by the 'tried and tested' method of immersing them in it:

> Traditionally, history undergraduates were offered no formal instruction in the nature of their chosen discipline; its time-honoured place in our literary culture and its non-technical presentation suggested that common sense combined with a sound general education would provide the student with what little orientation he or she required. This approach leaves a great deal to chance. (Tosh 2015, p. x)

These attitudes and practices are, however, changing, and there is now a growing, albeit still relatively small, literature on historical and archival research methods (see, for example, Trachtenberg 2006).

Compared to other social researchers, historical researchers are more closely dependent on documents (or sources), which may at least partly explain their lack of engagement with their methodology. Indeed, they would be lost without them:

> Despite multifarious changes in attitudes and approaches over the past hundred years ... historians are still source-based creatures; even those most 'modern' in outlook seek to reread and reinterpret sources; none would claim to do without them, although the nature of sources has changed greatly over the past century. (Black and MacRaild 2017, p. 83)

Not only that, historical researchers are wedded to the idea of producing texts or sources themselves for the use of future historians. Unlike in the other social sciences – where the refereed journal article largely holds sway – for historians the academic monograph or book, with the greater scope that it gives for the extended treatment of a topic, remains sovereign:

> academic history is defined primarily ... in terms of the heavyweight, textual monograph. This is produced in strict conformity to the basic epistemological precepts of reference, justified belief, incisive inference, apposite conceptualisation and lucid insight. But above all it is the result of the promotion of history as a mimetic (in the sense of imitation) form that is based on the correspondence theory of knowledge as opposed to the diegetic (narrative). (Munslow 2007, p. 66)

But historical research is not as straightforward and standardised as this would imply. There are increasing numbers of historical researchers, including some of a radical or feminist orientation, who are using more varied sources and approaches to research:

> modern students of the discipline are introduced to the idea of an engagement with documentary evidence, collected together in a particular kind of place, as a foundational and paradigmatic activity of historians. This is done despite the obvious fact that many modern historians simply never use ... archives. (Steedman 2001, p. x)

For example, in the move away from the archives to other sources, some have explored historical re-enactment for what it indicates about the nature of history and about who counts as a historian (Johnson 2015).

We shall explore the types of data and sources used by historical researchers further in the next section.

Types of Data and Sources

Tosh (2015) confirms that historical researchers have moved some way from a reliance on, or prioritisation of, written documents as their key sources: 'Historical sources encompass every kind of evidence that human beings have left behind of their past activities – the written word and the spoken word, the shape of the landscape and the material artefact, the fine arts as well as photography and film' (p. 71). As we have seen already, though (see Chapter 2), the kinds of evidence other than the 'written word' that Tosh identifies may all, in some sense, be regarded as documents as well, particularly when they have been recorded in some way. That is, each of the kinds of evidence that

Tosh identifies document aspects of human activity just as clearly and certainly – or not (as each will be subject to critical review) – as the written word does. Photographs, films, paintings, sculpture, household objects and the landscape itself are artefacts just as books and articles are, and they may, of course, be transferred to or summarised in written texts.

Purvis (1992) offers a different kind of categorisation, identifying three main kinds of sources or texts for historical research:

> I shall distinguish between three main categories that share certain characteristics in common – official texts, published commentary and reporting, and personal texts. *Official texts* includes state, bureaucratic, institutional and legal texts such as government reports, census data, court reports, official reports of societies and institutions, memoranda and official letters. *Published commentary and reporting* covers accounts of events that might be written or constructed without the direct help of the participants. Such texts include novels, films, photographs, advertisements, the writings of key political, social and literary figures, and newspapers. The approach in *personal texts* is in terms of a person's subjective experience. They include letters, diaries, photograph albums, autobiographies and life histories. (p. 275, emphasis in original)

This again brings up the distinction between primary and secondary sources or data, which we have already discussed in the previous chapter in the context of secondary data research (see Chapter 8). Whereas Purvis' first category, official texts, would be viewed as primary sources, her second and third categories, published commentary and reporting and personal texts, could be seen as incorporating elements of both primary and secondary sources. Thus, while photographs and letters might be treated as primary sources, novels and autobiographies would clearly be secondary sources.

McCulloch and Richardson (2000) seek to make the distinction clearer by taking a different approach:

> As a general rule, there are two major differences between the primary sources and secondary sources used in historical research. The first is about authorship: whereas primary sources are produced by those directly involved in or witnesses to a particular historical episode or issue, secondary sources are written after the event, usually by those who were not party to it ... The second key difference between primary and secondary sources, deriving from the first, concerns availability. While primary sources may take a range of forms and may be difficult to find, secondary sources are generally available in published form. (pp. 79–80)

This suggests a different kind of distinction between primary and secondary sources to that made by social scientists, and by documentary researchers in particular. What matters to the historian is whether the author of a document was a witness to or participant in the focus of the research; and we might also add the qualification that they should have produced the document shortly after the episode or event took place.

McCulloch and Richardson's second point highlights a key issue with historical research, namely the existence and availability of source material. The further back in time you go, less and less is likely to be available as primary source material. With fewer people around, there was less need for documentation, and what there was may well have been lost, destroyed or corrupted. With more recent periods this is less likely to be a problem, but even then sources may have been destroyed (e.g. in wartime, or deliberately to save storage space and cut costs; most institutions, including government departments, routinely cull their records) or access to them may be denied (e.g. for reasons of security or confidentiality).

Enfield (2006) makes the issue of availability clear in a distinctive context, in a discussion of languages as a living archive, languages which nowadays are under threat as never before:

> Languages are archives of a great deal of information of interest to many, if not all, disciplines of human science, as well as other branches of science such as agriculture, biology and medicine. Archives worldwide are endangered; when they are lost, they cannot be replaced. This is true not only for books, films and manuscripts, but for the very languages in which these are produced. Different storage media have radically different properties – compare the respective shelf life and modes of access of stone tablets, palm-leaf manuscripts, paper and living people. The living person seldom lasts a hundred years, and furthermore presents a wide range of access problems to the scientist (if the person is busy, disinterested, drunk, etc). For this and many other reasons, documenting comprehensive information about linguistic structure is a significant undertaking. (pp. 474–475)

Historians may thus also be seen as being responsible for producing documentation of existing social life, particularly those elements or aspects of it which may be under threat, in order to provide research materials for future researchers.

Returning to the primary/secondary distinction, Brundage (2002) divides primary sources into two categories, the second of which is then sub-divided into two further sub-categories:

> Written primary sources can be divided into two major categories: manuscript sources and published sources ... Published primary sources can be divided into two categories:
> 1) Manuscript materials such as letters, diaries, and memoranda, usually intended as private, sometimes intimate documents, often published after the death of their authors; 2) Materials that were intended from the outset to be printed and made public – for example newspaper articles, congressional debates, autobiographies, annual company reports, and reports of the United States Census. (pp. 16–17)

This shows, again, the way in which different authorities use different classification systems. For example, Brundage's second sub-category reads very much like Purvis' (1992) official texts, though it also includes some elements which Purvis classified as published commentary and reporting. His first sub-category corresponds well to Purvis' personal texts, though the latter would also accommodate much of Brundage's first category of manuscript sources (which itself becomes somewhat confused when

Brundage recognises published manuscript materials as a sub-category of published sources).

Brundage's (2002) 'manuscript materials' and Purvis' (1992) 'personal texts' both suggest that life stories – or aspects of them – represent one important, and perhaps a more contemporary, way in which historical research may be pursued. After all:

> The world is crammed full of human, personal documents. People keep diaries, send letters, make quilts, take photos, dash off memos, compose auto/biographies, construct websites, scrawl graffiti, publish their memoirs, write letters, compose CVs, leave suicide notes, film video diaries, inscribe memorials on tombstones, shoot films, paint pictures, make tapes and try to record their personal dreams. All of these expressions of personal life are hurled out into the world by the millions and can be of interest to anyone who cares to seek them out. They are all in the broadest sense 'documents of life'. (Plummer 2001, p. 17)

To Plummer's list we may, indeed must, add all of the burgeoning variety of online personal documents available on social media and more generally on the internet.

Of course, as with any other documents (see the discussion in Chapter 3), historical documents have to be approached with care once they have been identified and accessed:

> In approaching the sources, the historian is anything but a passive observer. The relevant evidence has to be sought after in fairly out-of-the-way and improbable places. The archives in which that evidence is found have to be scrutinised for political or ideological distortion. Ingenuity and flair are required to grasp the full range of uses to which a single source may be put. Of each type of evidence the historian has to ask how and why it came into being, and what its real import is. Divergent sources have to be weighed against each other, forgeries and gaps explained. No document, however authoritative, is beyond question. (Tosh 2015, pp. 118–119; see also Dibble 1963)

Indeed, authoritative documents might be regarded as being particularly questionable, given that authority is frequently used to deny or stifle questioning, while advancing one standard, 'accepted', point of view. Thus, government sources, to give one obvious example, have to be interrogated very carefully, as much as for what they don't say as for what they do, and placed in the context of the political debates of the day.

Darnton (2018) approaches this concern from the perspective of political science, and offers:

> eight suggestions for improving qualitative research with documentary primary sources. Scholars should cite their sources in detail for replication, but we should also clarify the main directions of sources explored but not cited. More broadly, we need to articulate a research strategy, why we headed in? one direction rather than another in search of evidence. Strategies might include following where others have worked, breaking new ground elsewhere, or following our knowledge of the policy process to target particular sources. When we have relevant sources in hand, we should clarify their specific relationship to our overall claims

about the causal process, and provide some robustness checks by probing the communicative context of key documents. (p. 124)

As well as reiterating the key point that published documentary research should detail how it was carried out to allow for process checking and replication by others, Darnton makes the valuable suggestion that researchers should also spell out what they did not do, and which documents they did not consult, and why. This calls for a good deal of honesty, openness and recognition (for example, some researchers may simply be unaware of particular documents, which they might have consulted had they known about them), but would enable a quicker and more cumulative expansion of research on the topic in question.

How the researcher treats archival and historical sources also depends, as Gidley (2018) makes clear, on their epistemological perspective:

we can identify two broad ways of working. These relate to the broad distinction between realism and constructionism ... The realist approach to archival work involves gathering as great a volume of texts as possible and scouring them for details of 'who', 'when', 'where' and 'what' – to use texts as evidence, as a representation of reality. This approach has often taken the documents themselves at face value – seeing them as a research resource ... The problem ... [is that] archived documentary sources are never perfect windows into the past. Rather, they are socially produced ... The social constructionist approach sees archived texts as *topic* rather than *resource* – as realities in themselves rather than a way of accessing some other reality. This approach is not concerned with the accuracy of the descriptions given in the documents, but in their social organization. That is, how are different discourses (and the different identities which emerge from them) produced? (pp. 293–294, emphasis in original)

Most social researchers approach the documents they use in their research from a realist or quasi-realist perspective; that is, they see them as valuable sources of data and information, though this does not mean they necessarily approach them uncritically, so Gidley's implied criticism may be a little harsh. The social constructionist approach he advocates is less popular but growing in influence (see the discussion of discourse analysis in Chapter 13).

Examples of Archival and Historical Research

Box 9.1 contains details of four contrasting examples of historical research. The variety of topics – early modern Norwegian witchcraft trials, the efficiency of the agricultural economy in early Norman Britain, the gender and occupation of English diarists in the period 1500–1700, and the living standards of English workers in the period 1770–1815 – is deliberate but also illustrative of the possibilities. Equally illuminating are the range of sources being used to answer the research questions: court books and fiscal records;

the Domesday Book; diaries; and indents from convict ships. All are written, indeed originally handwritten, sources.

BOX 9.1

Examples of Archival and Historical Research

1. There are two main series of sources to early modern Norwegian witchcraft trials: court books (tingbøker) and fiscal records (lensregnskaper) … Both … have strengths and weaknesses which need to be considered. The fiscal records are the sources which give us the longest time frame, since they are generally preserved in unbroken series from 1590 onwards. They are therefore the source best suited for studying trends in the chronology, scope and geography of trials. However, these records of witchcraft trials are the result of either expenses or income (or both) to the royal treasury that came as a consequence of the trials. Trials that were dropped or ended with acquittals therefore rarely made their way into the fiscal records, which means that they must be used with caution lest acquittals be misinterpreted as an absence of trials. At the other end of the scale, executions invariably incurred expenses and often small income from confiscated property as well (usually smaller than the expenses), which means that trials ending with a death sentence were much more likely to make their way into the fiscal records. This source, then, is thoroughly skewed in favour of the most serious cases … The court books in contrast contain much more information about each trial, and also about trials which ended in acquittals or were never brought to a conclusion and thus never made their way into the fiscal records. The main problem with the court books is that they are only sporadically preserved for the years before 1650. They are therefore of very limited use for the period in which the majority of the trials took place. (Knutsen 2003, p. 189)

2. Comprehensive information on production in 1086 is available for 333 Wiltshire lay estates. The data file was compiled from Domesday Book entries in the Victoria County History of Wiltshire (1955), which were checked against a facsimile of the Latin transcript and an English translation in the so called Phillimore edition and the Alecto Historical Editions translation. Phillimore and the Alecto Historical Editions translation were used to determine the hundred [a geographical division] locations of the estates. A general rule of thumb was developed that only entries for which (1) annual value is recorded, (2) either ploughteams or some meadowland, pasture or woodland are recorded and (3) some labour is recorded, were retained for analysis. In addition, 15 other entries were deleted because they were either implausible or incomplete. (McDonald 2010, p. 3233)

3. The diary is an immensely useful source for historians. As a record of specific events, an indicator of attitudes towards social, economic and religious trends, or simply acting as that connecting voice to the past, diaries have been described as 'the re-creation of a past age. The diarists are perhaps our richest source of detail: not only in the major historical events and personalities they depict, but in their social background of manners and morals, contemporary tastes and fashions in recreation and dress'. Yet there are some drawbacks to using diaries as historical source material. The main cause for concern is that the people who kept diaries

tended to come from the more prosperous, and obviously literate, sections of society. Given the high rate of illiteracy in early modern society, especially among the lower, labouring, sections of society, it can be argued that placing emphasis upon diaries limits the historical evidence to a small, rather privileged proportion of the population. Another concern for those undertaking research into early modern diaries is the possible unreliability of the source in terms of its factual accuracy. During the early modern period diaries were a developing genre and were not always the essentially private or spontaneous daily records which might be assumed. (McKay 2005, pp. 191–192; quoting Willy 1963)

4. Our sample comprised 11,303 English and, for comparative purposes, 5,005 Irish male convicts transported to New South Wales between 1817 and 1840 ... Accompanying each convict ship was an indent, a document that contained complete information on each convict, including age, gender, occupation, conjugal status, literacy status, town and county of birth, crime and previous convictions, as well as height. The fine grid of height measurements and the accompanying detailed information bolster our confidence in the accuracy and reliability of the convict records ... Height was typically recorded to the nearest quarter-inch. (Nicholas and Steckel 1991, pp. 940–941)

One common factor amongst the four examples given in Box 9.1 is that they all contain an assessment of the advantages and disadvantages of the sources being used, demonstrating the critical approach which historians take towards their sources. Thus, Knutsen (2003) notes that while the fiscal records are biased towards the more serious cases, notably those that led to a death sentence and had financial consequences, the court books are poorly preserved for the earlier periods of interest. McDonald (2010) uses a number of extant versions of the Domesday Book to cross-check data, and carefully excludes that which is incomplete or implausible.

McKay (2005) stresses that diaries are biased towards the prosperous and literate, and may contain factual inaccuracies. Nevertheless, the number of known diaries from her period and place of interest, 1500 to 1700 in England, is surprisingly high, 372, and increasing as more are identified or revealed. Nicholas and Steckel (1991), for their part, interpret 'The fine grid of height measurements and the accompanying detailed information' as evidence of their data's reliability.

Many more examples could, of course, be given, to further emphasise the variety of topics and sources in archival and historical research, and the care and consideration that has to be taken in pursuing such research. Thus, Tickell (2010) focuses on the prevention of shoplifting in eighteenth-century London. She:

uses evidence from Old Bailey transcripts to highlight the type of stock and businesses that were most commonly targeted by shoplifters and the most vulnerable locations for theft within these stores. It reveals how shopkeepers employed an ingeniously wide range of techniques to protect their goods and how these anti-theft strategies and devices were in many cases precursors of those familiar to us in the twenty-first century. The paper also draws attention to the role of staff in detecting potential offenders and suggests that concerns around customer theft may have been a factor in encouraging the withdrawal of women from the retail sector during this period ... many eighteenth-century shopkeepers developed the style and ambience of their shops to attract a wealthier class of leisure shopper: this paper argues that frequently, the associated new marketing techniques supported retail stock protection, either intentionally or fortuitously. It concludes by suggesting that this served to reinforce retailers' confidence in their chosen strategy for limiting losses and discouraging the illicit passage of their goods beyond the shop. (pp. 300–301)

Fernández-Montblanc, Izquierdo and Bethencourt (2018) combine documentary research with numerical modelling techniques so as to estimate the possible position of shipwreck remains:

The use of historical sources to identify a discovered shipwreck or to define a search area is an extended practice. In this case, the historical significance of the Battle of Trafalgar enables us to obtain a lot of valuable information. In our case, the documentary research has been extended to include information on the causes of the wreckage and to characterize the storm conditions that produced the stranding of *Fougueux*. Several documentary sources were considered, including ship logbooks, the *corpus documental* of the battle, watchtower weather observations, and a careful revision of previous works focused on the meteorological conditions during the storm following the battle. Finally, based on the results of the historical storm depiction, a systematic search within atmospheric re-analysis datasets was performed in order to select a recent storm with similar characteristics to the Battle of Trafalgar storm. The data of that analogous storm were used to simulate wind, waves, and current velocities during and immediately after the *Fougueux* stranding. (pp. 142–143)

Carmona and Renninger (2018):

focus on the work of the Royal Fine Art Commission (RFAC), which, for three quarters of a century, held the mantel of the UK Government's advisor on design in the built environment for England and Wales. The paper draws on archival and documentary evidence to explore the important work and concerns of the RFAC from its creation in 1924 and its early years, through to the post-war construction boom and into the 1980s and a new less paternalistic era of government. Analysis of the archives is supplemented by what the limited available literature tells us about the RFAC. (p. 53)

A final example is provided by Starck (2004, 2006), who carried out a content analysis of 1667 obituaries published in eight Australian newspapers in a six-month period during 2002/03, as well as more limited analyses of British and American newspapers, and interviews with obituarists and others concerned with the practice. While noting the obituary's recent revival as a newspaper art form, its role as a celebration of life as much as a marking of death, its often somewhat coded nature, its rather ambivalent attitude to detailing causes of death, gender imbalance and interest in the eccentric, he argues for its role as 'a valid instrument of historical record' (2006, p. 46).

Conclusion

Archival research and historical research have much to offer the documentary researcher. Physical archives can be comforting and comfortable places, where virtually all that is available on your topic is close to hand. You know where you will be researching for the foreseeable future, and can make yourself familiar with the staff and resources available.

Historical research more generally can be both challenging and limiting. It is challenging in terms of identifying and accessing the limited sources that will be available on a particular topic during a specific period, and in terms of then interpreting and using those sources as best you can. It is limiting in the sense that there will only be so many sources available to interpret, and you will always wish for access to that other source which no longer exists, or perhaps never existed.

KEY READINGS

McCulloch, G, and Richardson, W (2000) *Historical Research in Educational Settings*. Buckingham, Open University Press.

A text focused on the field of education, but also of more general interest.

Plummer, K (2001) *Documents of Life 2: An invitation to a critical humanism*. London, Sage.

A fascinating discussion of the diversity of documents that may be used in studying human lives.

Purvis, J (1992) Using Primary Sources when Researching Women's History from a Feminist Perspective. *Women's History Review*, 1, 2, pp. 273–306.

While particularly relevant for those interested in women's history, there is much of more general interest here as well.

Steedman, C (2001) *Dust*. Manchester, Manchester University Press.

A well-written account and critique of the use of archives.

Tosh, J (2015) *The Pursuit of History: Aims, methods and new directions in the study of history*. London, Routledge, sixth edition.

A popular textbook on historical method.

Trachtenberg, M (2006) *The Craft of International History: A guide to method*. Princeton, NJ, Princeton University Press.

A popular American textbook on historical method.

10
POLICY RESEARCH

CONTENTS

Introduction	122
The Nature of Policy and Policy Research	122
Types of Policy Research	125
Examples of Policy Research	126
Conclusion	130

Introduction

Policy research, the fifth major genre of documentary research that I have identified, shares with the other four the characteristic that it has been relatively little considered and written about, though much practised. Much policy research takes the form of a commentary on a particular, usually contemporary, policy or set of policies. The policy or policies in question may be national, international, local or institutional. The tone of the commentary is most commonly critical, evaluating the actual or potential impact of the policies concerned, identifying deficiencies in them, and recommending changes or improvements.

Higher education research, my own specialist field of research, offers a particularly interesting range of policy research. For everyone working in higher education has an opinion on the latest higher education policy, whatever their discipline or role (academic, administrative, student), and many are not shy of voicing and publishing it (Tight 2018). This tendency, while perhaps not quite so marked, is also evident in other fields.

Policy research also has similarities to historical research, the subject of the previous chapter (see Chapter 9), in that it has an obvious disciplinary home: in politics or political science departments in this case. But, just like historical research, it has a broader relevance as well, because policies – at local, regional, national or international level – affect all of the social sciences. Policy research is as relevant in sociology or social work as it is in education or psychology, business/management or law.

This chapter will consider:

- the nature of policy and policy research
- types of policy research
- examples of policy research.

Some conclusions will then be reached, and suggestions for further reading given.

The Nature of Policy and Policy Research

What is policy? One obvious, if slightly cynical, answer is that it is what politicians and their associates come up with and then impose upon the rest of the population: a set of proposals which they believe will improve education or health care or unemployment or some other area. Hence, as Ward et al. (2016, p. 45) note, 'the concept of policy is entangled with notions of public and social issues, the solutions to these, and the role of the state in providing these solutions'.

This is a reasonable if partial answer, as policies occur at local, regional and international levels as well as at national level, and may be enacted within institutions or societies as well as by government. There are many others involved in policy making besides politicians and their associates, including, for example, managers of all kinds; indeed, it might be said, all of us at some level.

So a broader, but somewhat circular, answer would be that policies are sets of proposals produced by those with the authority to act as policy-makers, who then seek to impose or practise those policies on those whom they have responsibility over or for. But policy may be seen as going much further than that, to include what is (deliberately or inadvertently) not done as well as what is proposed and done: 'Policy here is taken to be any course of action (or inaction) relating to the selection of goals, the definition of values or the allocation of resources. Fundamentally, policy is about the exercise of political power and the language that is used to legitimate that process' (Codd 1988, p. 235).

Trowler (2003, p. 96) takes a broad view of policy, arguing that:

> It is better to see policy as a process, something which is dynamic rather than static. This dynamism comes from a number of sources:
>
> - There is usually conflict among those who make policy, as well as those who put it into practice, about what the important issues or problems for policy are and about the desired goals.
> - Interpreting policy is an active process: policy statements are almost always subject to multiple interpretations depending upon the standpoints of the people doing the interpretative 'work'.
> - The practice of policy on the ground is extremely complex, both that being 'described' by policy and that intended to put policy into effect.

Policy-makers may be politicians – at national, local or international level – or they may be managers or leaders of organisations (such as companies or societies). They may be elected or appointed to their posts, or hold them by reason of their wealth, power or birth right. Yet, whoever makes the policies, they will be, as Trowler makes clear, subject to interpretation and practice by a multitude of others.

Most developed countries are awash with numerous policies, of most of which, most of their population will be unaware of (perhaps because many policies do not directly affect them), and will have had virtually no input in. In the words of Scott (1990, p. 59), 'Many of the most important public documents form a part of the systems of surveillance and social control that have become such an integral part of bureaucratic nation states'. This is what policies are designed to do, hopefully for the greater good, but by no means invariably so; which is why most policies are continually being critiqued, updated, altered, tweaked, repealed or replaced.

On the question of where policies come from, O'Connor (2007) states that:

> Policy may ... develop from three different, but compatible sources:
>
> - As an authoritative voice, responding to a public issue or problem...
> - As a hypothesis – policies develop in response to particular world-views, with inherent assumptions about human behaviour, to bias one behaviour against another...
> - As an objective of government action. (p. 231, emphasis in original)

As his second source suggests, policies are far from being objective responses to an agreed problem or problems; rather they are responses, often somewhat speculative, based on a particular perspective, such as that of a political party or a company owner or boss. Those who have to make the policies work, or who have to respond to them, may not, therefore, agree with them; they may, indeed, oppose them or work against them:

> Policy response is highly contextualized, complex and fragmented. There are no universal 'truths' about policy implementation: the journey from principle to practice, even if discursively framed in a particular way, is a contested one which involves institutions and individuals in a process of 'creative social action'. This is a crucial point, as contestation provides a political space in which dominant policy discourses are not simply accepted un-problematically at face value, but may be challenged, nuanced, reformulated and changed. (Ward et al. 2016, p. 47)

Saunders, in the context of higher education policy, has usefully developed the metaphor of the implementation staircase to help illustrate how policy may be practised:

> The implementation staircase provides an illustration of the systemic positions held by particular 'layers' within higher education systems, bringing a useful perspective on middle managers' strategic location. The implementation staircase metaphor suggests the importance of constructing the appearance of policy from the points of view of the main stakeholders within a policy environment. Further, it suggests these points of view may well differ significantly, and it is the task of analysis to 'construct' these differences. Another dimension to this metaphor is the way in which each group acts as both a receiver and an agent of policy messages, and, through this process, the message will undergo adaptation and be understood very differently according to the situated experience of each stake-holding group. (Saunders and Sin 2015, p. 139)

This, of course, makes it likely that the policies will not be implemented well or in the way intended; indeed, that they might be ignored or responded to only to the minimum level required. This, then, makes it likely that the policies will not work, or will not work in the way intended. Most policies usually end up having unintended and unforeseen, and perhaps deleterious, consequences. It can be extremely difficult for policy-makers overseeing the lives or work of hundreds, thousands or millions of people to exert sufficient oversight and foresight to push their policies through in the way desired. More typically, there is change and adaptation on the policy trajectory (or on the implementation staircase, as Saunders terms it) as it moves from enunciation through to enactment (and perhaps, if the policy-makers are really interested in the effects of their policies, evaluation).

And then, of course, if a policy does not work, the response from the policy-makers, or perhaps their successors, will likely be to develop and enact further policy to correct the errors of the previous policy and deal with its unforeseen consequences. Policy-making, whether in government (particularly if the parties are involved in government change) or an organisation (where new managers may wish to 'make their mark' by changing structures and practices), is essentially never-ending and always in flux. Practically, because societies are highly complex and ever evolving, it is almost impossible to get policy right, and certainly not at the first attempt.

It should be obvious by now, of course, if it wasn't already, why policy analysis is so important, and also why it is often so critical. Policy-makers have to be held to account, and we all (or, at least, all of us affected by the policies) need to know how well their policies are working and whether they are doing so in the way intended.

Types of Policy Research

We may, of course, recognise a considerable variety of types of policy and hence of policy research. To start with, there is the issue, already alluded to, of the level at which the policy operates or is pitched. This may be, for example, international, national, regional or local. Yet the level at which the policy is pitched and the level at which it is researched may be different; thus, the impact of a national policy may be researched at a local level, or an international policy may be researched at national level.

Then there is the question of what sort of policy it is, what field it belongs to. Policies stemming from national governments may, for example, relate to defence, education, finance, health care, immigration, industry, social care and countless other areas of interest. Typically, each field will have its own sets of both policy-makers and policy researchers – who may be well known to each other – specialising in just this field, or some aspect of it. These different sets of policy researchers will likely be based in different academic departments – for instance, business/management, economics, education, nursing, social work, sociology, as well as politics/political science – and, like academic specialists everywhere, will most likely have very little to do with each other.

Some researchers – more often based in politics/political science departments – will, however, attempt to produce a more generic and ongoing overview of policy developments at national, local or international level.

The underlying intention of the policy research may also be considered. Three basic intentions may be identified, though in practice these may well overlap:

- Policy research may aim to provide an account or description of the development and implementation of, and/or experience with, a particular policy or set of policies: how, for example, has a change in the retirement age impacted the economy?
- Or, and this is a common academic approach, it may set out to provide a critical review of a policy or set of policies: who, for example, has been disadvantaged by the change in retirement age, and in what ways?
- Or the intention may be to carry out an evaluation of the working of a policy or set of policies, and perhaps make recommendations for change: would, for example, the adoption of a different retirement age have had a greater impact?

The third variety of research identified is often organised and funded by the policy-makers themselves, though it may be carried out in-house or by external, usually academic, consultants.

A final distinction is particularly relevant to the concerns of this chapter, and it relates to how the policy research is carried out. In particular, we may ask what use of documents the research makes: after all, all policy involves documents, to set out the policy and how it will be implemented, and then perhaps to monitor this implementation. Is the research based wholly on some form of documentary analysis, or does it employ documentary analysis alongside other research methods? We will consider this further in the next section of the chapter.

Codd (1988, p. 235) offers an alternative typology for policy research, arguing that 'Policy analysis is a form of enquiry which provides either the informational base upon which policy is constructed, or the critical examination of existing policies'. This is an important distinction, as it indicates that policy research is not just about critiquing (usually) the expression and implementation of policy, but is also involved in providing the data and analysis upon which future policies may be based. Codd expands on this typology as follows:

> Analysis *for* policy can take two different forms: *(a) policy advocacy* which has the purpose of making specific policy recommendations; and *(b) information for policy* in which the researcher's task is to provide policy-makers with information and data to assist them in the revision or formulation of actual policies. Analysis *of* policy can also take two different forms: *(a) analysis of policy determination and effects*, which examines 'the inputs and transformational processes operating upon the construction of public policy' and also the effects of such policies on various groups; *(b) analysis of policy content*, which examines the values, assumptions and ideologies underpinning the policy process. (pp. 235–236, emphasis in original)

Of course, all social science academics might legitimately view themselves as being engaged – at least to some extent, and even if they have little or no direct contact with policy-makers – in analysis for policy, but only a minority engage in analysis of policy in their research role. This does, of course, bring out the policy/research link and nuance our discussion of policy research. While all policy will be based on some kind and level of research, the extent and source of this research will be highly variable.

In particular, the linkage between academic researchers and policy-makers who might make use of their research is not always as close as it might be. Academic researchers are not always highly competent at disseminating their research results – or sometimes even that interested in doing so, beyond their immediate peers – while policy-makers and their advisors, for their part, may not be thorough in seeking out the range of research relevant to their work.

Examples of Policy Research

Boxes 10.1 and 10.2 contain summaries of examples of published policy research. Those in Box 10.1 are examples based solely on documentary analysis, while those in Box 10.2 make use of another method (in each case, interviews) alongside documentary analysis.

BOX 10.1

Examples of Policy Research based Solely on Documentary Analysis

1. The content analysis of this study covers 91 circulars published by the Ministry of Education Malaysia between 1969 and 2011. The selection criteria included mention of disciplinary

matters, positive behavior, the roles of professionals, and the learning environment. Using pre-designated instruments, the analysis was carried out by the first author and another independent coder (an education officer with almost 10 years teaching experience). It involved the following steps: reading the documents, analyzing the documents and categorizing the information which was related to the theme, with a detailed discussion on the content of each circular. The concepts of positive and negative behavior, as well as strategies for promoting positive behavior and discouraging negative behavior were focused on. Inter-rater reliability scores indicate that both coders agreed on most items. (Awang, Jindal-Snape and Barber 2013, p. 204)

2. The department supplied the 32 successful applications selected for the NP [nurse practitioner] Program to the evaluation team as project documents ... We utilized a twofold analytic approach. First, we performed a content analysis of applications that were successfully funded to ascertain the key features and characteristics of the models. Second, we undertook textual analysis to provide insight into how applicants presented their proposed models. The information we captured under content analysis included the type of entity seeking funding (i.e., approved aged care provider, education provider, and so forth), key features of the proposed model of care, characteristics of the model, partnerships, financial models or employment arrangements proposed for the NP (i.e., employee or contractor), the proposed coverage of the model in terms of geography and population, and if the model had a broad aged care scope or a more specific scope ... For the textual analysis, we focused on the applicants' descriptions of their projects and their responses to the first assessment criterion: 'How does this model meet the program aims and objectives?' ... We analyzed the selected parts of the applications using an inductive analytic approach to identify recurrent and distinctive features of the proposed NP model. (Clark, Parker and Davey 2014, pp. 1594–1595)

3. This article focuses on electronic resources created by different levels of governmental institutions, political parties and individual politicians. It does not survey the many online media resources available since I am interested in the data created by political actors themselves and what this can tell us about elite political behaviour, preferences and attitudes. Access to elite-generated texts benefits from two trends. First, political parties and politicians in Taiwan have long demonstrated their enthusiasm for adopting various means of communicating with citizens and voters, most obviously as part of their campaign communications. Since the mid-1990s, this has taken the form of online communications, a practice that accelerated after the 2000 presidential campaign, and again after the popularization of Web 2.0 applications in the middle of the same decade. Secondly, since the Electronic Government Program was enacted in April 2001, governmental institutions at all levels have developed online infrastructures for improving internal efficiency, transparency and public services. Thousands of government agency websites have been created, and by November 2003, 'all government organizations were connected online'. This progress established Taiwan as one of the world's top-performing e-democracies, with the 'my e-gov' portal being cited as an example of global best practice. This laudable achievement is a boon for citizens and researchers alike. (Sullivan 2013, p. 174)

4. The documents being analysed covered disability policies which were initiated, developed and pursued by EU authorities over the last five decades. In order to study this material a

(Continued)

(Continued)

qualitative content analysis combining the steps of summarizing, explicating and categorizing was conducted. For a start, by way of using official European Internet archives 30 documents could be identified which explicitly dealt with disability related aspects in the broader sense. They had been published by different EU authorities between 1958 and 2005. Besides a summary of content and a categorization according to three policy objectives (social protection, labour market integration and equal rights) the content analysis looked at the following criteria: date of publication, document title, responsible EU authority, kind of document and legal relevance (binding/not binding for member states). In a second phase, 19 documents were selected for a more specific analysis going into more detail. These documents were chosen for these reasons: they were legally binding for the member states and/or marked a significant policy shift at the supranational level. This material was considered of high relevance as it represented policy measures which had great potential to influence the national level. The detail analysis [sic] also used a qualitative approach and included the steps of summarizing the content, exploring the historical context and categorizing the data along the following dimensions: disability definition, policy objective, actor and addressee, and type of policy instrument. An interpretative review of each document concluded this detail analysis. (Waldschmidt 2009, pp. 10–11)

BOX 10.2

Examples of Policy Research Using Documents and Other Methods

1. This article is the outcome of a comparative policy study conducted at the London School of Hygiene and Tropical Medicine, University of London. It is based on a qualitative and quantitative approach, using two complementary methods, documentary analysis and stakeholder analysis, which allowed for the triangulation of data. The documentary analysis was based on key EU, regional and national health and migration documents, as well as on national communicable disease acts and decrees and budgetary bills, and academic literature on the topic, identified through searches on Web of Knowledge, Embase, and Pubmed. The stakeholder analysis was founded on 20 semi-structured interviews with key national stakeholders in the communicable disease policy field in Finland, Norway and Sweden. The interviews were carried out during the autumn and winter of 2005. (Bernitz 2008, p. 876)
2. In addition, documentary analysis was carried out to consider the evidence of how universities link to government and national sports policy. The strategic plan of each university was analysed alongside key strategies for sport and higher education sport in England ... Qualitative content analysis was used, being one of many qualitative methods currently available for analysing data and interpreting its meaning. It was used as a means of describing and analysing the data. Key areas of thematic analysis included: (1) forming categories to identify the purpose for each university, grouping areas in common; (2) systematically identifying any mention of sport, physical activity, and health in university strategy; (3) systematically identifying any link and explicit mention of university sport in national sport policies. (Brunton and Mackintosh 2017, p. 382)

3. Issues of authenticity were unproblematic as most documents were deposited in state archives, but there were some concerns around the issue of representativeness as some private sector organisations were less inclined to archive documents than state agencies. Throughout the analysis of the documents, issues of form, structure, content and potential absences were brought to bear and documents were read as manifestations of the ideologies underpinning their source organisations. The interview and documentary data were organised across a time-ordered matrix of the sector's development between the late 1970s and 2007 and categorised according to their origin. Patterns and regularities as well as contradictions emerged as the data were coded, which posited a structure for the overall analysis. The findings from the documentary data were checked against interview data for correlations, verifications or disparities. (O'Brien 2010, pp. 567–568)

4. The study utilised a mixed-method approach guided by the interpretivist policy analysis perspective. The methods included analysis of secondary sources including government and sports policy documents, existing paperwork in the MoS [Ministry of Sport] and NOC [National Olympic Committee]. Secondary data sources included a limited survey of 200 people examining sports participation, physical activity levels, participation in physical education and perceptions of provision amongst the local population. Furthermore, 30 semi-structured interviews and observation utilising visual research methods (resulting in 100 photographs) for facility observation were also employed. Mixed-methods research designs have become more established in studies of physical activity and sports, and importantly sports policy evaluation. (Darko and Mackintosh 2015, pp. 375–376)

The four examples of policy research based solely on documentary analysis included in Box 10.1 illustrate some of the range of possibilities. While Awang, Jindal-Snape and Barber (2013) focus on education in Malaysia, Clark, Parker and Davey (2014) research nursing care in Australia, Sullivan (2013) examines Taiwanese politics, and Waldschmidt (2009) considers European Union disability policies. The documents researched are, respectively, government circulars, funded nurse-practitioner project proposals, electronic texts produced by politicians, and EU policy statements. All claim to have carried out forms of content analysis (see Chapters 12 and 13 for discussion of quantitative and qualitative approaches, respectively, to content analysis) on the documents studied. Clark, Parker and Davey also employed textual analysis (focusing on how the proposals were presented), and Waldschmidt carried out a 'detail analysis' of a more limited sample of the documents identified.

Of course, many other examples could have been given. To offer another four, Boholm (2014) examines Swedish parliamentary documents (including private members' motions, government bills, records of proceedings in the chamber, reports of parliamentary committee opinions, written communications from the government, factual memoranda on European Union (EU) proposals, stenographic records from meetings of the Committee on EU Affairs, interpellations and questions seeking written answers, answers to written questions, and statements of opinion from parliamentary committees) to uncover the political dimensions of nanotechnology. Jones and Symeonidou (2017) undertook a comparative study of inclusive education policy in Cyprus and England over the period 1899–2015, focusing in particular on 23 key documents.

Kaehne and Taylor (2016) researched the nature and content of consultation submissions to a Welsh parliamentary bill to 'provide an insight into the effectiveness of the consultation to citizen engagement in a newly devolved polity' (p. 86). They used a coding matrix for the analysis, comparing and reconciling the codes made by two independent raters. Finally, Prøitz (2015) considered the place of learning outcomes in Norwegian educational policy by analysing 'one particular type of Norwegian policy document from 1997 to 2011 ... the Annex for the Ministry of Education and Research in the Government's annual proposal for the national budget, known as Parliamentary Report no. 1 ... [which] provides rich information on the educational priorities and focus of the ministry as a part of the government's budget proposal presented to Parliament' (pp. 277–278).

The four examples of policy research given in Box 10.2 using documentary analysis and another method or methods all make use of interviews. Bernitz (2008) reports on a comparative analysis of policies in Finland, Norway and Sweden on communicable disease, combining analysis of policy documents with interviews with key national stakeholders to allow for triangulation of data. Brunton and Mackintosh (2017) focus on university sports policies in England, analysing strategy documents alongside data from interviews with those responsible for leading institutional policy.

O'Brien (2010) examined Irish tourism policy during the period 1987–2007, undertaking interviews with key players as well as an analysis of documents produced by the state and relevant public and private organisations. Darko and Mackintosh's (2015) interest was in the challenges and constraints impacting on sports policy and provision in the small island nations of Antigua and Barbuda. They used interviews, observation, surveys and photographs (the last two of which could also be regarded as documents) alongside more conventional documentary sources.

As with the examples of policy research based wholly on documentary analysis, it would be easy to multiply the number of examples of policy research using documentary analysis and another method or methods. Indeed, this would be much easier, as all policy research makes some use of documentary analysis, even if only at a minor level.

Conclusion

Policy research, like the other four genres of documentary research explored in this part of the book, is a broad area for research. It is engaged in by a wide variety of researchers from different disciplinary backgrounds, and makes use of a considerable range of techniques (which are discussed in more detail in Part 3 of the book). It offers many opportunities for those interested in policy.

KEY READINGS

Codd, J (1988) The Construction and Deconstruction of Educational Policy Documents. *Journal of Educational Policy*, 3, 3, pp. 235–247.

Though focused on education policy in particular, there is much in this article of general relevance.

O'Connor, M (2007) Documentary Analysis and Policy. pp. 229–245 in Addington-Hall, J, Bruera, E, Higginson, I, and Payne, S (eds) *Research Methods in Palliative Care*. Oxford, Oxford University Press.

While this chapter focuses on health care policy, its discussion of the use of documentary analysis in policy research is of more general interest.

Trowler, P (2003) *Education Policy*. London, Routledge, second edition.

An interesting analysis of both education policy and how it is researched.

Ward, S, Bagley, C, Lumby, J, Hamilton, T, Woods, P, and Roberts, A (2016) What is 'Policy' and what is 'Policy Response'? An illustrative study of the implementation of the leadership standards for social justice in Scotland. *Educational Management, Administration and Leadership*, 44, 1, pp. 43–56.

A good example of a policy analysis focusing on one particular policy.

PART 3

TECHNIQUES FOR DOCUMENTARY ANALYSIS

Part 3 contains four chapters, which together consider the varied ways in which documents may be analysed. While it adopts the conventional twofold categorisation of methods of analysis as either quantitative (i.e. involving numbers) or qualitative (not involving numbers) – in Chapters 12 and 13 – it does not accept this division as fundamental. Rather, quantitative and qualitative forms of analysis are viewed as complementary and suitable for combining together in a mixed methods approach (Chapter 14).

Chapter 11 provides a general overview to the analysis of documents and discusses approaches adopted towards the analysis of written texts and audio-visual texts.

Chapter 12 focuses on quantitative approaches to documentary analysis, considering simple quantitative analysis, quantitative content analysis and other forms of quantitative analysis. Illustrative examples are included.

Chapter 13 focuses on qualitative approaches to documentary analysis, including thematic analysis, qualitative content analysis, discourse analysis, conversation analysis and narrative analysis. Illustrative examples are included.

Chapter 14 examines the use of mixed methods approaches to documentary analysis, where quantitative and qualitative approaches are employed in conjunction with each other. It also considers the nature and importance of triangulation, whereby the results of more than one method of analysis are compared in order to strengthen the argument. Illustrative examples are included.

11
ANALYSING DOCUMENTS

CONTENTS

Introduction	136
Analysis of Written Texts	136
Analysis of Audio-Visual Texts	139
Conclusion	142

Introduction

The analysis of documents is, of course, the key part of the documentary research process. Identifying and accessing relevant documents is clearly critical, as there can be no analysis without this, and it is important to get hold of as much appropriate documentation as possible. The genre of documentary research which you choose to adopt is also important, as this will provide you with a wealth of examples with which to guide and compare your work. How you go about analysing the documents you have identified is, however, the most important factor, as upon this depends the overall quality of your research and thus how it is judged and received. That is the focus of this part of the book.

Just as there are genres of documentary research – literature reviews, systematic reviews and meta-analyses, secondary data research, archival and historical research, and policy research were identified as such in this book and were the subject of the previous five chapters – so there are different ways of going about the analysis of documents. For convenience, as with social research in general, these are most commonly divided into two categories – quantitative (see Chapter 12) and qualitative (see Chapter 13) approaches – which are the subjects of the next two chapters.

It has to be stressed, though, that dealing with documentary analysis methods in this way is simply a convenience. Quantitative and qualitative methods are best seen as complementary rather than opposed approaches, and may, of course, be used together in a pragmatic or mixed methods approach, and this will be discussed in Chapter 14.

This chapter takes an alternative, but also a more generic, approach to the processes involved in analysing documents. The two main sections focus on the analysis of written texts and the analysis of audio-visual texts. While these are arguably analogous processes, their different nature makes separate consideration worthwhile. The developing area of audio-visual textual analysis also merits particular attention.

Of course, as the discussion throughout this book should have made clear, other ways of organising the discussion would have been possible. However, even where the documents to be analysed might not be thought of as either written or audio-visual – as in the case, for example, of floods (Himmelsbach et al. 2015, discussed in Chapter 2) and languages (Enfield 2006, discussed in Chapter 9), both discussed as documents in other chapters – the processes used will be similar.

Some conclusions are reached, and some further reading is suggested, at the end of the chapter.

Analysis of Written Texts

Bowen (2009) provides a useful, but narrow and therefore thought-provoking, summary of documentary analysis as applied to written texts:

> The analytic procedure entails finding, selecting, appraising (making sense of), and synthesising data contained in documents. Document analysis yields data – excerpts, quotations, or

entire passages – that are then organised into major themes, categories, and case examples specifically through content analysis. (p. 28)

He identifies here two basic processes: (i) the identification of coherent pieces of text; and (ii) the attachment of appropriate labels to each of these pieces. Bowen recommends applying this technique to documentary analysis, and, at the end of the quotation, applies the term 'content analysis' to this. However, what he describes is actually the basic, or most common, approach taken towards qualitative research (see Chapter 13) in general, where it is commonly called thematic analysis (Braun and Clarke 2006) – note that Bowen refers to the identification of themes in the data – though it is also termed content analysis by some.

Thus, researchers analysing interview transcripts – which may, of course, also be thought of as documents, particularly if they are being analysed by someone other than the original interviewer, i.e. as secondary data (see Chapter 8) – typically follow this approach. The approach might proceed, particularly if the volume or size of the documents is large, with the assistance of qualitative data analysis software, or might, if the documents are more limited in number and scope, be essentially manual.

It is important here to stress again, therefore, that written texts can equally well be analysed quantitatively (see Chapter 12). The process would be analogous – i.e. pieces of the text, such as recurring words or phrases, would be identified, and their occurrence throughout the document then counted and compared – but nowadays it would be largely automatic, with the document digitised, and software driven. The researcher would not even need to identify which words or phrases to search for, as the software could do this for them as well.

The other point to emphasise about Bowen's account is his use of the term 'content analysis'. This term may be used in a generic sense – i.e. all documentary analysis (and many other types of research) is a form of content analysis, in that the content of the document(s) is being analysed – or more specifically, so it needs to be used with care. In particular, reinforcing the point made in the previous paragraph, content analysis may be either qualitative or quantitative (so it is considered further in both Chapters 12 and 13).

In an earlier piece of writing, Jupp and Norris (1993) discussed the major traditions or theoretical approaches for documentary analysis in the social sciences: 'Three main theoretical approaches have been examined in relation to the analysis of documents and texts and we have highlighted three forms of analysis – positivist content analysis, interpretative analysis of documents, and critical or discourse analysis' (pp. 49–50).

This categorisation is clearly different to, and broader than, that of Bowen (2009). Jupp and Norris explain the first of their categories, positivist content analysis, by reference to the earlier work of Holsti:

Holsti (1969) itemizes five key features of content analysis ... First, the procedures should be *objective*, that is, each step in the research process (for example, categorization and coding schemes) should be carried out on the basis of explicitly formulated rules ... Second, procedures must be *systematic*, that is the rules must be applied with consistency. Third, content analysis should have *generality* ... Fourth, content analysis is typically *quantitative* and can include counting the frequency with which certain themes or words appear ... Finally, content analysis is typically concerned with the *manifest* content and surface meaning rather than with deeper layers of meaning. (1993, pp. 40–41, emphasis in original)

What Jupp and Norris refer to as positivist content analysis might also be termed quantitative content analysis, following the rules of the scientific method in seeking to be objective, systematic and generalisable. Note the sting in their final comment, however, implying that such an approach – in contrast to their clearly preferred qualitative analysis – is superficial. This point, like much of the dispute between the proponents of qualitative versus quantitative forms of research (see Chapter 5), is highly debatable.

With interpretative analysis, by contrast, we are back in the mainstream of qualitative research:

[T]he interpretative tradition holds the basic assumption that social phenomena are of an essentially different order from natural ones. They are not objective, external and preordained but socially constructed by individuals. Therefore, it is argued, positivist approaches to the study of such phenomena are inappropriate. (1993, pp. 42–43)

This would align closely with Bowen's (2009) preferred approach to thematic and content analysis.

However, Jupp and Norris's preferred approach to documentary analysis is the critical tradition, which they also link with discourse analysis. A critical analysis approach to documents would involve:

A concern with analysis at a societal and social structural level ... An emphasis upon conflict between social groupings and on the dynamics of struggles between them ... An emphasis on power and control in the relation between social groupings ... An interest in ideology as a means by which existing structures and social arrangements are legitimated and maintained ... A commitment to not taking for granted what-is-said ... A commitment to changing the existing state of things. (1993, p. 46)

Discourse analysis is seen by Jupp and Norris as a particular development within the critical tradition, particularly associated with the work of Foucault and later Althusser, whereby what is said and written is treated and analysed as a discourse. This approach, together with qualitative content analysis, will be discussed in more detail in Chapter 13.

Clearly, then, the analysis of written texts may proceed in a variety of ways, depending on the researcher's epistemological position (i.e. their view of the world and how it may be known) and their methodological preferences. Alternatively, a mixture of analytical approaches may be adopted (see Chapter 14), potentially enabling a fuller understanding of the documents examined.

Analysis of Audio-Visual Texts

In recent years, the analysis of documents other than written texts has attracted more and more attention, in part due to the development of software to help in their analysis. A good deal of discussion and debate has focused on how the analysis of what may generically be termed audio-visual texts differs from that of written texts.

Figueroa (2008) gives the following advice on the analysis of audio-visual texts:

> when analysing audio-visual texts from an AVO-perspective [audio-visual data as an object of analysis], we should begin with a global analysis, view the whole programme, formulate hypotheses with regard to a generative question, analyse possible empirical examples of these hypotheses and concepts, and thereby slowly come to focus in on smaller sub-units of the audio-visual texts. The researcher thus moves from the global audio-visual text to its smaller units so as not to disrupt the structure of meaning of the text before she or he has had a chance to interpret it. It is important to compare, refine, confirm or reject every hypothesis with reference to the resulting theory about the AVO, to employ one's own contextual and scholarly knowledge, albeit in a flexible way, and to intertwine the hypothesis grounded in the observation of the data with one's contextual knowledge and a well-suited social theory about the empirical material under study, e.g. AVO. (p. 10)

This, again, reads very much like a classic approach to qualitative analysis: taking an overview at the start of the audio-visual text or texts that are to be analysed, assessing what is going on that is of interest (coming up with hypotheses or research questions), then exploring these ideas in detail while focusing on parts of the text, revising your ideas and continuing with the analysis. Figueroa's emphases on relating the analysis to what you already know (from the research literature on the topic), and utilising established theory, are also sensible but fairly standard advice.

Bohnsack (2009) focuses in particular on the analysis of pictures, which he sees as having both similarities and differences to written texts:

> When developing qualitative methods for the interpretation of pictures, it seems to be important not to explain pictures by texts, but to differentiate them from texts. Nevertheless, it seems equally important to develop common standards or methodological devices which are relevant for the interpretation of texts, as well as for the interpretation of pictures. Examples of common standards are: to treat the text as well as the picture as a self-referential system, to differentiate between explicit and implicit (atheoretical) knowledge, to change the analytic stance from the question What to the question How, to reconstruct the formal structures of texts as well as pictures in order to integrate single elements into the over-all context, and – last but not least – to use comparative analysis. The application or realization of these common standards and methodological devices in the field of the interpretation of pictures, however, has to be quite different from that of the interpretation of texts, if we intend to advance to iconicity as a self-contained domain, to its inherent laws and to its autonomy independent from texts. (p. 318)

Bohnsack aligns with Figueroa in the recommended use of a common methodology for analysis, and in noting the importance of the relationship between the overall picture and its parts. His emphasis on the use of comparative analysis is apt and might involve comparing what a picture suggests about the topic of interest with what written texts say (as well as what written texts say about the picture; see also the discussion of triangulation in Chapter 14), as well as with other pictures and interpretations of them.

Oleinik (2015) suggests an approach to the analysis of visual records which could be used either quantitatively or qualitatively, but then goes on to recommend a particular piece of qualitative data analysis software, QDA Miner:

> Content analysis of visual records commonly involves the transformation of images into a matrix with variables (such as date, sources, gender of the characters, etc.) in columns and cases (particular pictures) in rows. This approach allows for the use of standard statistics yet it involves the loss of a significant amount of data. QDA Miner enables the researcher to attribute codes to specific fragments of a picture, similarly to the coding of complex texts. Thus, multiple elements on images with a complex composition (common in street photography) can be coded separately without running the risk of losing data. QDA Miner makes it possible to retrieve fragments associated with a particular code at will. Also, the techniques of multidimensional scaling can be easily applied. The collection and analysis of visual records posted on the internet does not require free and informed consent either from their authors or from the people pictured on them. The main issue of research ethics arguably refers in this case to the protection of personal information. (p. 2209)

At the heart of the method being recommended – as compared to a matrix or tabular approach to analysis – is the coding of the elements of the picture, in much the same way that qualitative researchers would read and code a written text. As well as allowing as many codes to be identified as required, subject no doubt to some later revision and refinement, this approach also allows more than one code to be given to individual elements of the picture.

Oleinik touches on the ethical issues involved in the use of visual records available on the internet (see also the discussion of ethics in Chapter 3), suggesting that the researcher's key responsibility relates to keeping personal information safe. He emphasises that it is the identification of individuals that needs to be avoided:

> The researcher collects the information freely available on the internet. However, the analysis of this information enables the researcher to identify gender, age and some other personal information about the people pictured on visual records. Thus, the researcher must store the visual records in a secure place and eventually publish them in a form that prevents the identification of specific individuals. (2015, p. 2209)

While this guidance sounds rather dogmatic, it seems a sensible strategy to adopt, avoiding possible later disputes.

Also focusing on data available online, Salmons (2016) distinguishes two kinds of approach, preferring the term materials analysis to document analysis as, for her, it doesn't carry the connotation of a sole concern with written texts:

Two types of online extant data collection are *materials analysis* and *unobtrusive observation*. While the term 'document analysis' has been commonly used to describe the review of written texts, here the term 'materials analysis' is used in acknowledgment of the diverse visual media as well as written materials available to review online. (p. 116)

The other approach identified, unobtrusive observation, is sometimes – in an online context – termed more pejoratively 'lurking', as when the observer signs up to, for example, an online discussion forum, observes and saves the discussion, but does not directly participate.

Salmons also usefully breaks down the materials analysis category to recognise three types of materials:

- Historical materials. Materials from the pre-Internet era scanned into digital formats and posted online.
- Contemporary materials. Materials described as contemporary are those created for electronic access.
- Emergent materials. Materials described as emergent are those being created now in current discussions, blogs, and/or social networking sites. (p. 117)

The first of these is obviously of particular relevance for those undertaking archival or historical research (see Chapter 9). The last type is also suitable for study through unobtrusive observation. Note, however, that Salmons takes a particular approach to delimiting historical, contemporary and emergent materials – which reads much like a past/present/future distinction – by using the advent of the internet as a borderline.

Box 11.1 illustrates some of the possibilities for analysing audio-visual texts by quoting three examples. Cooper and Hughes (2015) present the audio-visual equivalent of an in-depth interview in their examination of videotapes of the philosophies and autobiographies of noted scholars. Lyon (2016) provides an examination of the everyday rhythms of Billingsgate Fish Market in London through an audio-visual montage of photography and sound recordings, effectively offering both a synthesis and an analysis. And Jacobsson (2017) discusses possible approaches to the intercultural analysis of film. Many more examples could be offered.

BOX 11.1

Examples of Audio-Visual Text Analysis

1. We invited international scholars in the field of the social sciences and humanities to document their philosophies and autobiographies on videotape. We asked the following questions: What are the overarching themes or theories that unite the scholars' methodological and conceptual frameworks? How have the scholars' unique lived experiences contributed to their interpretivist or critical viewpoints? What autobiographical stories rise to the forefront? Can

(Continued)

(Continued)

> these stories be linked or connected to represent an unfolding narrative through both space and time? Through the course of narrative analysis, significant themes such as poverty, social inequality, classism, oppression, and colonization emerged from the videotaped dialogues. The scholars' unique narratives coalesced into a single narrative that traced and documented the history of qualitative research. (Cooper and Hughes 2015, p. 28)

2. This article documents, shows and analyses the everyday rhythms of Billingsgate, London's wholesale fish market. It takes the form of a short film based an [sic] audio-visual montage of time-lapse photography and sound recordings, and a textual account of the dimensions of market life revealed by this montage. Inspired by Henri Lefebvre's *Rhythmanalysis*, and the embodied experience of moving through and sensing the market, the film renders the elusive quality of the market and the work that takes place within it to make it happen. The composite of audio-visual recordings immerses viewers in the space and atmosphere of the market and allows us to perceive and analyse rhythms, patterns, flows, interactions, temporalities and interconnections of market work, themes that this article discusses. The film is thereby both a means of showing market life and an analytic tool for making sense of it. (Lyon 2016, p. 1)

3. The most frequent aspect of the intercultural perspective on film that can be found in previous research is a focus on what might be called 'Intercultural themes and motifs'. This is also the most obvious way of applying an intercultural perspective on film; to look at moving images and the stories told and evaluate if the portrayals of cultures, cultural differences and intercultural encounters are positive or negative or possible to relate to what is going on in contemporary societies. Numerous films from different film cultures around the world contain intercultural encounters of different kinds, from minor parts of the storyline such as cultural misunderstandings to linguistic mishaps and communication breakdown as comic relief. But cultural differences described as problems and obstacles also frequently figure as major themes in serious dramas and melodramas depicting intercultural encounters and social relationships in multicultural societies. (Jacobsson 2017, p. 61)

Nowadays, more and more research is focusing on online data and materials (Kosciejew 2010), and their analysis. Nevertheless, there is still a huge amount of material available for analysis in the form of pictures (Bale 1999, Meyer 2018, Wright and Sharpley 2018), television (Johnson and Johnson 1993), videotapes (Koohzadi and Keyvanpour 2014), audiotapes and media in general (Altheide and Schneider 2013, Burn and Parker 2003). While we might question the rather tired old adage that 'a picture is worth a thousand words', we should still recognise the possibilities here.

Conclusion

This chapter has examined the analysis of both textual and audio-visual data. The processes involved in these research designs are analogous, but make different demands on the researcher. Audio-visual material has great potential for expanding research away from conventional written texts, either to complement it or as a focus for research on its own.

KEY READINGS

Bohnsack, R (2009) The Interpretation of Pictures and the Documentary Method. *Historical Social Research*, 34, 2, pp. 296–321.

The author adopts and applies a particular interpretation of what he terms documentary method.

Figueroa, S (2008) The Grounded Theory and the Analysis of Audio-visual Texts. *International Journal of Social Research Methodology*, 11, 1, pp. 1–12.

A good introductory guide to audio-visual analysis.

Jupp, V, and Norris, C (1993) Traditions in Documentary Analysis. pp. 37–51 in Hammersley, M (ed.) *Social Research: Philosophy, politics and practice*. London, Sage.

A dated but still useful discussion of alternative approaches to documentary analysis.

Oleinik, A (2015) On Content Analysis of Images of Mass Protests: A case of data triangulation. *Quality and Quantity*, 49, pp. 2203–2220.

A thoughtful methodological and ethical discussion.

Salmons, J (2016) *Doing Qualitative Research Online*. London, Sage.

The second edition of a popular textbook.

12

QUANTITATIVE APPROACHES

CONTENTS

Introduction	146
Simple Quantitative Analysis	146
Quantitative Content Analysis	148
Other Forms of Quantitative Documentary Analysis	153
Conclusion	154

Introduction

This chapter focuses on quantitative approaches to the analysis of documents; it is complemented by the following chapter (Chapter 13), which focuses on qualitative approaches. Chapter 14 then considers mixed methods approaches, combining elements of both quantitative and qualitative approaches, and triangulation.

This organisation is both a convenience and an acceptance of the standard binary way in which forms of social analysis are categorised. It should not be read as implying that quantitative and qualitative approaches to analysis are fundamentally different or oppositional; rather, they are seen as complementary ways of interpreting documents or, more generally, data.

At the core of quantitative approaches to documentary analysis are the varied forms of quantitative content analysis which are practised (just as qualitative content analysis accounts for the bulk of qualitative documentary analysis). Quantitative content analysis will, therefore, be considered in the main and middle section of this chapter. Before then we will look at simpler forms of quantitative documentary analysis, with a later section focusing on other and more complex forms of quantitative analysis that have been applied to documents.

These distinctions are not, of course, hard, unchanging and immutable. In particular, it has to be recognised that content analysis may be defined in such broad and varied ways that it could be seen as encompassing nearly all forms of documentary analysis – after all, documentary analysis primarily focuses on the content of the document(s) being researched – whether quantitative, qualitative or both. In this chapter and the following one, however, we will use the term content analysis in a specific way, as pertaining to the analysis of the entire content, or specific parts of the content, of the document or documents in question.

But, first, we will consider simpler forms of quantitative documentary analysis.

Simple Quantitative Analysis

The simplest forms of quantitative documentary analysis involve the examination of relevant documents for the numerical data they contain – or the creation from those documents of numerical data – relating to the topic of interest (Dale 1939). A good example of this is provided by Tickell's (2010) study of the prevention of shoplifting in eighteenth-century London. In common with many historical studies, the article does not include a specific section detailing the methodology and methods adopted, but the reader does find the following explanation part way through the text:

> To establish the type and form of these operational practices [measures designed to prevent shoplifting] around 1,200 shoplifting trials have been examined, a substantial majority of those heard at the Old Bailey between 1730 and 1790 as recorded in the commercially licensed Proceedings of the Old Bailey. Although these are edited transcripts, comparison with other

contemporary accounts has confirmed the accuracy and reliability of the record as a source. This broad survey was supplemented by a more detailed analysis of all trials during two sample periods, 1743–1749, the earliest during which shoplifting trials are consistently recorded in some detail, and 1773–1779, a period of similar length later in the century. This served to provide a systematic quantitative analysis of the material and thus to show any indication of change or trend. The Proceedings are a rich source of evidence of retailer behaviour that have been underused for this purpose. Whilst nominally relating to cases prosecuted, they disclose practices which were clearly in more general operation. (p. 303)

What Tickell (2010) has done is to methodically go through the records of shoplifting trials at the Old Bailey during the periods selected, noting down details, which are then turned into numerical data. Thus, the article contains tables detailing the types of stolen goods, where in the shop they were stolen from, the gender of the shop staff who were present at the time of the theft, and the modus operandi and value of the thefts. Using this data, together with a qualitative analysis of the same records (i.e. this is a mixed methods analysis), Tickell is able to present a convincing account of trends in shoplifting behaviour and prevention.

Of course, Tickell (2010) had to undertake quite a bit of work in the archives in order to gather this data. Other kinds of quantitative documentary analysis can be much less time-consuming and more straightforward. An obvious example of this is the use of official statistics, produced by governments and their agencies, and by other bodies (Levitas and Guy 1996). Official statistics can be an extremely useful source of quantitative data, and – given their scale and coverage – it would be foolish to ignore them if they related to your research topic (and there can be few research topics on which official statistics can shed no light). At the very least they should provide valuable contextual information: for example, of the national picture within which your local case study is located.

It is especially important in using official statistics, therefore, not to be blinded by their 'official' nature and treat them as if they were 'objective facts' (see also the discussion in Chapter 8). Rather, like any other document, they should be interrogated as to who compiled them and why, and why they compiled them in the particular way that they did. Thus, May (2001; see also Seale 2018) draws attention to:

the problems associated with the construction of criminal statistics. From the decision to report a crime, through the police decision to pursue an investigation, to the courts' decision to sanction offenders – if they are caught – a number of different practices leads to a variable outcome. For these reasons, we should treat official statistics on crime with considerable caution. (p. 80)

While crime statistics may appear to be particularly liable to selective interpretation and misuse, all official statistics should, therefore, be treated with care. Other forms of statistics which are publicly available – such as those compiled by private companies or interest groups – should probably be approached with even more caution. For, all other things being equal, it is in the compiler's interest to present the statistics in as favourable a light as possible.

Quantitative Content Analysis

While, as we have already noted, content analysis may be either quantitative or qualitative in nature (or both of course), it was first developed as a quantitative approach and, for some authors, remains exclusively so. Thus, for example, Neuendorf (2002, p. 1) defines it in the following way: '*Content analysis* may be briefly defined as the systematic, objective, quantitative analysis of message characteristics'. That, by any measure, is a very positivist definition.

Quantitative content analysis has been developing for around a century, having, like many methods, expanded from a particular discipline to be applied more widely: 'Content analysis, originally used in communication sciences but increasingly utilised in public health, is a research method used to generate objective, systematic, and quantitative descriptions of a topic of interest' (Ash et al. 2017, p. 2; see also Krippendorff and Bock 2009).

While we may query both Neuendorf and Ash et al.'s use of the term 'objective' – can any research methods be truly objective? – the emphasis on a systematic and quantitative approach is clear. Leaving aside the objection that content analysis may be qualitative instead or as well, quantitative content analysis is clearly presented as an attempt to bring rigour and system to the analysis of documents.

Beyond that, however, opinions and practices fragment, and we may recognise different approaches to quantitative content analysis. Thus, Indulska, Hovorka and Recker (2012) identify two main strategies for analysis:

> Content analysis is concerned with the semantic analysis of a body of text, to uncover the presence of dominant concepts. In general, content analysis approaches fall into two categories, viz., conceptual and relational. In conceptual analysis, text material is examined for the presence, frequency, and centrality of concepts. Such concepts can represent words, phrases, or more complex constructs. Relational analysis, on the other hand, tabulates not only the frequency of concepts in the body of text, but also the co-occurrence of concepts, thereby examining how concepts (pre-defined or emergent) are related to each other within the documents. These relationships may be based on contextual proximity, cognitive mapping, or underlying emotion, to name just a few. (pp. 50–51)

By contrast, Tartz and Krippner (2017), not unreasonably, see these two approaches as part of the same overall strategy: 'Content analysis employs an explicit, organised plan for assembling data, quantifying them to measure the concepts under study, examining their patterns and interrelationships' (p. 195).

Quantitative context analysis is not, therefore, just a simple or simplistic strategy:

> Content analysis ... should not just be about producing simple counts of things, but should also involve an attempt to take in issues of meaning and context. This can sometimes work by combining content analysis with other methods, or by using it as a framework for the more interpretive analysis of texts. (Seale and Tonkiss 2018, p. 410)

Indulska, Hovorka and Recker (2012) compare two specific computational techniques for large-scale quantitative content analysis (they examined over 8,500 journal article abstracts in this way). First, latent semantic analysis: 'a content analysis method that uncovers latent semantic relationships within a corpus of text through statistical computations, to extract a quantification of the meaning of text units' (p. 51). Second, data mining: 'an automated approach to identifying patterns in sets of data. While many data mining algorithms exist, applications suitable for text content analysis typically follow a three-step approach of (a) parsing text, (b) identification of concepts, and (c) clustering' (p. 52).

Using these techniques, Indulska et al. showed:

> how the results from the two analyses can be used together to extend our understanding of *what* dominant high-level themes are in the published literature of selected journals, *how* these themes are composed, and *how* they contribute to the thematic movement of ideas published in the journals over time. (2012, p. 65)

While they applied these techniques to academic journals, there is no reason why they could not be applied to the analysis of other kinds of documents.

While the intention of quantitative content analysis to offer a systematic and rigorous quantitative approach (or approaches) to the analysis of documents seems clear, in practice it may not always be carried out as carefully and critically:

> Examples of QCA [quantitative content analysis] research in which a coding protocol is developed methodically and validated systematically are rare. Consequently, the qualities that define QCA, distinguish it from qualitative forms of content analysis, and endow it with its appeal as a research technique fade away. (Rourke and Anderson 2004, p. 15)

What Rourke and Anderson are calling for here is for researchers to make clear how and why they undertook quantitative content analysis – though the same point might be made about all and any kinds of research – in the way that they did, so that those subsequently reading the results may check and/or replicate the approach taken.

Box 12.1 summarises four examples of quantitative content analysis being applied in social science research. The examples concern research into state domestic violence coalitions in the USA, the NewsHour programme broadcast by the Al-Jazeera English-language television station, senior online communities worldwide, and portrayals of men and women on primetime American television, illustrating something of the diversity of topics that can be researched in this way.

BOX 12.1

Examples of Quantitative Content Analysis

1. We conducted a quantitative content analysis of websites of state domestic violence coalitions. A complete list of all state domestic violence coalitions, and links to their official websites, was obtained through the federal U.S. Department of Justice, Office on Violence

(Continued)

(Continued)

    Against Women website in 2010. This list included coalitions in all 50 states, the District of Columbia, and the U.S. territories Guam and Puerto Rico (N = 53). As website information was not available for Guam and Puerto Rico, they were excluded from the present study, resulting in a total sample of 51 websites. Available website text publicly posted in 2010 was printed and served as the primary text for analysis ... The final coding scheme ... included the creation of a word frequency list (with each word indicative of a construct of interest). The PI [principal investigator] of the project and the graduate-level RA [research assistant] each then independently coded all documents for indicators of words on this list. Frequency counts were then tabulated for each word, and the corresponding categories, and presented as descriptive statistics (percentages). (Barrett et al. 2016, pp. 362–363)

2. The programme selected for analysis, the *NewsHour* at 18.00 GMT [Greenwich Mean Time] is the flagship news program for the channel, linking up the Doha headquarters with the London broadcasting center and the Washington broadcasting center ... This makes *NewsHour* a particularly interesting program to analyse in order to discuss the channel's coverage of world events. The material on which this study was based was recorded every second day over two periods of two months (October–December 2007 and May–July 2008). Sixty newscasts are included in the study. The news item most often distinguished by an introductory statement from the studio is the basic unit of analysis ... multiple coders (the author and two research assistants) coded a total of 1324 news items. The coders were carefully trained in operationalizing the codebook, and an intercoder reliability test, testing measurement consistency, was assessed by recoding 10 percent of the news items. Intercoder agreement ranged from kappa 0.89 at categories region and news format, to main source visibility 0.87, presence on the ground 0.85, main source 0.80 and subsidiary sources 0.78, to main topic 0.68. (Figenschou 2010, p. 90)

3. The research team searched the web and identified more than 40 online communities, which, according to their names, home pages, and welcome posts, explicitly target seniors. Each forum and chat was reviewed, and those that were relatively new or nonactive (less than a few hundred posts) and/or required registration were screened out (to avoid ethical issues). Given the public nature of online forums, the study was approved as exempted from human subjects review. The final sample consisted of 14 established communities. Seven of the communities were from the United States, four were British, two were Canadian, and one was Australian. However, all of them except for one (Florida Retirement Forums) targeted a global audience. Two communities had both a forum and a chat room, and the rest had a forum only. The study followed a full year of activity in these communities, between April 1, 2007, and March 31, 2008. The overall database included 19,963 threads (i.e., discussions, stream of posts concerning the same topic and with the same opening post) and 686,283 posts (i.e., messages). The number of authors was 79,665. (Nimrod 2009, pp. 384–385)

4. To document current portrayals of women and men on primetime television, a quantitative content analysis was conducted. A 1-week composite of primetime television programming across nine broadcast and cable networks was randomly sampled, yielding 89 programs and 1,254 characters. Consistent with prior findings, women were significantly underrepresented on primetime TV when compared with men. Analyses examined representations of gender in the realms of occupation, aggression, sexualization, and stereotypically masculine and feminine attributes, with comparisons drawn across different age groups. Contrary to popular belief, these findings suggest that the

current state of primetime television does not represent a 'golden age' for women. Although it appears that some gender stereotypes have declined when compared to previous decades, others (e.g., dominant men, sexually provocative women) have persisted. Implications are discussed in terms of cultivation and social cognitive theories. (Sink and Mastro 2017, p. 3)

The examples also illustrate diversity in the scale of the analyses being carried out. Thus, Barrett et al. (2016) focused on the mission (or equivalent) statements found on 51 websites; Figenschou (2010) examined 1,324 news items contained in 60 newscasts; Nimrod (2009) analysed a database containing 19,963 threads and 686,283 posts from 79,665 authors; while Sink and Mastro (2017) considered nine television networks, 89 programmes and 1,254 characters. Clearly, the scope of quantitative content analysis is potentially huge, and it may be applied to audio-visual media as well as to written texts.

Many more examples of the use of quantitative content analysis across the social sciences may be identified. Forrest et al. (2017) carried out an analysis of clinical guidelines, public health guidelines and technology appraisals in the UK to examine the nature of age-related references in them:

We tabulated the total number of age-extracts overall, and within each theme and subtheme, across document types. We used Poisson regression (after checking that assumptions were met) to compare the total number of age-extracts across document type, using the log number of documents as the offset. (pp. 501–502)

Also in the general field of health care, Ash et al. (2017) examined family-based childhood obesity prevention interventions published between 2008 and 2015, and written in English, across the globe (see also Gicevic et al. 2016).

Quantitative content analysis is frequently used in the analysis of academic publications (often referred to as bibliometric studies). For example, as already mentioned, Indulska, Hovorka and Recker (2012) searched core journals in the information systems, management and accounting disciplines, accumulating a database of over 8,500 abstracts, 'to extend our understanding of what dominant high-level themes are in the published literature of selected journals, how these themes are composed, and how they contribute to the thematic movement of ideas published in the journals over time' (p. 65).

Other examples of such bibliometric studies are Nilsson et al.'s (2007) analysis of articles published in the *Journal of Counseling and Development* between 1991 and 2000, Parker, Chang and Thomas's (2016) analysis of quantitative research in the *Journal of Marital and Family Therapy* over the period 2005–2014, and Naganathan and Islam's (2015) study of the use of South Asian ethnic categorisation in Canadian health research.

The content analysis of academic publications may also be more focused in nature, as in citation analysis, where the references given in the text and listed at the end of each paper are analysed for what they reveal about relative article popularity and academic networks. Examples include Brunn's (2018) analysis of the citation impacts of American Association of Geographers' presidential addresses; Tight's (2009) study of what citations tell us about the structure of higher education research; and Foster et al.'s (2007) examination of citation patterns and citation behaviour in economic geography. Lin (1996) employed citation analysis alongside a broader quantitative content analysis.

As we have seen from the examples given in Box 12.1, quantitative content analysis is also commonly used to study more popular media: printed, online and broadcast. Thus, O'Brien, Myles and Pritchard (2016) examined how infant feeding was portrayed in five popular women's magazines in the UK: 'Content was classified using five different categories ... Codes were generated after a preliminary review of the data and revising them as greater familiarity with the data was achieved ... the frequency of each code was recorded per magazine title. Descriptive statistical analysis was performed' (p. 222).

Other examples include Bond's (2015) study of the portrayals of sex and sexuality in gay- and lesbian-oriented media, Hou, Chang and Sung's (2010) examination of teachers' knowledge sharing in blogs, Patterson et al.'s (2015) research into UK newsprint coverage of proposed legislation to prohibit smoking in private vehicles carrying children, Tillery and Chresfield's (2012) analysis of Black newspapers' coverage of the first wave of Afro-Caribbean immigration to the United States, and van Leuven, Heinrich and Deprez's (2015) study of how the Arab Spring was covered in the Belgian news media.

Beyond the academic and popular media, quantitative content analysis has been employed to study many other types of text, as in Lin's (1996) research into negative political advertising, Lock and Seele's (2016) analysis of 237 corporate social responsibility reports in 11 European countries, Poldner et al.'s (2014) study of student teachers' reflective writing, Proksch, Slapin and Thies's (2011) examination of party electoral pledges in post-war Japan, Roessger's (2017) analysis of meaning-making language in adult education, and Ruggiero and Green's (2017) study of secondary school students' digital game designs.

Indeed, it is difficult to imagine a topic that cannot be researched using quantitative content analysis. For example, Tartz and Krippner (2008, 2017) have employed it to research gender differences in dreaming in both Argentina and Japan, 'using an established coding system for the quantitative study of dream content ... that uses nine empirically derived categories, such as characters, social interactions, activities, environmental press, physical surroundings, and descriptive elements' (2017, p. 195). Goldey, Avery and van Anders (2014) have used it to examine sexual fantasies and their relation to gender/sex, while Janghorban et al. (2015) have explored sexual and reproductive rights from a Qur'anic perspective.

Quantitative content analysis has also been used to examine documents in combination or in parallel with other methods. Both Naganathan and Islam (2015) and Oleinik (2011) used it together with qualitative content analysis to provide triangulation (a mixed methods approach and quite a common combination); Shea et al. (2013) combined it with social network analysis; and Williams and Shepherd (2017) used it together with inductive concept development and secondary data.

Documentary research employing quantitative content analysis raises a number of issues. For a start, there are still some nagging doubts for some regarding ethical concerns (see also the discussion in Chapter 3). Is it enough that the data you are researching already exists, in a published and accessible form, and that the quantitative analysis undertaken will not reveal any individual details, or is some form of ethical clearance still desirable? Or does this depend on whether the topic being studied is sensitive in some way, in which case how do you determine what is sensitive?

Then there are coding issues, which need to be taken seriously if the research is to be seen as rigorous and replicable. Codebooks or guidelines need to be drawn up and agreed, and inter-rater reliability has to be measured and addressed (as it would be unwise to rely on the accuracy and consistency of a single rater or coder). And then there are the issues involved in using software to analyse huge amounts of data, using techniques such as latent semantic analysis or data mining, and the associated concerns that this removes the researcher too far from the data.

Sjøvaag and Stavelin (2012) offer nine guidelines for quantitative content analysis of online news: operationalise research questions or hypotheses, design the coding scheme, define the sample, write the selectors, run a pilot study, start the coding process, review the codebook continuously, perform coding spell-check and establish inter-coder agreement. They conclude that:

> The main methodological findings emerging from the quantitative content analysis of the news content of nrk.no in 2009 relate to the need to adjust the design of the methodology to the medium. Analyzing the content of an online news publication quantitatively is not the same as analyzing the news output of a traditional news broadcaster. Traditional news media – whether a print newspaper, nightly news programming on television or a radio program – have limited publication space but the online environment does not. As a result, online news tends to be more varied thematically than traditional news that undergoes stricter editorial procedures due to space and time limitations. (p. 226)

Sjøvaag and Stavelin's guidelines appear to be fairly generic in nature, so they could be usefully applied to other quantitative content analyses of documents.

Other Forms of Quantitative Documentary Analysis

There are, of course, other forms of quantitative documentary analysis in addition to the simpler forms and varieties of content analysis that have been discussed so far. These forms are typically both more complex and more specialised, though they could – in general terms – be viewed as simply more sophisticated versions of quantitative content analysis.

For example, Chen, Dooley and Rungtusanatham (2016) make use of process research and event analysis. This involved the secondary data analysis of 1,544 collected documents: congressional hearing statements, academic journal articles, statements in the press, annual reports, electronic (safetyforum.com) and print media (*Wall Street Journal, St Petersburg Times, Washington Post*) regarding the Ford/Firestone company breakup:

The objective of the quantification strategy is to examine the dissolution process and answer the question 'How does relationship dissolution unfold over time?' Because the focus is on the process of relationship dissolution in a broader auto industry context, we confine our analytical chronology between February 7, 2000, when the tread separation issue became public knowledge (involving other network players), and May 21, 2001, when the relationship formally dissolved. The quantification strategy transforms the raw data into events for statistical analysis using three steps. Step 1 identified relevant events from the raw text data resulting in a systematic list of events. Step 2 characterizes event properties by coding events, reducing the mass of qualitative text data to a quantitative time series ready for statistical methods. Step 3 analyzes events to test for temporal dependencies in order to uncover patterns and sequences. (2016, p. 328)

Rather than analysing a given document or set of documents in the same way, as in quantitative content analysis, this approach involves creating a quantitative document (the time series) for analysis from a large number of other documents of relevance. As the authors make clear:

the basic unit of analysis in process research is an event, generally defined as a non-routine, collective and public act that marks the transition from one system or time state to another ... 158 events were identified from the sources ... By coding in this systematic manner, we were able to identify six major 'event types' ... We sought *accuracy* by assessing inter-coder reliability ... We performed event time series regression analysis. (2016, pp. 328, 331)

In a similar way, Lam and Chan (2017) employ process-tracing techniques to study harbour protection in Hong Kong during the transition from British to Chinese rule (discussed further in Chapter 14).

Both of these studies used rigorous techniques to interrogate the available documents to reconstruct chronologies of events in detail, with, in a second stage, the chronology itself then becoming the subject of further analysis (alongside, in the Hong Kong example, a qualitative analysis of the same data set). These studies also illustrate well how the original qualitative data (i.e. the newspaper reports and other documents studied) may be used to produce quantitative data for analysis.

Conclusion

Various forms of quantitative content analysis of documents have been widely exploited to date. They have considerable potential as a methodology to be applied to the analysis of a huge range of topics. Simpler and more complex quantitative techniques may also be employed.

With the use of the appropriate software, substantial volumes of data may be quickly analysed in these ways. However, there is always a need to ensure the rigour and transparency of the process, and to bear in mind possible ethical issues.

KEY READINGS

Indulska, M, Hovorka, D, and Recker, J (2012) Quantitative Approaches to Content Analysis: Identifying conceptual drift across publication outlets. *European Journal of Information Systems*, 21, pp. 49–69.

A good example of a quantitative content analysis, in this case of bibliometric data.

Neuendorf, K (2002) *The Content Analysis Guidebook*. Thousand Oaks, CA, Sage.

A popular textbook, adopting a rigidly quantitative approach.

Rourke, L, and Anderson, T (2004) Validity in Quantitative Content Analysis. *Educational Technology Research and Development*, 52, 1, pp. 5–18.

A useful article focusing on validity issues.

Sjøvaag, H and Stavelin, E (2012) Web Media and the Quantitative Content Analysis: Methodological challenges in measuring online news content. *Convergence*, 18, 2, pp. 215–229.

Here the focus is on measurement, in the particular context of online news output.

13
QUALITATIVE APPROACHES

CONTENTS

Introduction	158
Thematic Analysis	158
Qualitative Content Analysis	160
Discourse Analysis	163
Conversation Analysis	167
Narrative Analysis	169
Conclusion	172

Introduction

This chapter follows on from the previous one, which considered quantitative approaches, by focusing on qualitative approaches to documentary analysis. Qualitative and quantitative approaches to analysis are viewed as complementary, and their use in combination is discussed in Chapter 14 which follows.

The chapter is organised in terms of five main sections – successively examining thematic analysis, qualitative content analysis, discourse analysis, conversation analysis and narrative analysis – which are identified as the major qualitative strategies for analysing documents.

Other forms of qualitative analysis are, of course, recognised. Thus, Neuendorf (2002) identifies rhetorical analysis, structuralist or semiotic analysis, interpretative analysis, critical analysis and normative analysis as well as the forms identified here, but does not include thematic analysis (though this is essentially what she calls interpretative analysis). This indicates a certain flexibility in terminology, which is – as we have seen – fairly common in academic research.

To give another example, Wertz et al. (2011) identify five ways of doing qualitative analysis (of documents and other forms of qualitative data): phenomenological psychology, grounded theory, discourse analysis, narrative research and intuitive inquiry; only two of which figure explicitly in this chapter. It is clear, then, that there is only partial agreement between authors, and no general agreement overall, regarding the forms and terminology of qualitative research and analysis.

It is also, of course, debatable just how distinct these different forms of qualitative analysis really are. As we noted in the previous chapter, content analysis on its own can be interpreted so broadly that it could incorporate all of the other analytical techniques identified; and, as we shall see, qualitative forms of content analysis are also increasingly popular. Yet each of the five types of qualitative documentary analysis recognised here has its own literature and advocates, so they will be treated separately and sequentially, before some conclusions are reached.

Thematic Analysis

Thematic analysis is undoubtedly the most common contemporary approach – indeed, it might be called the standard or underlying approach – to qualitative analysis, whether of documents or other forms of data. Indeed, it is so ubiquitous that – like documentary analysis – it is often not formally identified as the methodology being used by qualitative researchers. It is, in short, the obvious strategy to take.

In thematic analysis, the researcher examines the data collected, in written or other format, and seeks to summarise it and draw out key points by identifying recurrent themes (which may change and develop, and be re-labelled and amalgamated, as the analysis proceeds). Examples (quotations) are then typically selected to illustrate these themes. Ryan and Bernard (2003) describe the process in documentary research as follows:

Analyzing text involves several tasks: (1) discovering themes and subthemes, (2) winnowing themes to a manageable few (i.e., deciding which themes are important in any project), (3) building hierarchies of themes or code books, and (4) linking themes into theoretical models. (p. 85)

Ryan and Bernard also helpfully identify a list of things to look for in identifying themes, including repetitions, indigenous typologies or categories, metaphors and analogies, transitions, similarities and differences, linguistic connectors, missing data and theory-related material. They then detail the processing techniques – cutting and sorting, word list and keywords in context, word co-occurrence, metacoding – involved in carrying out the task.

While this sounds much like the processes recommended in the previous chapter for quantitative analysis, Guest, MacQueen and Namey (2012) distinguish the approach from quantitative techniques (see Chapter 12):

Thematic analyses move beyond counting explicit words or phrases and focus on identifying and describing both implicit and explicit ideas within the data, that is, themes. Codes are then typically developed to represent the identified themes and applied or linked to raw data as summary markers for later analysis. (p. 10)

Rather than producing a precise numerical account, therefore, thematic analysis seeks to inductively identify and illustrate the key themes in a document.

It has to be recognised, of course, that thematic analysis is unlikely to be as replicable as a quantitative analysis of a document. If the thematic analysis is sufficiently well described and exemplified, another researcher should be able to see how the themes chosen were arrived at, and make a judgement as to the overall quality of the research. However, another qualitative researcher conducting a fresh thematic analysis of the same document – even with the same purpose in mind – would probably identify a different set of themes, though there might be some overlap and shared terminology.

Box 13.1 summarises two examples of thematic analysis being used in documentary research, one from health care and one from education. Filho et al. (2017) present a thematic analysis of Brazilian national curricular guidelines for dentistry, medicine and nursing, with a particular focus on what these have to say about interprofessional education.

BOX 13.1

Examples of Thematic Analysis of Documents

1. The data gathered for this study (research corpus) were obtained from the 2001 NCGs [National Curricular Guidelines] for medicine and nursing, the 2002 NCGs for dentistry and the recently approved NCGs for medicine ... these are important documents in informing professions education [sic] in Brazil. Specifically, the NCGs outline key features for curricular design as well as teaching/learning methodologies that are used in undergraduate health

(Continued)

(Continued)

education across the entire country. Therefore, an in-depth investigation of these NCGs would constitute a key step to understand the potential role of IPE [interprofessional education] in shaping the education of medicine, nursing, and dentistry students ... The analysis of data was based on a thematic approach ... After downloading the official documents, an initial reading was made to become familiarised with these materials. During this phase, the NCGs contents were examined to gather general impressions and to compose the corpus for the analysis. In the next phase, relevant text extracts from the NCGs were grouped together to form a series of themes. Finally, data in each of themes [sic] was summarised to allow a critical interpretation. (Filho et al. 2017, p. 755)

2. The corpus consists of two sets of data: field notes and data from documents ... The documentary sources were of different kinds: documents related to the programme, minutes from meetings, evaluation sheets and similar sources. Of special importance were the final master's theses, which are openly accessible at UiO [the University of Oslo]. Analysing students' master's theses to study the qualities of higher education programmes has certain merits that have been overlooked by researchers in this field. Theses are high-stakes documents, meaning they represent a strong involvement on the part of the students, who engage in partly self-regulated activity for extended periods of four to eight months with variations in thematic focus and research design. As objects for summative and integrative assessment, the theses represent a number of dimensions or learning objectives that may be coherent or contradictory. At the same time, however, one has to consider the fact that theses represent a specific genre written for a targeted reader group (the examination board). Similar assessment of credibility, representativeness and meaning was done for all the documentary sources. The analytical strategies we used were a combination of narrative approaches and thematic analysis. (Lahn and Erikson 2016, pp. 688–689)

In the second example, Lahn and Erikson (2016) examine documentation from a Norwegian university, focusing on the master's theses produced by students following a specific programme. Interestingly, their analysis involved elements of narrative analysis (e.g. constructing the stories of particular students' thesis experience) and content analysis as well as thematic analysis (see the later sections in this chapter). They also use a second source of data – their own field notes made during the project – alongside the collected documents.

Qualitative Content Analysis

Content analysis began its life as a specifically quantitative set of techniques (see the discussion in Chapter 12), but latterly expanded to incorporate qualitative approaches as well. While some prominent authors still treat it as an exclusively quantitative approach (e.g. Neuendorf 2002), it is now well established as a qualitative documentary analysis technique.

A key point about qualitative content analysis is its relation to other kinds of qualitative and documentary analysis. As Holsti (1969), an early writer on the topic, recognises:

> Nearly all research in the social sciences and humanities depends in one way or another on careful reading of written materials. Given the ubiquity of this process in research, what characteristics distinguish content analysis from any careful reading of documents? (p. 2)

Clearly, the confusion and overlap between different named forms of analysis is of long standing. What Holsti's comment also reveals, however, is the desire of many qualitative researchers to move beyond a simple 'careful reading of documents' to engage in a more rigorous analysis (and one which might stand up better to some of the criticisms made by quantitative researchers).

Holsti continues to provide his own definition:

> Content analysis is any technique for making inferences by objectively and systematically identifying specified characteristics of messages ... this definition incorporates the three criteria discussed earlier: content analysis must be objective and systematic, and, if it is to be distinguished from information retrieval, indexing, or similar enterprises, it must be undertaken for some theoretical reason. Our definition does not include any reference to quantification because a rigid qualitative-quantitative distinction seems unwarranted for the purposes of defining the technique, for excluding certain studies from consideration as examples of systematic analysis of documentary data, or, by itself, for praise or condemnation of content analysis. (p. 14, emphasis in original)

Like Neuendorf (2002, quoted in Chapter 12), then, Holsti specifies objectivity as one of three identifying criteria. However, since he extends content analysis to include qualitative as well as quantitative approaches, it is even more difficult to see how this position can be sustained in the present day. For, no matter how rigorously qualitative research (or, for that matter, quantitative research) is pursued, there will always be subjective elements involved. However, Holsti's other two criteria – systematic and theoretical – seem reasonable.

A leading contemporary authority on the technique, Krippendorff (2013), offers another definition: 'Content analysis is a research technique for making replicable and valid inferences from texts (or other meaningful matter) to the contexts of their use' (p. 24). This does not appear to be in conflict with the definition provided by Holsti. Krippendorff also recognises three underlying characteristics for the approach, but here he diverges somewhat in not stressing objectivity, systematicity or theory:

> Contemporary content analysis has three distinguishing characteristics. **First**, content analysis is an *empirically grounded method*, exploratory in process, and predictive or inferential in intent ... **Second**, contemporary content analysis *transcends traditional notions of symbols, contents, and intents* ... **Third**, contemporary content analysis has been forced to develop a methodology of its own. (Krippendorff 2013, pp. 1–4, emphases in original)

Krippendorff is not, however, denying Holsti and Neuendorf's analyses, but rather emphasising another set of factors, which, to him, set content analysis (whether qualitative or quantitative) apart from other methods.

Altheide and Schneider (2013) focus in particular on qualitative content analysis, which they term ethnographic content analysis (ECA), and on how it differs from quantitative content analysis (QCA):

> ECA follows a recursive and reflexive movement between concept development – sampling – data collection – data coding – data analysis – interpretation. The aim is to be systematic and analytic but not rigid. Categories and variables initially guide the study, but others are allowed and expected to emerge throughout the study, including an orientation towards *constant discovery* and *constant comparison* of relevant situations, settings, styles, images, meanings and nuances. To this end, ECA involves focusing on and collecting numerical and narrative data rather than following the positivist convention of QCA of forcing the latter into predefined categories of the former. (p. 26, emphases in original)

Curiously, despite the implied harsh critique of quantitative forms of content analysis, this allows a quantitative element in qualitative content analysis, as both narrative and numerical data may be collected. The emphasis on being systematic and analytical remains.

Box 13.2 summarises three varied examples of the use of qualitative content analysis in documentary research, relating to health care, education and journalism. Evans (2014) reports on an analysis of English health research and development documents, focusing on patient and public involvement in research, and resulting in a qualitative synthesis of the findings.

BOX 13.2

Examples of Qualitative Content Analysis

1. The approach to documentary analysis adopted here was primarily a qualitative content analysis ... A systematic approach was adopted to identifying relevant English health R&D [research and development] documents over the period of interest. The search strategy had four stages. First, inclusion and exclusion criteria were identified. The key decision here was to include only generic R&D policy documents ... Second, the search strategy was developed to identify English DH [Department of Health] or NHS [National Health Service] R&D policy documents relevant to PPI [patient and public involvement] in research from the publication of the first R&D strategy in 1991 through to 2010. These documents were categorised into two types: (a) documents expressing overall R&D policy, and (b) documents specifically focused on PPI in research. The sites chosen for searching were the DH, NHS Evidence and INVOLVE websites. References to other official documents were followed up ... Third, a data extraction pro forma was developed to capture (a) content of the document, (b) the extent to which it addressed PPI in research, (c) the rationale given (if any) for supporting PPI in research, including any explicit reference to research evidence ... The fourth stage of the process was a

critical assessment of the context, nature and extent of evidence referenced to underpin any commitment to PPI in each policy document. Finally a qualitative synthesis was undertaken, looking at the overall story that emerged of the evolving approach by English health research policy makers to the question of an evidence base for PPI in research across all the documents surveyed. (Evans 2014, pp. 365–366)

2. We conducted a qualitative content analysis of print media coverage of the early years of the charter school debate. We analyzed 145 articles about public charter schools and public alternative schools that appeared in the New York Times and Los Angeles Times between 1994 and 2006. We developed two types of coding categories: descriptive and interpretive. The descriptive coding categories captured the following information about each article in our dataset: the publisher, the type of school described and the student population. The interpretive coding categories captured reporters' descriptions of the students, teachers, resources, and institutional cultures of charter and alternative schools. (Rooks and Munoz 2015, p. 1)

3. We conducted a qualitative content analysis of 20 journalistic comics (print and digital), most of which were published by English-language and German-language media outlets over the last few years ... In our qualitative analysis, we focused on the graphic devices concerning authenticity. We used an exploratory inductive approach searching for visually striking techniques (comparable to on-the-scene-reports on TV), positive deviants of patterns (e.g. multi-layered storytelling), visual elements (e.g. infographics, photographs), and surprising cases concerning the stylistic devices such as lettering, colour design, page layout, or size and shape. (Weber and Rall 2017, p. 380)

Rooks and Munoz (2015) examined print media coverage of the Charter School debate in the USA, analysing 145 newspaper articles published between 1994 and 2006, and carrying out both descriptive and interpretive coding. Weber and Rall (2017) looked at 20 journalistic comics, published in English or German, focusing on the graphic devices used concerning authenticity.

Discourse Analysis

Discourse analysis has witnessed a considerable growth in interest in recent years, and there are many competing texts available (e.g. Chouliaraki and Fairclough 1999, Fairclough 1992, Gee 1999, 2011, Georgakopoulou and Goutsos 1997, Hyland and Paltridge 2011, Johnstone 2008, Locke 2004, Machin and Mayr 2012, Rogers 2004, Scollon 2008, Van Leeuwen 2008, Widdowson 2007, Wodak and Meyer 2016, Wooffitt 2005). Most of these texts focus primarily on the analysis of talk, but some also deal with texts (including documents). Talk, particularly when it has been recorded and transcribed, may also, of course, be regarded as a document (see also the discussion of conversation analysis in the following section).

A distinction is made by some practitioners between discourse analysis and critical discourse analysis (CDA), with the latter seen as 'especially concerned with language and power' (Hafner 2017, p. 818). But, as Hafner (p. 818, emphasis in original) goes on to point out, 'many discourse analysts who are concerned with issues of social justice *do not* identify their work as CDA' and 'all discourse analysis is ultimately "critical"'. We will then stick to the basic term discourse analysis.

A simple definition of the term is provided by Gee (2011): 'Discourse analysis is the study of language-in-use. Better put, it is the study of language at use in the world, not just to say things, but to do things' (p. ix). This suggests that a key difference between discourse analysis and other forms of qualitative documentary analysis is its origins in, and focus on, the literary or linguistic element in talk or text. Tonkiss (2018) confirms this in offering two definitions of discourse:

> Discourse can refer to a single utterance or speech act (from a fragment of talk to a private conversation to a political speech) or to a systematic ordering of language involving certain rules, terminology and conventions (such as legal or medical discourse). This second definition allows researchers to analyse how discourses shape specific ways of speaking and understanding. (p. 478)

Of course, as ever, the reality of discourse analysis is more complex than that. As O'Connor (2007) notes:

> Discourse analysis may take many forms. It assists the researcher to view beyond the words, as more than tools for communication, and to examine the context of their usage, the meanings understood; what is symbolized within the community, and implied values. Language is highly symbolic, rarely politically neutral, and illustrates the world-view of the user to the listener, thus language is never just descriptive, but often shapes the way a community views an issue or a phenomenon. (p. 235)

O'Connor also offers some practical guidance for undertaking discourse analysis:

> Before commencing analysis, objective questions that may set the scene for more detailed questioning of the text itself include:
>
> - What is the status of the text?
> - Is the text part of a wider text?
> - Who is the author of the text?
> - Who is the intended audience?
> - Are there stakeholders in what has been written?
> - Who are the people with the power to make decisions and how are they using their power?
> - Are there hidden agendas/biases, hidden issues or aspects of a bigger issue?
> - What sort of authority has been given to the document?
> - What sorts of decisions have been made, with what level of authority and influence? (p. 238)

While I would, again, question, regret and reject the use of the word 'objective', this does suggest that the processes involved in discourse analysis are very similar to those in other forms of documentary analysis (see Chapters 3 and 11). What differs, of course, is the focus on discourse.

As with other forms of documentary research and analysis, documentary researchers interested in discourse are not short of types and sources of data. Thus, Goddard and Carey (2017, pp. 179–180) identify the following:

> There are many different genres of writing that could potentially form part or all of the data for a discourse-analytic project. Here are some examples:
>
> *Written stories* (not part of professional publications) – e.g. children's writing
>
> *Magazine advertisements* – e.g. for products aimed at a particular group
>
> *Magazine features* – e.g. problem pages, celebrity stories, 'real-life' stories
>
> *Special interest publications* – e.g. cookery, property
>
> *Promotional material* – e.g. flyers, freesheets, junk mail
>
> *Newspaper articles* – e.g. news reports, editorials, features, obituaries
>
> *Literary texts* – e.g. where a particular group is represented or theme explored
>
> *Comics and graphic novels* – as above
>
> *Non-fiction texts* – as above
>
> *Organisational documents* – e.g. policy documents, instructions, handbooks, business memos, agendas and minutes, written texts from particular occupations such as education, medicine or law
>
> *Writing that marks social customs* – e.g. greetings cards such as birthday cards

In short, the discourse analyst interested in exploring documents has a vast plethora of readily available examples available for interrogation.

Box 13.3 contains details of three contrasting examples of discourse analysis being applied in documentary research. In the first of these, Chonka (2016; cf. Richards 2017) undertakes a critical discourse analysis of three Somalian propaganda videos, while, in the second, Hopewell (2017) provides a critical discourse analysis of a single, but arguably key, World Trade Organisation document, focusing on its positioning, framing and silences. The third example (Friedman 2017) offers an analysis of selected international conflict-resolution documents, in this case relating to the Arab–Israeli conflict, pointing out how constructive ambiguity may lead to positional interpretation and possible progress.

BOX 13.3

Examples of Discourse Analysis in Documentary Research

1. This paper interrogates the cultural, religious and historical narratives which are wrapped up in the content of pro-HSM (Harakat Al Shabaab Al Mujaahidiin) propaganda videos – often prosaic, domestic or idyllic themes seemingly far removed from the violence of much of the Islamist propaganda which receives greater scholarly or journalistic attention. Here I apply Alshaer's 'culture of communications' methodology as utilised in his analysis of media/literary products of Hamas in the Occupied Palestinian Territories ... Building on Said's notions of the inseparability of language and culture and a Saussurian conception of language as sign, this ... 'cultural' framing of the methodology speaks to a core feature of critical discourse analysis approaches: the treatment of language as a social practice in itself and an emphasis on the dialectical relationship existing between a context and a 'discursive event' ... My own selection of 'texts' is based on professional and research experience in the Somali media environment since 2012 and my wider Ph.D. research focuses on the relationship between a transnational Somali-language public sphere of news media and the continuing deployment of ethno-nationalist discourses. As such, I identify in the analysis narrative overlaps between these pro-HSM propaganda videos and material in the wider media environment across Somalia. The paper primarily engages with three videos from the same media network (Al Furqaan media), which, although of different lengths, all share numerous stylistic features. The analysis moves between a fine-grained examination of particular elements of the discourses and an attempt to situate the recurring themes of the material in the broader contexts of both the struggle for the reconfiguration of the Somali state and wider debates in the Somali-language public sphere. (Chonka 2016, p. 249)

2. This study draws on a large data corpus, incorporating a wide range of WTO [World Trade Organisation] documents pertaining to its relationship with civil society, such as public relations materials, speeches, press releases, information on its website, internal memoranda and policy directives, and materials from the annual WTO Public Forums ... The analysis presented here pays particular attention to one specific document – an official document in which the WTO attempts to address concerns from civil society, entitled 'Top 10 Reasons to Oppose the World Trade Organization: Criticism, yes ... misinformation, no!' In this text, the WTO sets out 10 concerns raised by civil society and responds to each one ... Despite its age, this remains a critical document for understanding the WTO's orientation toward civil society. First, what makes this text unique and particularly fruitful for analysis is its dialogic quality: it is structured as a dialogue between the WTO and civil society ... Second, this is a foundational text that shaped the future trajectory of WTO discourse directed at the public and civil society... Consequently, the discourse contained ... is highly representative of that found elsewhere in the data corpus ... To examine the discourse of the WTO, I employ CDA [critical discourse analysis]. As an approach that looks at discourse within larger social and political structures and in its relationship to inequality, power, and domination, CDA is particularly well-suited to the analysis of global governance institutions. CDA views discourse as a form of social action, produced by actors rooted in the social world, with specific intents and strategies. It thus provides a valuable means of examining the productive aspects of discourse and the work that

it does. I center my analysis on three key aspects of the WTO's discourse: its use of positioning, framing, and silences. (Hopewell 2017, pp. 54–55)

3. Analysis of these conflict resolution documents is based on an assortment of discourse analysis tools, specifically utilizing tools developed by discourse pragmatics that relate to how meanings are created and interpreted through indirect language. Utilizing this body of literature as well as the ... literature dealing with equivocation and vagueness strategies, this approach will utilise the following steps to identify evasion strategies and their interpretations:

   i. Identify discursive resources which avoid taking a definitive stand on a sensitive issue.
   ii. Examine how each discursive resource is implemented in various conflict resolution documents.
   iii. Examine whether this discursive resource is identified by the media and how it is interpreted through media coverage of the document.

This approach is applied to the following corpus: (a) the four conflict resolution documents described above; (b) newspaper coverage of each of the documents, attempting to identify how evasion strategies are interpreted by one of the central actors in the conflict. The corpus includes print media coverage of each document one week before its publication (to examine interpretation of document leaks) and three weeks following its publication. (Friedman 2017, p. 388)

Other examples include Choudhury and Haque's (2018) study of Canadian newspaper discourse on natural disasters, concluding that:

> newspapers play a crucial role in constructing meaning and social consensus regarding metaphors and rhetoric related to resilience to natural disasters. Newspaper framing helps develop a shared understanding by, for example, arguing that extreme weather is a new norm and that resilience is a necessary way of thinking in the face of these emerging conditions. (p. 245)

These examples demonstrate again that discourse analysis, just like documentary analysis in general, may be applied to audio-visual as well as textual documents.

Conversation Analysis

Conversation analysis, like discourse analysis, largely stems from linguistics. While there are numerous texts available (e.g. Drew and Heritage 2006, Have 1999, Hutchby and Wooffitt 1998, Liddicoat 2011, Richards and Seedhouse 2005, Sidnell 2010), it is probably fair to say that it has had a lesser impact on documentary research across the social sciences to date – that is, outside of linguistics – than discourse analysis (to which it has been compared: Wooffitt 2005). In part, this is because conversation analysis is much more directed towards the spoken word, and spoken language has a different set of conventions to written language. We may again, of course, make the point, though, that once spoken language is written down, as it normally is for conversation analysis purposes, it may be treated as another document.

Bruhn and Ekstrom (2017) offer the following explanation:

> CA [conversation analysis] is an approach for the detailed examination of talk in social interactions. The main objects of analyses are the participants' design of actions and the sequential turn-by-turn organization and dynamics of interaction. It is based on a conviction that this is best understood through the study of actual conversations made available for analyses in recordings and transcriptions. CA understands institutions (roles, norms and rules) as oriented to and (re)shaped in activities of interaction. Interaction in institutional contexts is organized for specific tasks. Tasks such as offering good service, making assessments and decisions are considered as practical achievements in interaction. (p. 196)

Gosen and Koole (2017) offer an alternative approach to conversation analysis through a discussion of its aims:

> The enterprise of Conversation Analysis is to unearth the methods that participants use to accomplish their conversations as social projects. To get to these 'methods', CA focuses on what participants make observable for each other since social interaction can only be accomplished when participants index interactional issues such as 'what are we doing' or 'what are we talking about' for their co-participants. As analysts then, we use the observable materials that also participants use to conduct their interaction, and to do an analysis of these materials is to establish a systematic relation between an observable feature – a form – and the meaning attributed to this form. (p. 791)

Gosen and Koole then identify, in the area of educational research, major topics for conversation analysis, including turn-taking, sequence organisation, classroom order, second-language education, and learning and understanding.

Conversation analysis is a very precise and detailed approach, following accepted guidelines and practices, where particular conversations (or parts of conversations) are set out on the page in a prescribed fashion. Indeed, while it is considered here as a qualitative approach to documentary analysis, it could be said to be semi-quantitative or mixed mode in nature.

Box 13.4 illustrates two examples of the use of conversation analysis. Bruhn and Ekstrom (2017) offer an analysis of what they call 'frontline interactions in the public sector', in their case involving the Swedish Board for Study Support, which offers grants and loans to students. They undertake a detailed analysis of 67 telephone calls, from a database of over 1,400, to show how rules were applied in practice.

QUALITATIVE APPROACHES | 169

BOX 13.4

Examples of Conversation Analysis in Documentary Research

1. The interactional data comes from a larger corpus of audio recordings of 1,400 telephone calls. We recorded calls from four regional offices and 62 different call-takers during 2011 and 2012. For this study we selected 300 calls for rough transcription. The sample was selected randomly, except that we made sure to include calls to all offices, several call-takers and calls related to both the application and repayment of loans. Sixty-seven calls containing rule-applications on individual cases were selected for detailed analyses ... The relevant parts of the calls were transcribed according to CA conventions and translated into English. (Bruhn and Ekstrom 2017, pp. 199–200)

2. The primary database includes the main U.S. news programs broadcasting live interviews nightly (ABC's *Nightline*, PBS's *NewsHour*) and on Sunday mornings (NBC's *Meet the Press*, CBS's *Face the Nation*, ABC's *This Week*). This database (n = 65 interviews) includes a systematic sample of one week of news broadcasts as well as some intentional oversampling of interviews with more liberal and conservative politicians to address the constitutive puzzle at the heart of the paper ... Some additional interview materials (n = 12) were drawn from various other sources: nightly network news programs, cable news programs, public radio news, and presidential news conferences. The database is temporally broad, spanning a three-decade period of relative stability in journalistic question design (mid-1980s through mid-2010s). It emphasizes traditional questioning conducted by professional journalists over other varieties of broadcast talk ... The materials were recorded and transcribed using conversation analytic conventions. All materials were subject to analytic induction, with attention to both general patterns and deviant cases in pursuit of a comprehensive analysis of the database. (Clayman 2017, pp. 45–47)

The second example (Clayman 2017) involved analyses of American television news broadcasts, looking for both 'general patterns and deviant cases' in interview practices. It was concluded that:

> The findings shed light on how politicians balance appeals to centrist and partisan viewers, how journalists police the boundaries of mainstream politics, and how both parties contribute to a process of legitimation that enacts and at times modifies the parameters of the sociopolitical mainstream. (p. 41)

Narrative Analysis

Narrative analysis, in essence, is the academic version of storytelling; it aims to identify and analyse the stories or accounts regarding the topic of interest presented by one or more people: orally, in writing or in other media. Griffin and May (2018, p. 513) put it this way:

> Although the definition of the term *narrative* is under some dispute, key characteristics that are included in many definitions are that a narrative is an account of a non-random sequence of events that conveys some kind of action and movement through time. Thus, narratives are generally understood to have some form of chronology.

Alongside classic accounts of narrative analysis (e.g. Connelly and Clandinin 1990), we can find more recent and specialised versions. Thus, Webster and Mertova (2007) discuss critical event narrative analysis, while Holstein and Gubrium (2012) examine dialogical narrative analysis and quantitative narrative analysis amongst other themes. Franzosi (2004) illustrates the use of story grammars, relational data models and network models in socio-historical research. Practitioners of narrative analysis are as likely, therefore, as other researchers to develop and follow their own specialist techniques and directions.

Webster and Mertova (2007) offer the following summation of narrative analysis or inquiry:

> Narrative inquiry attempts to capture the 'whole story', whereas other methods tend to communicate understandings of studied subjects or phenomena at certain points, but frequently omit the important 'intervening' stages. Narrative research aims for its findings to be well grounded and supportable – it aims for verisimilitude, producing results that have appearance of truth or reality. (p. 10)

In other words, narrative analysis aims not just to produce stories, but good or convincing stories, for academic analysis.

Webster and Mertova also offer a framework for narrative inquiry:

> At the highest levels of the framework are two factors that both govern and justify the methodology: the themes of *human centredness* and the *complexity* of human experience. The methodology contains four constituent parts: research *processes*, *negotiations* that occur, *risks* that may arise, and preparation and auditing of *results*. (p. 104, emphases in original)

This confirms that the processes that the researcher goes through to compile the narrative are broadly similar to those involved in other forms of social research.

Griffin and May (2018) divide narrative analyses into two main types:

> Within this disparate methodological field, one key distinction can be made, namely between studies that focus mainly on the 'textual' elements of the narrative itself (be this oral, written or visual) and those studies that also focus on the interactional context within which the narrative is told. The first group ... can further be divided along two axes: first, from *thematic* to *holistic* analyses, and second, from analysing the *content* of what is said to analysing *how* it is said. (p. 515)

The analysis may, therefore, be more or less complex, depending on the aspects of the narrative and its context that are included in the research.

Box 13.5 contains two examples of the use of narrative analysis in documentary research. In the first of these, Deerman (2017) carries out an analysis of publications produced by the Christian Right in the United States. Her analysis 'shows that the movement's core narrative of redemption split into two narratives that emphasized either of two meanings of redemption: (1) to reform society, and (2) to save sinners through prayer' (p. 561).

BOX 13.5

Examples of Narrative Analysis in Documentary Research

1. I approached the publications of the Christian Right as packages of stories to be contextualized and examined as narrations taking place in particular institutional contexts, operating within known narrative conventions, and having a role in orienting and directing action. Analysis of the first ten years of publication of the *Moral Majority Report* and *CWA Newsletter* began by identifying and compiling the regularly named protagonists and settings, with the finding that both varied little across the two publications. I then identified and compiled repeatedly mentioned events, finding partial overlap across the two organizations. For analytic convenience I termed a unit of data a 'piece' and defined it as an individual article, letter (from a reader), editorial, announcement, news report, and the like of at least 100 words in length ... Identifying a shared and demarcated set of narrative elements (protagonists, settings, and events), made it possible to delineate the core narrative and to separate it from the many stories circulating throughout the documents. Though perhaps not known to individual actors, nor present in individually told stories, the core narrative is stable and connects narrative elements in a meaningful way by providing an internal logic. I selected fifty pieces from each organization for closer analysis. This subset of data developed through a series of analytic decisions to achieve narrative richness. Length matters. Though 100 words is an arbitrary parameter, conducting narrative analysis with chunks of text facilitates examination of the purpose, function, and recounting of movement narratives. I selected pieces to reflect the ten-year period and the range of topics addressed. I also selected pieces to represent the entire (though narrow) range of authors. (Deerman 2017, p. 570)

2. In this article, the main media genre under scrutiny is the TV documentary. Therefore, the three chronological documentary episodes are the most important textual corpus to be examined. Narrative analysis will be deployed in unraveling the underlying structuring of each episode and in addressing voice as a communicative resource allocated to each manifested or latent narrator ... the first analytical step is to exhibit the temporality of the media narrative, in which the voices of multiple subjects are disproportionately allocated in temporal lengths. Second, the allocation of subjects' voices can imply the documentary's narrative structure ... The relationship between voice and narrative is seemingly equated with the intermeshing

(Continued)

(Continued)

> of the narrators' agency and the narrative's structure. Therefore, employing narrative analysis resonates with the theoretical tenet of this article, as it attempts to unravel the implementation of voice and its limitation in modern media and institutional logic. Within each episode, voice is interwoven in the narrative fabric presented as monologue, conversation, or commentary. Thus, in determining the narrative pattern of each documentary episode, various techniques, such as conversation analysis (CA), are deployed to capture the featured voices interwoven in each episode. Conversations in documentaries contribute to the formation of the narrative by wielding an interactive way of storytelling. Therefore, the limited usage of CA will not blemish the coherence of the 'overall narrative analysis'. (Li 2016, pp. 407–408)

The second example, Li (2016), carries out an analysis of three television documentaries which sought to destigmatise severe mental health patients (SMPs) in Hong Kong. Li notes that:

> SMPs' voices steadily increase in length and prominence in the narrative's temporal line, yet they are strictly orchestrated within the sealed narrative that is subject to the institutional interest of promoting the rehabilitation mode of mental health care in Hong Kong. The voice/narrative inequality between SMPs and mental institutions leads to the 'dependent destigmatization' that indicates a dependent power relation between SMPs and powerful institutions. (p. 403)

Note that Li also engages in conversation analysis (discussed in the previous subsection) as part of this research.

Both these studies demonstrate the usefulness of adopting a narrative approach, while illustrating that it is not totally distinct from other forms of qualitative analysis.

Conclusion

Qualitative approaches to documentary analysis involve, in addition to the standard qualitative approach of thematic analysis, a range of different analytical approaches – focusing on content, conversation, discourse or narrative – which share many characteristics in common and overlap to a certain degree. Some of these approaches – as in the case of both content analysis and narrative analysis – also allow for a quantitative alternative or complementary analysis (see also Chapter 12), while others, notably conversation analysis, follow a clear set of guidelines which can become semi-quantitative in its interpretation. Clearly, then, qualitative and quantitative strategies are not as distinct as some would wish or believe. This forms the focus for the discussion in the next chapter, on mixed methods approaches and triangulation.

KEY READINGS

Altheide, D, and Schneider, C (2013) *Qualitative Media Analysis*. Thousand Oaks, CA, Sage.

A useful textbook discussing a range of strategies.

Braun, V, and Clarke, V (2006) Using Thematic Analysis in Psychology. *Qualitative Research in Psychology*, 3, 2, pp. 77–101.

A much cited article on thematic analysis.

Gee, J (2011) *How to do Discourse Analysis: A toolkit*. London, Routledge.

A helpful and practical guide.

Gosen, M, and Koole, T (2017) Conversation Analysis. pp. 791–811 in Wyse, D, Selwyn, N, Smith, E, and Suter, L (eds) *The BERA/SAGE Handbook of Educational Research*. London, Sage, two volumes.

Provides a clear introduction in the educational context.

Krippendorff, K (2013) *Content Analysis: An introduction to its methodology*. Thousand Oaks, CA, Sage, third edition.

A popular and voluminous textbook on the topic.

Liddicoat, A (2011) *An Introduction to Conversation Analysis*. London, Continuum, second edition.

As it indicates, a useful introductory overview.

Ryan, G, and Bernard, R (2003) Techniques to Identify Themes. *Field Methods*, 15, 1, pp. 85–109.

A very helpful discussion of some of the practical issues involved in thematic analysis.

Webster, L, and Mertova, P (2007) *Using Narrative Inquiry as a Research Method: An introduction to using critical event narrative analysis in research on learning and teaching*. London, Routledge.

A very readable introduction to one approach to narrative analysis.

14
MIXED METHODS APPROACHES

CONTENTS

Introduction	176
Triangulation and Mixed Methods	176
Why and How to Combine Quantitative and Qualitative Approaches in Documentary Research	177
Examples of Mixed Method Documentary Research	178
Conclusion	180

Introduction

The previous two chapters focused on quantitative (Chapter 12) and qualitative (Chapter 13) approaches to documentary analysis. As we have already argued, the quantitative/qualitative distinction has been hugely emphasised – indeed, over-emphasised (see the discussion in Chapter 5) – in discussions of social research methodology. The approach taken in this book has, therefore, been to view quantitative and qualitative methods as complementary rather than oppositional.

Documents may be researched using mixed methods, in particular by combining quantitative and qualitative analyses of the same document or documents. This will enable the confirmation or questioning of results, as well as providing a fuller and more multi-faceted analysis (Oleinik 2011). The use of mixed methods is seen here, therefore, as a key way of achieving triangulation. While the employment of mixed methods will inevitably require more time and effort, the benefits – even in relatively small-scale research – are likely to be considerable.

This chapter starts by considering the relation between the general principle of triangulation and the use of mixed methods approaches in documentary analysis. The issues involved in combining quantitative and qualitative approaches in documentary research are then examined. Finally, some examples of mixed methods documentary research are reviewed to illustrate some of the possibilities and benefits.

Triangulation and Mixed Methods

The idea of triangulation and the notion of mixed methods research are closely related. Triangulation as a principle implies that it is advisable to carry out more than one analysis – of the same or of related data sets, by the same or different researchers, on the same topic or case – in order to have greater confidence in one's findings, or to make those findings more comprehensive. Employing a mixed methods approach is one obvious strategy through which to achieve triangulation.

Triangulation may lead to what is termed convergent validation; that is, the analysis of the topic or case of interest using two or more methods, or by two or more researchers, results in essentially the same findings. This allows the researchers involved to have greater confidence in the veracity of their findings and interpretation. Their findings have, at least for the time being, been confirmed or validated.

There are other possible results from triangulation, however, which are perhaps even more useful or interesting. Thus, the application of alternative research methods, by the same or different researchers, may suggest an interpretation of the data that is rather more complicated or comprehensive than had initially been thought. This is to be welcomed, as it will typically lead to a fuller understanding of the topic or case under research.

However, triangulation may also lead to a divergence or even contradiction in results and their interpretation. In other words, the findings from the application of different methods of analysis, or from analyses by different researchers, to the same or related data sets may be distinctly different. Assuming that the research has been carried out competently, this also suggests that matters are more complex than originally thought, and that some further thinking, and probably further research, is needed. This should not, though, be too disheartening; after all, what it suggests is that the topic or case in question is worth researching.

Adopting and applying a mixed methods approach will always lead to some degree of triangulation. As we have seen, documentary research is commonly used in mixed methods studies alongside other methodologies, such as interviews or surveys (see, in particular, the examples included in Boxes 2.2, 5.1 and 10.2). Indeed, as I have remarked elsewhere in this book, this usage may be seen as endemic. What is of interest in this chapter is the use of mixed methods within documentary research.

Mixed methods approaches may, of course, be applied to the analysis of documents on a wholly quantitative or qualitative basis. Thus, for example, within qualitative analysis, narrative analysis might be carried out alongside conversation analysis (Li 2016; discussed in Box 13.5). The focus in the remainder of the chapter, however, is on the combination of quantitative and qualitative methods in documentary research.

Why and How to Combine Quantitative and Qualitative Approaches in Documentary Research

One obvious response to the question 'why combine quantitative and qualitative approaches in documentary research?' is, of course, 'why not?' If the document or documents you are researching contain both qualitative and quantitative data, it makes little sense – unless you have other, overriding reasons, such as lack of time or the need to focus – to reject available data which may have a key bearing on your research topic and questions.

Where this is not the case, or only marginally so – and this will most typically be the case where the document being analysed is essentially qualitative in nature – it still makes sense to employ quantitative methods as well if and where you can. The qualitative and quantitative analyses of the same document(s) will likely complement each other, each shedding some fresh light on the conclusions derived from the other.

Or it may be that – as already suggested in the discussion of triangulation – the qualitative and quantitative analyses do not simply complement each other, but suggest different or extended interpretations. These will also be valuable findings, perhaps leading you to reject your initial understanding, and carry out further research.

Combining quantitative and qualitative approaches in documentary analysis is perhaps most obvious as a strategy when a content analysis is being undertaken, as parallel forms of quantitative and qualitative content analysis have been developed. However, thematic analysis – probably the most common form of qualitative analysis employed, both in documentary research and more generally – though regarded as a qualitative approach, may readily become pseudo-quantitative in nature when the relative frequency of the different themes identified is considered. Such a complementary, quantitative analysis can easily be made explicit and rigorous.

While this is not either common or standard, it is not difficult to envisage a quantitative element being added to other qualitative documentary analysis approaches, such as discourse, conversation and narrative analysis. And, turning the perspective around, qualitative elements may also be readily added to quantitative documentary analyses. For example, where the document being analysed is a quantitative database or a statistical report, maintaining a contextual critical edge demands that the authorship, origins and purpose of the document are considered (see also Chapter 3), which can only really be achieved in a qualitative fashion.

Examples of Mixed Method Documentary Research

Some examples of the use of quantitative and qualitative approaches in combination in analysing documents have already been identified in this book. Thus, Naganathan and Islam (2015), Oleinik (2011) and Tickell (2010), each of which were discussed in Chapter 12, all combined forms of quantitative and qualitative analysis in their research. This is a fairly common mixed method approach to documentary analysis; after all, if you start examining a particular document or set of documents from a qualitative perspective, it is quite difficult to avoid drawing out quantitative data as well if it is included in the document or readily compiled from it. The same applies if one starts from a quantitative perspective when qualitative data is also present in the document(s). So mixed methods approaches are really very widespread, at least at a basic level, in documentary analysis.

Box 14.1 includes two further examples of mixed method use in documentary analysis, to illustrate some of the possibilities. Lam and Chan (2017) examine harbour protection in Hong Kong over the 1992–2006 period (a time of political transition, during which the territory was returned to China by the UK). Having collected 588 news articles from one newspaper, they analyse this data set using both qualitative and statistical techniques. They conclude that:

> Our case narrative of issue framing is supported by the quantitative topic modelling of the published discourse on harbour reclamation. Tracking the shifting popularity of different policy frames in a corpus of news articles on the harbour protection advocacy ... shows that competing aspects came to dominate the policy process in rapid succession. At the first wave of reclamation construction in the early 1990s, attention first fell on shipping safety but then shifted quickly to the harbour as a natural asset as the support of green groups was solicited. After that, the legality of reclamation construction took over as the TPB [Town Planning Board] was brought to court during the early 2000s. Finally, the theme of citizen participation came into focus in the harbour protection debate. Consistent with the qualitative analysis, the pattern is suggestive of a highly experimental approach to issue framing in which, in contrast to the common strategy of deepening identification with a policy frame, different issue frames were adopted in a relatively short period of time. (pp. 64–65)

BOX 14.1

Examples of Mixed Method Documentary Analysis

1. For the analysis, we adopted process-tracing techniques, as venue shopping and issue framing are both sequential in nature and are traditionally studied using case-based, longitudinal methods. Process tracing preserves the chronology of choice making as advocates move between venues and issue frames so that particular choices can be directly linked to co-occurring developments in regime transition. In terms of data sources, we drew on news articles, memoirs, and other archival data to identify and describe major events in the advocacy history as well as any important developments connecting these events. For a stronger empirical basis, we include a statistical analysis of the same textual dataset on which the qualitative analysis of issue framing was performed. We compiled a corpus of 588 news articles on the harbour protection controversy published in the South China Morning Post between 1992 and 2006. Using these articles, we identified and estimated the probability that alternative frames were used to define harbour protection using the R package 'lda' for Latent Dirichlet Allocation (LDA) topic modelling. Intuitively, the LDA algorithm captures the underlying 'topics' in a body of texts through a reverse-engineering process. It is assumed that each document is drawn from a mix of topics with different probability distribution of words, so that meaningful frames can be identified as groups of words that occur across documents in a non-random fashion. A set of probabilities reflecting the year-to-year likelihood of observing the constituent words of these frames is then computed as a measure of the changing importance of different issue frames for harbour reclamation. (Lam and Chan 2017, pp. 57–58)

2. To explore the questions outlined above, this study relies on the textual and graphical data contained on university home pages ... To compile this desired home page data, Import.IO, a data-scraping software, was first used to extract the web addresses of all 80 English-speaking institutions listed on the Universities Canada directory ... Import.IO gathered the links to each of these institutions' home pages from the Universities Canada directory by following a series of steps, including 'clicks' and 'copy-and-paste' style functions, coded by the author. Rapidminer Studio, a software package with data-scraping capabilities, was then used to follow each extracted hyperlink to each university home page and extract their textual content. Since university home pages also commonly contain rich graphical content (e.g. pictures, insignia), screenshots of each were manually captured using an extension for the Google Chrome browser ... The procedure outlined above resulted in the generation of a textual data set with over 31,800 words, the rough equivalent of 64 single spaced pages of content. In addition, 80 unique home page screenshots were also gathered ... To analyse this data, a mixed-methodological form of content analysis used within multiple higher education marketing studies was employed. First, Rapidminer Studio was used to generate counts for every word and two-word combination ('bigram') present in the text contained across all university home pages ... Following this preliminary step ... each home page screenshot was inputted into QSR NVivo, and the author proceeded to examine and manually code all text and images present within them ... This second step permitted a more in-depth exploration of how high-frequency words and phrases identified earlier were used on home pages. It also allowed for an analysis of the content of graphical material communicated through home pages, to which previous counts were completely insensitive. (Milian 2017, pp. 59–61)

In the second example, Milian (2017) extracts textual and graphical data from Canadian university home pages on the internet using data-scraping software. A data set of over 31,800 words and 80 screenshots is the result, which he then analyses both quantitatively (simple word counts) and qualitatively (text coding): note that this is also an interesting example of using both written and visual texts. Milian argues that:

> Methodologically, this study employs a unique blend of data-scraping techniques, textual and graphical empirical sources, and mixed methods that has yet to gain prominence within higher education research. This approach could serve as a template for future researchers to similarly map promotional behaviour across other higher education sectors, allowing them to expediently examine vast amounts of data. (2017, p. 69)

Undoubtedly, data analysis software is of considerable help in undertaking both quantitative and qualitative research, and particularly if the two are combined, as in these examples, in mixed methods research. The use of software, and of secondary data (see Chapter 8), allows much larger data sets to be assembled and analysed. But even in smaller-scale studies, there is much to be said for utilising as many forms of data and analysis as possible.

Conclusion

Mixed methods approaches to documentary analysis, combining quantitative and qualitative elements, have much to offer in developing expanded and complementary analyses – that is, enabling triangulation – of the same documents or data sets. Rather than, falsely in my view, regarding quantitative and qualitative approaches as being based on inherently opposed paradigms, it makes much more sense to use them pragmatically in parallel (Bryman 2015, Scott 2007, Tashakkori and Teddlie 1998, 2010), thereby getting as much as possible out of the analysis of any particular document or documents.

KEY READINGS

Bryman, A (2015) *Social Research Methods*. Oxford, Oxford University Press, fifth edition.

A popular research methods textbook, in which the final part focuses on mixed methods research.

Tashakkori, A, and Teddlie, C (eds) (2010) *Sage Handbook of Mixed Methods in Social and Behavioral Research*. Thousand Oaks, CA, Sage, second edition.

A substantial edited handbook compiled by two of the most widely published authors on this topic.

PART 4

WHERE NEXT?

Part 4, the final part of this book, contains just two chapters.

Chapter 15 considers how to approach sharing and disseminating your research, including through seminars, conference presentations and publications, and how to go about planning further research.

Chapter 16 concludes the book by re-emphasising its key messages.

15

SHARING AND DISSEMINATING YOUR RESEARCH

CONTENTS

Introduction	184
Evaluating Your Research	184
Seminars and Conference Presentations	185
Writing Up for Publication	186
Planning Further Research	188
Conclusion	189

Introduction

This chapter considers what you might do once you've finished, or nearly finished, a documentary research project (though much the same issues are relevant for other kinds of research project). It is based on the premise that you will wish or need to share and disseminate your research and its findings. After all, doing research and keeping it to yourself is a fairly pointless exercise, unless it is highly confidential and/or extremely personally satisfying.

So you really owe it to yourself to get your findings out there into the wider world. After all, by now you must have read a significant number of publications of relevance to your research. These will almost certainly be of variable quality, yet all of them have been published in some form and have been of some use to fellow researchers (including you). Don't you think that your research has also been worthwhile, and that you can do at least as well in terms of publishing it?

The chapter is organised in four main sections:

- first, we consider how you might evaluate or assess the worth of your research before you go public with it
- the options of presenting your research in public at a seminar or a conference are reviewed
- the processes involved in writing up your research as an article, report or book are considered, along with those involved in getting published
- the question of what to do next, or planning for further research, is discussed.

Finally, some conclusions are reached.

Evaluating Your Research

It's sensible to have an idea of the quality and worthwhileness of your research before you seek to present it publicly or try and get it published. Being able to argue its worth, and having some confidence in its quality, is critical if you want others to take you seriously. So it is a good idea to start by evaluating or assessing your research yourself.

Before considering how you might evaluate your own research – which may initially seem to be too much of a challenge – it is worth briefly considering how you evaluate other people's research. I would suggest that there are four key questions to bear in mind when doing, or attempting to do, this:

- Can you understand what the researchers have done and why?
- Does their interpretation of their findings seem reasonable and defensible?
- Can you relate their research to other research on the topic?
- Does their research suggest plausible change actions and/or further research directions?

If you have been carrying out your research competently, these are the kinds of questions you will have been asking – whether explicitly or implicitly – about other people's research. They underlie, for example, the processes involved in carrying out a literature review (see Chapter 6), as well as, more generally, those involved in undertaking any kind of documentary research (see especially Chapters 3, 5 and 11). The trick now is to be able to turn these questions around and ask them of your own research, as, after all, other researchers will do.

Ask yourself these sorts of questions:

- Why did you do your research in the way that you did?
- How can you explain and/or justify this?
- If you were starting your research again now, what might you do differently, and why?
- What did you think you were going to find out, and what have you found out?
- What are your key findings, and how strong is the evidence for them?
- Are other interpretations of your data possible, and, if so, why do you favour the one you have advanced?
- Where does your research fit alongside other research; what similarities and differences are there in your findings?
- What is your research contribution, and how significant a contribution is this?
- What does your research suggest should be done now (in terms of changes in practice or further research)?

Of course, you don't have to carry out this evaluation entirely on your own. Most obviously, you could turn to fellow researchers in your field; perhaps those you have been working alongside, or with whom you have developed useful relationships during the course of your research. If there are particular aspects of your research you are less confident about, focus on them, getting advice on how your research might be added to or strengthened.

In addition, if you have friends, colleagues or family members who are interested in your research, you could run it past them. Explain to them what you have been researching and what you have found, show them any draft materials you have already produced and get their opinions and assessment. Being able to explain your research to non-specialists, without using lots of jargon and overlong sentences, is, after all, an important and useful skill.

Seminars and Conference Presentations

Once you are reasonably confident that your research has been worthwhile, and that you have something to contribute to the field, an obvious next step is to give a seminar or present at a relevant conference. If you have no previous experience of public speaking, this is the time to start developing it. Don't be too nervous: if you can talk about your research with your colleagues, friends and family, you can surely talk about it more publicly to a slightly larger group and in a somewhat more formal fashion.

Remember also that, if people come to your seminar or presentation, it's probably because they are interested in what you have to say, so you shouldn't have to work too hard. Many of them will be at a similar stage to you in their research development, so they are likely to be sympathetic, supportive and helpful (and you might return the compliment by taking an interest in their research findings).

Seminars can be very informal – often over a 'brown bag' lunch (beware 'mayonnaise mouth') – and you might be able to organise one yourself in your organisation or department and invite colleagues and fellow researchers. If you have good contacts, you might also offer to give a seminar elsewhere, perhaps the same seminar more than once. This should be very useful to you in getting a range of varied opinions and suggestions on your research, as well as in developing your speaking and presentational abilities.

Conference presentations can be more formal and will usually involve you submitting a proposal – perhaps just an abstract or one side of A4 – ahead of the conference to the organising committee. They will then get back to you, accepting or rejecting your proposal, or perhaps suggesting some changes to your plans. Clearly, it's important to select a conference or conferences that is/are relevant for your research, but other factors may also come into play (e.g. national or international, time of year, numbers of participants, cost, length). Spending a few days in a warm, welcoming and interesting city, while giving your presentation and listening to several others of interest, can be a pleasant experience.

Once you've been accepted as a presenter, it's a matter of working up and practising your presentation. You will have a defined amount of time in which to present (often 30 minutes or less), some of which may be reserved for questions and general discussion, so it's important not to try to deliver too much. People will not thank you for eating into their lunch break or delaying the start of the next session; but they may well think of you for future presentations if you have been punctual and entertaining.

Having some visual or audio-visual aids is often a good idea but try not to get sucked into a lengthy and tedious PowerPoint presentation. If you do use visual aids, don't simply repeat what is on the slides; your audience should be able to read them far quicker than you can speak them, and will be looking for additional insights. Less is often more, and it's what you have got to say, and your audience's responses to it, that are of key importance.

Don't be too disappointed if your audience is relatively small; however small your audience, if they engage with you and your research, it will have been worthwhile. If they don't, there's always next time. Few speakers at academic conferences in the social sciences, unless they are delivering invited keynote sessions, attract large numbers. You will need to build up a reputation over time – for having something interesting and useful to say – to grow your audience.

Writing Up for Publication

Writing up and seeking to publish your research is also, of course, another way of assessing its quality, as it usually involves the judgement of your work by one or more people, or reviewers, who have specialist expertise and knowledge of your research area or methodology. Academic publishing is a competitive practice, and almost always requires the author(s) to undertake some significant revision of what they originally drafted, in light of the comments made by reviewers, if they are to proceed to publication.

Successful publication in a reputable academic journal is a significant achievement and a strong (if by no means foolproof) indication of the quality and value of a piece of work. However, even if you can't get your article published in one of the highest rated journals, it is still worthwhile pursuing publication elsewhere.

One obvious way to get a grip on what is involved in writing up your research for publication is to examine previous examples. If you are unsure about how to proceed, numerous examples of different kinds of documentary research have been referred to and discussed in earlier chapters. Identify a few that seem of particular interest or relevance to you, access copies of the articles and study how the authors have structured and presented their arguments.

Whatever genre of publication you are attempting – for example, an academic journal article, a book chapter, a report, a conference paper or perhaps a dissertation – there will be existing, more or less successful, examples you can access and study. Get advice, if you can, on particularly good examples (and, perhaps, also on particularly bad ones). If you can't get any advice, focus on those which are highly cited (typically for positive, but also sometimes negative, reasons) by other researchers. You can get information on citation rates from many academic database search engines (see Chapter 3).

Look at the way in which the writing up of the research has been organised, how it has been divided into sections, and the balance of space devoted to the different sections. Note the kind of language used, the way references to other publications are brought in and how the author(s) put forward their argument. There are also a number of guides available to writing up (see, for example, Murray 2013).

If you are seeking academic publication, and have identified a journal – or, perhaps, a small number of possible journals – that you would like to target with an article, there are two further things that you must do before you submit your article for consideration.

First, visit the journal's website, as this will contain useful guidance on all kinds of relevant matters, from the journal's focus and coverage, and its editors and editorial board, through to details of permissible word lengths, expected section headings and approved referencing style. There will probably be a pdf document entitled *Guidance for Authors*, or something similar, which you can download and study. Read all of this carefully and take the guidance on board. The editor or editors may also be open to direct queries from potential authors.

Second, access and read recent copies of the journal in question, ideally going back at least a decade. This is essential to check what they have published that is of relevance to your research, and to ensure that you refer to relevant articles from the journal in your article and reference them. If you don't do this, it will both seem impolite and cast doubt on your thoroughness as a researcher. After all, why would you be targeting a journal unless it published material directly relevant to your topic and interests? And, if it did, why would you not then refer to it?

One final point if you are seeking academic publication: be prepared for some knock-backs, but don't let them put you off. Academic reviewers can be pretty tough, and many journals have high rejection rates. However, if you persevere and take the comments made on your article on board, there is a good chance you will get it published somewhere in time. There is an ever increasing number of academic journal outlets out there, and the newer ones, in particular, are likely to be relatively short of decent quality material.

Planning Further Research

It is a cliché of any piece of social research that one of the main conclusions is always that 'more research is needed'. A single research project, no matter how extensive it is or how much previous related research it builds upon, will never answer all of the questions it set out to do with finality. Indeed, it is most likely – in another cliché of social research – to identify yet more questions. Social research is an ongoing cycle of discovery and interpretation.

It may be more constructive, however, to turn this around, and argue that the most useful conclusions from any piece of research concern what we don't know, rather than what we do (or what we have just found out). Research is very useful for refining our thinking and helping to make it clear what else needs to be researched. So, rather than thinking of this as a somewhat self-indulgent way of trying to ensure continuing funding and/or employment, it's better to see it as central to social research.

Bearing in mind that the conclusion of a research project can also be a rather deflating time – What do I do now with all of this spare time? Where is my next contract coming from? – it's probably sensible, then, to view any research project as part of a continuing cycle. So, if you're serious about research – and not just doing a piece of documentary research as a one-off, never-to-be-repeated exercise – you should always be planning further research.

This might be a relatively simple or obvious process: for example, now that I've finished researching this document, I'll move on to research this related document, and so forth, until an overall picture is built up of what can be learned from a particular set of documents. Or it may be more complicated: for instance, you might move on to re-analyse the document in a different way, or to employ a different research design to gather and analyse related data.

Whichever direction you take, and assuming that the piece of documentary research you are engaged in isn't a one-off, the advice would be to be planning further research, and looking for additional research opportunities, all of the time. Note down ideas as they come to you and work them up when you have the opportunity. You may not be able to undertake all of the research projects you develop, but this should both include some fun elements and help in your continuing development as a researcher.

Conclusion

This chapter has argued that, having successfully completed a documentary research project, you owe it to yourself, and to the broader research community, to do what you can to share and disseminate your findings and ideas. The obvious ways of doing this are through presentations and/or publications of one sort or another. Your target audience may be people working or practising in the area you have been researching, or those academics who also research it, or both.

Nowadays, of course, a lot of this can be done online as well as, or instead of, the more conventional face-to-face or in-print alternatives. You could even set up your own website to report on your project as it proceeds, perhaps providing blogs of what the research experience feels like as well as final reports and papers. Whatever way(s) you choose, don't keep it to yourself; research is much more useful and interesting if it is shared.

KEY READINGS

The 'self-help' literature on presenting, writing and disseminating research is mainly orientated towards students. Here, however, are three books which take these issues further:

Murray, R (2013) *Writing for Academic Journals*. Maidenhead, Open University Press, third edition.

Shephard, K (2005) *Presenting at Conferences, Seminars and Meetings*. London, Sage.

Silvia, P (2014) *Write It Up: Practical strategies for writing and publishing journal articles*. Washington, DC, American Psychological Association.

16

CONCLUSIONS

It seems most appropriate to use this concluding chapter to re-emphasise a series of key points about the nature and potential of documentary research in the social sciences (and beyond).

First, we may start by stressing the broad nature of documentary research. A document may simply be a text (printed or online), which is the most commonly understood meaning of the term. But a document can also be an audio recording, a video recording, a picture, a map or some other kind of artefact. Any set of data that you have not recently collected yourself (i.e. through an interview, a survey or an observation) may be considered to be a document.

Second, as this understanding of documents suggests, documentary research is endemic in nature, throughout the social sciences and beyond. Indeed, it is difficult to conceive of doing a piece of social research that does not involve some documentary analysis, if perhaps on a fairly small scale. You will, for example, almost certainly read and analyse some academic articles or policy statements, and refer to this literature in your report.

Third, documentary research may then, most commonly, be carried out in combination with other forms of research, such as interviews, surveys or observations. Documentary and other forms of analysis may be used to contextualise, deepen, extend and triangulate each other, resulting in a more comprehensive and convincing set of findings.

Fourth, documentary research may also be carried out on its own. There are so many documents available, on just about any subject or topic you can think of, that the possibilities for documentary research are huge. In many cases, there is simply no pressing need to collect more data (at considerable expense in terms of time and money). Rather, research into existing documentary sources – including, of course, data sets collected through previous interview, survey or observation-based studies – can be used to identify where precisely it would be most useful to target further empirical data collection.

Fifth, and finally, the accessibility and low cost of the vast majority of documentary research have to be underlined. With the increasing amount of documentary material available online – which, in most fields, is already way more than a single researcher or small team could analyse in their research career – there is so much documentary research that can be done by the researcher without even leaving the comfort of their own home or office.

The future of social research is documentary research!

REFERENCES

Aaltonen, J, and Kortti, J (2015) From Evidence to Re-enactment: History, television and documentary film. *Journal of Media Practice, 16, 2*, pp. 108–125.

Abbott, S, Shaw, S, and Elston, J (2004) Comparative Analysis of Health Policy Implementation: The use of documentary analysis. *Policy Studies, 25, 4*, pp. 259–266.

Abdullah, A (2016) An Islamic Monetary Theory of Value and Equation of Exchange: Evidence from Egypt (696–1517). *Humanomics, 32, 2*, pp. 121–150.

Allport, G (1942) *The Use of Personal Documents in Psychological Science*. New York, Social Science Research Council.

Altheide, D, and Schneider, C (2013) *Qualitative Media Analysis*. Thousand Oaks, CA, Sage.

Angell, R (1945) A Critical Review of the Development of the Personal Document Method in Sociology. In Gottschalk, L, Kluckhohn, C, and Angell, R, *The Use of Personal Documents in History, Anthropology and Sociology*. New York, Social Science Research Council.

Arreman, I, and Weiner, G (2007) Gender, Research and Change in Teacher Education: A Swedish dimension. *Gender and Education, 19, 3*, pp. 317–337.

Ash, T, Agaronov, A, Young, T, Aftosmes-Tobio, A, and Davison, K (2017) Family-based Childhood Obesity Prevention Interventions: A systematic review and quantitative content analysis. *International Journal of Behavioral Nutrition and Physical Activity, 14, 1*, 113.

Atkinson, P, and Coffey, A (1997) Analysing Documentary Realities. pp. 45–62 in Silverman, D (ed.) *Qualitative Research: Theory, method and practice*. London, Sage.

Avby, G, Nilsen, P, and Ellström, P-E (2017) Knowledge Use and Learning in Everyday Social Work Practice: A study in child investigation work. *Child and Family Social Work*, 22, pp. 51–61.

Awang, M, Jindal-Snape, D, and Barber, T (2013) A Documentary Analysis of the Government's Circulars on Positive Behavior Enhancement Strategies. *Asian Social Science*, 9, 5, pp. 203–208.

Azorin, C, and Muijs, D (2017) Networks and Collaboration in Spanish Education Policy. *Educational Research*, 59, 3, pp. 273–296.

Bagley, C, and Hillyard, S (2011) Village Schools in England: At the heart of their community? *Australian Journal of Education*, 55, 1, pp. 37–49.

Bakari, W, Bellot, P, and Neji, M (2017) A Logical Representation of Arabic Questions towards Automatic Passage Extraction from the Web. *International Journal of Speech Technology*, 20, 2, pp. 339–353.

Baker, W, and Hüttner, J (2017) English and More: A multisite study of roles and conceptualisations of language in English medium multilingual universities from Europe to Asia. *Journal of Multilingual and Multicultural Development*, 38, 6, pp. 501–516.

Bale, J (1999) Foreign Bodies: Representing the African and the European in an early twentieth century 'contact zone'. *Geography*, 84, 1, pp. 25–33.

Balmer, B (2010) Keeping Nothing Secret: United Kingdom chemical warfare policy in the 1960s. *Journal of Strategic Studies*, 33, 6, pp. 871–893.

Barbic, F, Hidalgo, A, and Cagliano, R (2016) Governance Dynamics in Multi-partner R&D Alliances. *Baltic Journal of Management*, 11, 4, pp. 405–429.

Barrett, B, Almanssori, S, Kwan, D, and Waddick, E (2016) Feminism within Domestic Violence Coalitions: A quantitative content analysis. *Affilia*, 31, 3, pp. 359–371.

Bearman, M, Smith, C, Carbone, A, Slade, S, Baik, C, Hughes-Warrington, M, and Neumann, D (2012) Systematic Review Methodology in Higher Education. *Higher Education Research and Development*, 31, 5, pp. 625–640.

Benton, D, Fernández-Fernández, M, González-Jurado, M, and Beneit-Montesinos, J (2015) Analysis of a Global Random Stratified Sample of Nurse Legislation. *International Nursing Review*, 62, pp. 207–217.

Berdan, F (2009) Mesoamerican Ethnohistory. *Ancient Mesoamerica*, 20, pp. 211–215.

Beretvas, N (2010) Meta-Analysis. pp. 255–263 in Hancock, G and Mueller, R (eds) *The Reviewer's Guide to Quantitative Methods in the Social Sciences*. New York, Routledge.

Bernitz, B (2008) Communicable Disease Policy Development in Response to Changing European Political Frontiers in Finland, Norway and Sweden. *Scandinavian Journal of Public Health*, 36, pp. 875–878.

Bishop, D (2008) The Small Enterprise in the Training Market. *Education + Training*, 50, 8–9, pp. 661–673.

Black, J, and MacRaild, D (2017) *Studying History*. Basingstoke, Palgrave Macmillan, fourth edition.

Blaxter, L, Hughes, C, and Tight, M (2010) *How to Research*. Maidenhead, Open University Press, fourth edition.

Bohnsack, R (2009) The Interpretation of Pictures and the Documentary Method. *Historical Social Research*, 34, 2, pp. 296–321.

Boholm, M (2014) Political Representations of *Nano* in Swedish Government Documents. *Science and Public Policy*, 41, pp. 575–596.

Bond, B (2015) Portrayals of Sex and Sexuality in Gay and Lesbian-oriented Media: A quantitative content analysis. *Sexuality and Culture*, 19, pp. 37–56.

Boon, H, Hirschkorn, K, Griener, G, and Cali, M (2009) The Ethics of Dietary Supplements and Natural Health Products in Pharmacy Practice: A systematic documentary analysis. *International Journal of Pharmacy Practice*, 17, pp. 31–38.

Bowen, G (2009) Document Analysis as a Qualitative Research Method. *Qualitative Research Journal*, 9, 2, pp. 27–40.

Branley, D, Seale, C, and Zacharias, T (2018) Doing a Literature Review. pp. 63–78 in Seale, C (ed.) *Researching Society and Culture*. London, Sage, fourth edition.

Braun, V, and Clarke, V (2006) Using Thematic Analysis in Psychology. *Qualitative Research in Psychology*, 3, 2, pp. 77–101.

Bridger, A (2014) Visualizing Manchester: Exploring new ways to study urban environments with reference to situationist theory, the dérive and qualitative research. *Qualitative Research in Psychology*, 11, 1, pp. 78–97.

British Educational Research Association (BERA) (2018) *Ethical Guidelines for Educational Research*. London, BERA, fourth edition.

Bruce, C (1994) Research Students' Early Experiences of the Dissertation Literature Review. *Studies in Higher Education*, 19, 2, pp. 217–229.

Bruhn, A, and Ekstrom, M (2017) Towards a Multi-Level Approach on Frontline Interactions in the Public Sector: Institutional transformations and the dynamics of real-time interactions. *Social Policy and Administration*, 51, 1, pp. 195–215.

Brundage, A (2002) *Going to the Sources: A guide to historical research and writing*. Wheeling, IL, Harlan Davidson.

Brunn, S (2018) Citation Impacts of AAG Presidential Addresses. *The Professional Geographer*, 70, 2, pp. 209–218.

Brunton, J, and Mackintosh, C (2017) Interpreting University Sport Policy in England: Seeking a purpose in turbulent times? *International Journal of Sport Policy and Politics*, 9, 3, pp. 377–395.

Bryman, A (2004) *Social Research Methods*. Oxford, Oxford University Press, second edition.

Bryman, A (2015) *Social Research Methods*. Oxford, Oxford University Press, fifth edition.

Buckland, M (1997) What is a Document? *Journal of the American Society for Information Science*, 48, 9, pp. 804–809.

Bunn, F, Trivedi, D, Alderson, P, Hamilton, L, Martin, A, Pinkney, E, and Iliffe, S (2015) The Impact of Cochrane Reviews: A mixed-methods evaluation of outputs from Cochrane Review Groups supported by the National Institute for Health Research. *Health Technology Assessment*, 19, 28, pp. 1–99.

Burn, A, and Parker, D (2003) *Analysing Media Texts*. London, Continuum.

Burns, R (2000) *Introduction to Research Methods*. London, Sage.

Cabot, H (2012) The Governance of Things: Documenting limbo in the Greek asylum procedure. *Political and Legal Anthropology Review*, 35, 1, pp. 11–29.

Canonico, P, De Nito, E, Esposito, V, Martinez, M, and Iacono, M (2017) The Adoption of Knowledge Integration Mechanisms in an Interdisciplinary Research Project. *Management Research Review*, 40, 5, pp. 604–622.

Carmona, M, and Renninger, A (2018) The Royal Fine Art Commission and 75 Years of English Design Review: The first 60 years, 1924–1984. *Planning Perspectives*, 33, 1, pp. 53–73.

Carruthers, B, and Halliday, T (2006) Negotiating Globalization: Global scripts and intermediation in the construction of Asian insolvency regimes. *Law and Social Inquiry*, 31, 3, pp. 521–584.

Carta, S (2015) Documentary Film, Observational Style and Postmodern Anthropology in Sardinia. *Visual Anthropology*, 28, 3, pp. 227–247.

Cevasco, R, Moreno, D, and Hearn, R (2015) Biodiversification as an Historical Process: An appeal for the application of historical ecology to bio-cultural diversity research. *Biodiversity and Conservation*, 24, 13, pp. 3167–3183.

Chen, Y-S, Dooley, K, and Rungtusanatham, J (2016) Using Text Analysis and Process Modeling to Examine Buyer–Supplier Relationship Dissolution: The Ford–Firestone breakup. *Journal of Purchasing and Supply Management*, 22, pp. 325–337.

Chonka, P (2016) Spies, Stonework, and the Suuq: Somali nationalism and the narrative politics of pro-Harakat Al Shabaab Al Mujaahidiin online propaganda. *Journal of Eastern African Studies*, 10, 2, pp. 247–265.

Choudhury, M, and Haque, E (2018) Interpretations of Resilience and Change and the Catalytic Roles of Media: A case of Canadian daily newspaper discourse on natural disasters. *Environmental Management*, 61, pp. 236–248.

Chouliaraki, L, and Fairclough, N (1999) *Discourse in Late Modernity: Rethinking critical discourse analysis*. Edinburgh, Edinburgh University Press.

Chu, D (2009) Making Claims for School Media: A study of teachers' beliefs about media in Hong Kong. *Asia Pacific Journal of Education*, 29, 1, pp. 1–15.

Ciasullo, M, and Troisi, O (2013) Sustainable Value Creation in SMEs: A case study. *The TQM Journal*, 25, 1, pp. 44–61.

Clark, J, Jones, A, Potter, C, and Lobley, M (1997) Conceptualising the Evolution of the European Union's Agri-environment Policy: A discourse approach. *Environment and Planning A*, 29, pp. 1869–1885.

Clark, S, Parker, R, and Davey, R (2014) Nurse Practitioners in Aged Care: Documentary analysis of successful project proposals. *Qualitative Health Research*, 24, 11, pp. 1592–1602.

Clayman, S (2017) The Micropolitics of Legitimacy: Political positioning and journalistic scrutiny at the boundary of the mainstream. *Social Psychology Quarterly*, 80, 1, pp. 41–64.

Clubine-Ito, C (2004) Multilevel Modelling for Historical Data. *Historical Methods, 37*, 1, pp. 5–22.

Codd, J (1988) The Construction and Deconstruction of Educational Policy Documents. *Journal of Educational Policy, 3*, 3, pp. 235–247.

Cohen, L, Manion, L, and Morrison, K (2011) *Research Methods in Education*. London, Routledge, seventh edition.

Cohen, L, Manion, L, and Morrison, K (2017) *Research Methods in Education*. London, Routledge, eighth edition.

Collins, S, Durington, M, Daniels, G, Demyan, N, Rico, D, Beckles, J, and Heasley, C (2013) Tagging Culture: Building a public anthropology through social media. *Human Organization, 72*, 4, pp. 358–368.

Conn, K (2017) Identifying Effective Education Interventions in Sub-Saharan Africa: A meta-analysis of impact evaluations. *Review of Educational Research, 87*, 5, pp. 863–898.

Connelly, M, and Clandinin, J (1990) Stories of Experience and Narrative Inquiry. *Educational Researcher, 19*, 5, pp. 2–14.

Cooper, H (2010) *Research Synthesis and Meta-analysis: A step-by-step approach*. Thousand Oaks, CA, Sage, fourth edition.

Cooper, K, and Hughes, N (2015) Thick Narratives: Mining implicit, oblique and deeper understandings in videotaped research data. *Qualitative Inquiry, 21*, 1, pp. 28–35.

Cope, E, Partington, M, and Harvey, S (2017) A Review of the Use of a Systematic Observation Method in Coaching Research between 1997 and 2016. *Journal of Sports Sciences, 35*, 20, pp. 2042–2050.

Crawshaw, R, and Fowler, C (2008) Articulation, Imagined Space and Virtual Mobility in Literary Narratives of Migration. *Mobilities, 3*, 3, pp. 455–469.

Dale, A, Arber, S, and Procter, M (1988) *Doing Secondary Analysis*. London, Unwin Hyman.

Dale, E (1939) Quantitative Analysis of Documentary Materials. *Review of Educational Research, 9*, 5, pp. 466–471.

Darko, N, and Mackintosh, C (2015) Challenges and Constraints in Developing and Implementing Sports Policy in Antigua and Barbuda: Which way now for a small island state? *International Journal of Sport Policy and Politics, 7*, 3, pp. 365–390.

Darnton, C (2018) Archives and Inference: Documentary evidence in case study research and the debate over US entry into World War II. *International Security, 42*, 3, pp. 84–126.

Davis, G (2012) A Documentary Analysis of the Use of Leadership and Change Theory in Changing Practice in Early Years Settings. *Early Years, 32*, 3, pp. 266–276.

Deerman, E (2017) Spillover Effects: Explaining narrative divergences of the Christian Right, 1979–1989. *Journal of Historical Sociology, 13*, 3, pp. 561–586.

Del Río, P, Peñascoa, C, and Mir-Artigues, P (2018) An Overview of Drivers and Barriers to Concentrated Solar Power in the European Union. *Renewable and Sustainable Energy Reviews*, pp. 1019–1029.

Devlin, R (2015) 'Teenage Traumas': The discursive construction of young people as a 'problem' in an Irish radio documentary. *Young: Nordic Journal of Youth Research*, 13, 2, pp. 167–184.

Dew, K (2005) Documentary Analysis in CAM Research: Part 1. *Complementary Therapies in Medicine*, 13, pp. 297–302.

Dew, K (2006) Documentary Analysis in CAM Research: Part 2. *Complementary Therapies in Medicine*, 14, pp. 77–80.

Dibble, V (1963) Four Types of Inference from Documents to Events. *History and Theory*, 3, 2, pp. 203–221.

Dolowitz, D, Buckler, S, and Sweeney, F (2008) *Researching Online*. Basingstoke, Palgrave Macmillan.

Donet, F, Pallares, A, and Burillo, S (2017) Bibliometric Characteristics of Articles on Key Competences Indexed by ERIC from 1990 to 2013. *European Journal of Teacher Education*, 40, 2, pp. 145–156.

Drabble, S, O'Cathain, A, Thomas, K, Rudolph, A, and Hewison, J (2014) Describing qualitative research undertaken with randomised control trials in grant proposals: A documentary analysis. *BMC Medical Research Methodology*, 14, 24, 11pp.

Drew, P, and Heritage, J (eds) (2006) *Conversation Analysis*. London, Sage, *four* volumes.

Dwyer, C, and Davies, G (2010) Qualitative Methods III: Animating archives, artful interventions and online environments. *Progress in Human Geography*, 34, 1, pp. 88–97.

Enfield, N (2006) Languages as Historical Documents: The endangered archive in Laos. *South East Asia Research*, 14, 3, pp. 471–488.

Evans, D (2014) Patient and Public Involvement in Research in the English NHS: A documentary analysis of the complex interplay of evidence and policy. *Evidence and Policy*, 10, 3, pp. 361–377.

EzzelArab, A (2009) The Fiscal and Constitutional Program of Egypt's Traditional Elites in 1879: A documentary and contextual analysis of 'al-Lā'iḥa al-Waṭaniyya' ('The National Programme'). *Journal of Economic and Social History of the Orient*, 52, 2, pp. 301–324.

Fairclough, N (1992) *Discourse and Social Change*. Cambridge, Polity Press.

Fernández-Kranz, D, Lacuesta, A, and Rodríguez-Planas, N (2013) The Motherhood Earnings Dip: Evidence from administrative records. *Journal of Human Resources*, 48, 1, pp. 169–197.

Fernández-Montblanc, T, Izquierdo, A, and Bethencourt, M (2018) Scattered Shipwreck Site Prospection: The combined use of numerical modelling and documentary research. *Archaeological and Anthropological Sciences*, 10, pp. 141–156.

Figenschou, T (2010) A Voice for the Voiceless? A quantitative content analysis of Al-Jazeera English's flagship news. *Global Media and Communication*, 6, 1, pp. 85–107.

Figueroa, S (2008) The Grounded Theory and the Analysis of Audio-Visual Texts. *International Journal of Social Research Methodology*, 11, 1, pp. 1–12.

Filho, J, Da Costa, M, Forster, A, and Reeves, S (2017) New National Curricula Guidelines that Support the Use of Interprofessional Education in the Brazilian Context: An analysis of key documents. *Journal of Interprofessional Care, 31*, 6, pp. 754–760.

Fink, A (2005) *Conducting Research Literature Reviews: From the internet to paper.* Thousand Oaks, CA, Sage, second edition.

Fitzgerald, T (2007) Documents and Documentary Analysis: Reading between the lines. pp. 278–294 in Briggs, A and Coleman, M (eds) *Research Methods in Educational Leadership and Management.* London, Sage, second edition.

Foley, C, Droog, E, Healy, O, McHugh, S, Buckley, C, and Browne, J (2017) Understanding Perspectives on Major System Change: A comparative case study of public engagement and the implementation of urgent and emergency care system reconfiguration. *Health Policy, 121*, pp. 800–808.

Forrest, L, Adams, J, Ben-Shlomo, Y, Buckner, S, Payne, N, Rimmer, M, Salway, S, Sowden, S, Walters, K, and White, M (2017) Age-related References in National Public Health, Technology Appraisal and Clinical Guidelines and Guidance: Documentary analysis. *Age and Ageing, 46*, pp. 500–508.

Foster, J, Muellerleile, C, Olds, K, and Peck, J (2007) Circulating Economic Geographies: Citation patterns and citation behaviour in economic geography, 1982–2006. *Transactions of the Institute of British Geographers, 32*, pp. 295–312.

Fox, A (2010) Printed Questionnaires, Research Networks and the Discovery of the British Isles, 1650–1800. *The Historical Journal, 53*, 3, pp. 593–621.

Franzosi, R (2004) *From Words to Numbers: Narrative, data and social science.* Cambridge, Cambridge University Press.

Friedman, E (2017) Evasion Strategies in International Documents: When 'constructive ambiguity' leads to oppositional interpretation. *Critical Discourse Studies, 14*, 4, pp. 385–401.

Frisch, S, Harris, D, Kelly, S, and Parker, D (eds) (2012) *Doing Archival Research in Political Science.* Amherst, NY, Cambria Press.

Froggatt, K (2007) The 'Regulated Death': A documentary analysis of the regulation and inspection of dying and death in English care homes for older people. *Ageing and Society, 27*, pp. 233–247.

Galan, J, Sanchez, M, and Zuniga-Vicente, J (2005) Strategic and Organizational Evolution of Spanish Firms: Towards a holding network form? *British Journal of Management, 16*, pp. 279–292.

Galvan, J, and Galvan, M (2017) *Writing Literature Reviews: A guide for students of the social and behavioral sciences.* New York, Routledge.

Gee, J (1999) *An Introduction to Discourse Analysis: Theory and method.* London, Routledge.

Gee, J (2011) *How to Do Discourse Analysis: A toolkit.* London, Routledge.

Georgakopoulou, A, and Goutsos, D (1997) *Discourse Analysis: An introduction.* Edinburgh, Edinburgh University Press.

Gerstl-Pepin, C (2015) Popular Media Portrayals of Inequity and School Reform in The Wire and Waiting for 'Superman'. *Peabody Journal of Education, 90*, 5, pp. 691–710.

Gicevic, S, Aftosmes-Tobios, A, Manganello, J, Ganter, C, Simon, C, Newlan, S, and Davison, K (2016) Parenting and Childhood Obesity Research: A quantitative content analysis of published research 2009–2015. *Obesity Reviews, 17*, pp. 724–734.

Gidley, B (2018) Doing Historical and Documentary Research. pp. 285–304 in Seale, C (ed.) *Researching Society and Culture*. London, Sage, fourth edition.

Gilbert, A, Stanley, D, Penhale, B, and Gilhooly, M (2013) Elder Financial Abuse in England: A policy analysis perspective related to social care and banking. *Journal of Adult Protection, 15*, 3, pp. 153–163.

Giovannini, A (2016) Towards a 'New English Regionalism' in the North? The case of Yorkshire First. *Political Quarterly, 87*, 4, pp. 590–600.

Goddard, A, and Carey, N (2017) *Discourse: The basics*. London, Routledge.

Goldey, K, Avery, L, and van Anders, S (2014) Sexual Fantasies and Gender/Sex: A multimethod approach with quantitative content analysis and hormonal responses. *Journal of Sex Research, 51*, 8, pp. 917–931.

Gomez, L, Sarmiento, R, Ordonez, M, Pardo, C, de Sa, T, Mallarino, C, Miranda, J, Mosquera, J, Parra, D, Reis, R, and Quistberg, D (2015) Urban Environment Interventions Linked to the Promotion of Physical Activity: A mixed methods study applied to the urban context of Latin America. *Social Science and Medicine, 131*, pp. 18–30.

Gosen, M, and Koole, T (2017) Conversation Analysis. pp. 791–811 in Wyse, D, Selwyn, N, Smith, E, and Suter, L (eds) *The BERA/SAGE Handbook of Educational Research*. London, Sage, *two* volumes.

Gottschalk, L (1945) The Historian and the Historical Document. In Gottschalk, L, Kluckhohn, C, and Angell, R (eds) *The Use of Personal Documents in History, Anthropology and Sociology*. New York, Social Science Research Council.

Grazioli, S, and Jarvenpaa, S (2003) Consumer and Business Deception on the Internet: Content analysis of documentary evidence. *International Journal of Electronic Commerce, 7*, 4, pp. 93–118.

Greer, C, and McLaughlin, E (2013) The Sir Jimmy Savile Scandal: Child sex abuse and institutional denial at the BBC. *Crime, Media, Culture, 9*, 3, pp. 243–263.

Griffin, A, and May, V (2018) Narrative Analysis and Interpretative Phenomenological Analysis. pp. 511–532 in Seale, C (ed.) *Researching Society and Culture*. London, Sage, fourth edition.

Grosvenor, I (2018) 'What do they know of England who only England know': A case for an alternative narrative of the ordinary in twenty-first-century Britain. *History of Education, 47*, 2, pp. 148–168.

Guest, G, MacQueen, K, and Namey, E (2012) *Applied Thematic Analysis*. Thousand Oaks, CA, Sage.

Guggenheim, M (2015) The Media of Sociology: Tight or loose translations? *British Journal of Sociology, 66*, 2, pp. 345–372.

Haas, V, and Levasseur, E (2013) Rumour as a Symptom of Collective Forgetfulness. *Culture and Psychology, 19,* 1, pp. 60–75.

Hafner, C (2017) Discourse Analysis/Critical Discourse Analysis. pp. 812–829 in Wyse, D, Selwyn, N, Smith, E, and Suter, L (eds) *The BERA/SAGE Handbook of Educational Research.* London, Sage, two volumes.

Hak, T (1998) 'There are Clear Delusions': The production of a factual account. *Human Studies, 21,* pp. 419–436.

Hakim, C (1982) *Secondary Analysis in Social Research: A guide to data sources and methods with examples.* London, George Allen & Unwin.

Halabi, S, Smith, W, Collins, J, Baker, D, and Bedford, J (2012) A Documentary Analysis of HIV/AIDS Education Interventions in Ghana. *Health Education Journal, 72,* 4, pp. 486–500.

Hamilton, M, and Hillier, Y (2007) Deliberative Policy Analysis: Adult literacy assessment and the politics of change. *Journal of Education Policy, 22,* 5, pp. 573–594.

Hargreaves, J (2008) The Under-used Resource of Historical Research. *Nurse Researcher, 15,* 3, pp. 32–44.

Harkin, M (2010) Ethnohistory's Ethnohistory: Creating a discipline from the ground up. *Social Science History, 34,* 2, pp. 113–128.

Harrisson, T, and Madge, C (1939/1986) *Britain by Mass-Observation.* London, Cresset Library.

Hart, C (1998) *Doing a Literature Review: Releasing the social science research imagination.* London, Sage.

Hart, S (2010) Self-Regulation, Corporate Social Responsibility and the Business Case: Do they work in achieving workplace equality and safety? *Journal of Business Ethics, 92,* 4, pp. 585–600.

Hattie, J (2009) *Visible Learning: A synthesis of over 800 meta-analyses relating to achievement.* London, Routledge.

Have, P ten (1999) *Doing Conversation Analysis: A practical guide.* London, Sage.

Hay, I, Bochner, D, and Dungey, C (2002) *Making the Grade: A guide to successful communication and study.* Melbourne, Oxford University Press, second edition.

Heaton, J (2004) *Reworking Qualitative Data.* London, Sage.

Heaton, J (2008) Secondary Analysis of Qualitative Data: An overview. *Historical Social Research, 33,* 3, pp. 33–45.

Heavens, S (2016) Brian Roberts and the Origins of the 1959 Antarctic Treaty. *Polar Record, 52,* 267, pp. 717–729.

Hengstermann, C (2017) Pre-existence and Universal Salvation: The Origenian renaissance in early modern Cambridge. *British Journal for the History of Philosophy, 25,* 5, pp. 971–989.

Henjewele, C, Sun, M, and Fewings, P (2012) Analysis of Factors Affecting Value for Money in UK PFI Projects. *Journal of Financial Management of Property and Construction, 17,* 1, pp. 9–28.

Henninger, M, and Scifleet, P (2016) How are the New Documents of Social Networks Shaping our Cultural Memory? *Journal of Documentation, 72*, 2, pp. 277–298.

Herkenrath, M, and Knoll, A (2011) Protest Events in International Press Coverage: An empirical critique of cross-national conflict databases. *International Journal of Comparative Sociology, 52*, 3, pp. 163–180.

Hertz, S, and Krettenauer, T (2016) Does Moral Identity Effectively Predict Moral Behavior? A meta-analysis. *Review of General Psychology, 20*, 2, pp. 129–140.

Hight, C, and Coleborne, C (2006) Robert Winston's *Superhuman*: Spectacle, surveillance and patient narrative. *Journal of Health Psychology, 11*, 2, pp. 233–245.

Himmelsbach, I, Glaser, R, Schoenbein, J, Riemann, D, and Martin, B (2015) Reconstruction of Flood Events Based on Documentary Data and Transnational Flood Risk Analysis of the Upper Rhine and its French and German Tributaries since AD 1480. *Hydrology and Earth System Sciences, 19*, pp. 4149–4164.

Hirschauer, S (2006) Putting Things into Words: Ethnographic description and the silence of the social. *Human Studies, 29*, 4, pp. 413–441.

Holstein, J, and Gubrium, J (eds) (2012) *Varieties of Narrative Analysis*. Los Angeles, CA, Sage.

Holsti, O (1969) *Content Analysis for the Social Sciences and Humanities*. Reading, MA: Addison-Wesley.

Hopewell, K (2017) Invisible Barricades: Civil society and the discourse of the WTO. *Globalizations, 14*, 1, pp. 51–65.

Hordosy, R (2014) Who Knows What School Leavers and Graduates are Doing? Comparing information systems within Europe. *Comparative Education, 50*, 4, pp. 448–473.

Hou, H-T, Chang, K, and Sung, Y (2010) What Kinds of Knowledge do Teachers share on Blogs? A quantitative content analysis of teachers' knowledge sharing on blogs. *British Journal of Educational Technology, 41*, 6, pp. 963–967.

Houle, F (1994) The Credibility and Authoritativeness of Documentary Information in Determining Refugee Status: The Canadian experience. *International Journal of Refugee Law, 6*, 1, pp. 6–33.

Hubbard, P, and Colosi, R (2015) Respectability, Morality and Disgust in the Night-time Economy: Exploring reactions to 'lap dance' clubs in England and Wales. *Sociological Review, 63*, pp. 782–800.

Hudler, M, and Richter, R (2002) Cross-national Comparison of the Quality of Life in Europe: Inventory of surveys and methods. *Social Indicators Research, 58*, 1–3, pp. 217–228.

Hutchby, I, and Wooffitt, R (1998) *Conversation Analysis: Principles, practices and applications*. Cambridge, Polity Press.

Hyland, K, and Paltridge, B (eds) (2011) *Continuum Companion to Discourse Analysis*. London, Continuum.

Indulska, M, Hovorka, D, and Recker, J (2012) Quantitative Approaches to Content Analysis: Identifying conceptual drift across publication outlets. *European Journal of Information Systems, 21*, pp. 49–69.

Jacobsson, A (2017) Intercultural Film: Fiction film as audio-visual documents of interculturality. *Journal of Intercultural Studies*, 38, 1, pp. 54–69.

Janghorban, R, Roudsari, R, Taghipour, A, and Abbasi, M (2015) Sexual and Reproductive Rights from Qur'anic Perspective: A quantitative content analysis. *Asian Social Science*, 11, 3, pp. 182–187.

Jesson, J, Matheson, L, and Lacey, F (2011) *Doing Your Literature Review: Traditional and systematic techniques*. London, Sage.

Johnson, C, and Johnson, B (1993) Medicine on British Television: A content analysis. *Journal of Community Health*, 18, 1, pp. 25–35.

Johnson, K (2015) Rethinking Re(doing): Historical re-enactment and/as historiography. *Rethinking History*, 192, 2, pp. 193–206.

Johnstone, B (2008) *Discourse Analysis*. Malden, MA, Blackwell, second edition.

Jones, C, and Symeonidou, S (2017) The Hare and the Tortoise: A comparative review of the drive towards inclusive education policies in England and Cyprus. *International Journal of Inclusive Education*, 21, 7, pp. 775–789.

Jupp, V, and Norris, C (1993) Traditions in Documentary Analysis. pp. 37–51 in Hammersley, M (ed.) *Social Research: Philosophy, politics and practice*. London, Sage.

Kaehne, A, and Taylor, H (2016) Do Public Consultations Work? The case of the Social Services and Well-being (Wales) Bill. *Public Policy and Administration*, 31, 1, pp. 80–99.

Kamberi, D (1999) A Survey of Uyghur Documents from Turpan and their Importance for Asian and Central Eurasian History. *Central Asian Survey*, 18, 3, pp. 281–301.

Kiselev, G (2008) L D Landau in the Soviet Atomic Project: A documentary study. *Physics – Uspekhi*, 51, 9, pp. 911–954.

Kluckhorn, C (1945) The Personal Document in Anthropological Science. In Gottschalk, L, Kluckhohn, C, and Angell, R, *The Use of Personal Documents in History, Anthropology and Sociology*. New York, Social Science Research Council.

Knutsen, G (2003) Norwegian Witchcraft Trials: A reassessment. *Continuity and Change*, 18, 2, pp. 185–200.

Koohzadi, M, and Keyvanpour, M (2014) An Analytical Framework for Event Mining in Video Data. *Artificial Intelligence Review*, 41, pp. 401–413.

Kort, F (1960) The Quantitative Content Analysis of Judicial Opinions. *Political Research, Organization and Design*, 3, 7, pp. 11–14.

Kosciejew, M (2010) Crossing the Print to Digital Rubicon: A documentary analysis of media migrations. *International Journal of Technology, Knowledge and Society*, 6, 1, pp. 219–226.

Kosciejew, M (2015) Disciplinary Documentation in Apartheid South Africa: A conceptual framework of documents, associated practices and their effects. *Journal of Documentation*, 71, 1, pp. 96–115.

Krippendorff, K (2013) *Content Analysis: An introduction to its methodology*. Thousand Oaks, CA, Sage, third edition.

Krippendorff, K, and Bock, M (eds) (2009) *The Content Analysis Reader*. Thousand Oaks, CA, Sage.

Kynaston, D (2008) The Uses of Sociology for Real-time History. *Historical Social Research*, *33*, 3, pp. 68–74.

Lahn, L, and Erikson, T (2016) Entrepreneurship Education by Design. *Education + Training*, *58*, 7–8, pp. 684–699.

Lam, W, and Chan, K (2017) Policy Advocacy in Transitioning Regimes: Comparative lessons from the case of harbour protection in Hong Kong. *Journal of Comparative Policy Analysis*, *19*, 1, pp. 54–71.

Lampe, K, Mulder, E, Colins, O, and Vermeiren, R (2017) The Inter-rater Reliability of Observing Aggression: A systematic literature review. *Aggression and Violent Behavior*, *37*, pp. 12–25.

Laxton, P (1999) The Evidence of Richard Horwood's Maps for Residential Building in London, 1799–1819. *The London Journal*, *24*, 1, pp. 1–22.

Lekgoathi, S (2009) 'Colonial' Experts, Local Interlocutors, Informants and the Making of an Archive on the 'Transvaal Ndebele'. *Journal of African History*, *50*, pp. 61–80.

Lemov, R (2009) Towards a Data Base of Dreams: Assembling an archive of elusive materials, c. 1947–61. *History Workshop Journal*, *67*, pp. 44–68.

Leonardi-Bee, J, Nderi, M, and Britton, J (2016) Smoking in Movies and Smoking Initiation in Adolescents: Systematic review and meta-analysis. *Addiction*, *111*, pp. 1750–1763.

Leston-Bandeira, C (2016) Why Symbolic Representation Frames Parliamentary Public Engagement. *British Journal of Politics and International Relations*, *18*, 2, pp. 498–516.

Levitas, R, and Guy, W (eds) (1996) *Interpreting Official Statistics*. London, Routledge.

Lew-Levy, S, Reckin, R, Lavi, N, Cristobal-Azkarate, A, and Ellis-Davies, K (2017) How Do Hunter-Gatherer Children Learn Subsistence Skills? A meta-ethnographic review. *Human Nature*, *28*, 4, pp. 367–394.

Li, Y (2016) From 'Whom to Blame' to 'Nothing to Fear': Documentary narratives, voices and 'dependent distigmatization' of severe mental patients in Hong Kong. *Chinese Journal of Communication*, *9*, 4, pp. 403–421.

Liddicoat, A (2011) *An Introduction to Conversation Analysis*. London, Continuum, second edition.

Light, R, and Pillemer, D (1982) Numbers and Narratives: Combining their strengths in research reviews. *Harvard Educational Review*, *52*, 1, pp. 1–26.

Lin, Y (1996) Empirical Studies of Negative Political Advertising: A quantitative review using a method of combined citation and content analysis. *Scientometrics*, *37*, 3, pp. 385–399.

Lincoln, Y (1980) *Documentary Analysis and Record Utilization: New uses for old methods*. Paper presented at the Annual Meeting of the American Educational Research Association, Boston, April.

Lock, I, and Seele, P (2016) The Credibility of CSR (Corporate Social Responsibility) Reports in Europe: Evidence from a quantitative content analysis in 11 countries. *Journal of Cleaner Production*, *122*, pp. 186–200.

Locke, T (2004) *Critical Discourse Analysis*. London, Continuum.

Locock, L, Robert, G, Boaz, A, Vougioukalou, S, Shuldham, C, Fielden, J, Ziebland, S, Gager, M, Tollyfield, R, and Pearcey, J (2014) Using a National Archive of Patient Experience Narratives to Promote Local Patient-centered Quality Improvement: An ethnographic process evaluation of accelerated experience-based co-design. *Journal of Health Services Research and Policy*, 19, 4, pp. 200–207.

Lopes-Fernandes, M, Soares, F, Frazão-Moreira, A, and Queiroz, A (2016) Living with the Beast: Wolves and humans through Portuguese literature. *Anthrozoös*, 29, 1, pp. 5–20.

Lundy, L (2012) Children's Rights and Educational Policy in Europe: The implementation of the United Nations Convention on the Rights of the Child. *Oxford Review of Education*, 38, 4, pp. 393–411.

Lyon, D (2016) Doing Audio-Visual Montage to Explore Time and Space: The everyday rhythms of Billingsgate Fish Market. *Sociological Research Online*, 21, 3, pp. 1–12.

Macfarlane, B, Zhang, J, and Pun, A (2014) Academic Integrity: A review of the literature. *Studies in Higher Education*, 39, 2, pp. 339–358.

Machin, D, and Mayr, A (2012) *How to Do Critical Discourse Analysis*. London, Sage.

Maclure, M (2005) 'Clarity Bordering on Stupidity': Where's the quality in systematic review? *Journal of Education Policy*, 20, 4, pp. 393–416.

McCulloch, G (2004) *Documentary Research in Education, History and the Social Sciences*. London, Routledge.

McCulloch, G (2011) Historical and Documentary Research in Education. pp. 248–255 in Cohen, L, Manion, L, and Morrison, K (eds) *Research Methods in Education*. London, Routledge, seventh edition.

McCulloch, G, and Richardson, W (2000) *Historical Research in Educational Settings*. Buckingham, Open University Press.

McCullough, P (2008) Print, Publication and Religious Politics in Caroline England. *The Historical Journal*, 51, 2, pp. 285–313.

McDonald, J (2010) Efficiency in the Domesday Economy, 1086: Evidence from Wiltshire estates. *Applied Economics*, 42, 25, pp. 3231–3240.

McGrattan, C, and Williams, S (2017) Devolution and Identity: Multidirectionality in 'Welshness' and 'Northern Irishness'. *Regional and Federal Studies*, 27, 4, pp. 465–482.

McKay, E (2005) English Diarists: Gender, geography and occupation, 1500–1700. *History*, 90, 298, pp. 191–212.

McKenzie, P, and Davies, E (2010) Documentary Tools in Everyday Life: The wedding planner. *Journal of Documentation*, 66, 6, pp. 788–806.

May, T (2001) *Social Research: Issues, methods and process*. Buckingham, Open University Press, third edition.

Meyer, M (2018) In the Eye of the Storm: Photographs of Russian prisoners of war in Denmark during the First World War. *Photography and Culture*, 11, 1, pp. 61–90.

Michelini, L, and Fiorentino, D (2012) New Business Models for Creating Shared Value. *Social Responsibility Journal*, 8, 4, pp. 561–577.

Mifsud, D (2016) 'Decentralised' Neoliberalism and/or 'Masked' Recentralisation? The policy to practice trajectory of Maltese school reform through the lens of neoliberalism and Foucault. *Journal of Education Policy, 31*, 4, pp. 443–465.

Milian, R (2017) What's for Sale at Canadian Universities? A mixed-method analysis of promotional strategies. *Higher Education Quarterly, 71*, 1, pp. 53–74.

Milla, M, Faturochman, and Ancok, D (2013) The Impact of Leader–Follower Interactions on the Radicalization of Terrorists: A case study of the Bali bombers. *Asian Journal of Social Psychology, 16*, pp. 92–100.

Milligan, C, Bingley, A, and Gatrell, A (2005) Digging Deep: Using diary techniques to explore the place of health and well-being amongst older people. *Social Science and Medicine, 61*, pp. 1882–1892.

Moher, D, Liberati, A, Tetzlaff, J, Altman, D, and the PRISMA Group (2009) Preferred Reporting Items for Systematic Reviews and Meta-Analyses: The PRISMA statement. *Annals of Internal Medicine, 151*, 4, pp. 264–269.

Momeni, P, Jirwe, M, and Emami, A (2008) Enabling Nursing Students to become Culturally Competent: A documentary analysis of curricula in all Swedish nursing programs. *Scandinavian Journal of Caring Science, 22*, pp. 499–506.

Morrison, A, Bickerstaff, D, and Taylor, B (2009) Referrals to a Learning Disability Social Work Team 1996 to 2005. *British Journal of Learning Disabilities, 38*, pp. 168–174.

Mpinga, E, Verloo, H, London, L, and Chastonay, P (2011) Health and Human Rights in Scientific Literature: A systematic review over a decade (1999–2008). *Health and Human Rights, 13*, 2, pp. 102–129.

Munslow, A (2007) *Narrative and History*. Basingstoke, Palgrave Macmillan.

Murray, R (2013) *Writing for Academic Journals*. Maidenhead, Open University Press, third edition.

Naganathan, G, and Islam, F (2015) What is 'South Asian'? A quantitative content analysis evaluating the use of South Asian ethnic categorization in Canadian health research. *South Asian Diaspora, 7*, 1, pp. 49–62.

Neuendorf, K (2002) *The Content Analysis Guidebook*. Thousand Oaks, CA, Sage.

Neufeld, M (2011) The Politics of Anglican Martyrdom: Letters to John Walker, 1704–1705. *Journal of Ecclesiastical History, 62*, 3, pp. 491–514.

Nicholas, S, and Steckel, R (1991) Heights and Living Standards of English Workers during the Early Years of Industrialization, 1770–1815. *Journal of Economic History, 51*, 4, pp. 937–957.

Nilsson, J, Love, K, Taylor, K, and Slusher, A (2007) A Content and Sample Analysis of Quantitative Articles Published in the *Journal of Counseling and Development* between 1991 and 2000. *Journal of Counseling and Development, 85*, pp. 357–363.

Nimrod, G (2009) Seniors' Online Communities: A quantitative content analysis. *The Gerontologist, 50*, 3, pp. 382–392.

O'Brien, A (2010) Beyond Policy-making: Institutional regimes, the state and policy implementation in the Irish case. *Current Issues in Tourism, 13*, 6, pp. 563–577.

O'Brien, E, Myles, P, and Pritchard, C (2016) The Portrayal of Infant Feeding in British Women's Magazines: A qualitative and quantitative content analysis. *Journal of Public Health, 39*, 2, pp. 221–226.

O'Connor, M (2007) Documentary Analysis and Policy. pp. 229–245 in Addington-Hall, J, Bruera, E, Higginson, I, and Payne, S (eds) *Research Methods in Palliative Care*. Oxford, Oxford University Press.

Oleinik, A (2011) Mixing Quantitative and Qualitative Content Analysis: Triangulation at work. *Quality and Quantity, 45*, pp. 859–873.

Oleinik, A (2015) On Content Analysis of Images of Mass Protests: A case of data triangulation. *Quality and Quantity, 49*, pp. 2203–2220.

Oliver, S, and Tripney, J (2017) Systematic Review and Meta-Analysis. pp. 452–476 in Wyse, D, Selwyn, N, Smith, E, and Suter, L (eds) *The BERA/SAGE Handbook of Educational Research*. London, Sage, two volumes.

Pan, M (2017) *Preparing Literature Reviews: Qualitative and quantitative approaches*. London, Routledge.

Parker, E, Chang, J, and Thomas, V (2016) A Content Analysis of Quantitative Research in *Journal of Marital and Family Therapy*: A 10-year review. *Journal of Marital and Family Therapy, 42*, 1, pp. 3–18.

Patterson, C, Semple, S, Wood, K, Duffy, S, and Hilton, S (2015) A Quantitative Content Analysis of UK Newsprint Coverage or Proposed Legislation to Prohibit Smoking in Private Vehicles Carrying Children. *BMC Public Health, 15*, 760, 7pp.

Paul, S, and Hill, M (2013) Responding to Self-harm: A documentary analysis of agency policy and procedure. *Children and Society, 27*, pp. 184–196.

Payne, G, Williams, M, and Chamberlain, S (2004) Methodological Pluralism in British Sociology. *Sociology, 38*, 1, pp. 153–163.

Peelo, M (1994) *Helping Students with Study Problems*. Buckingham, Open University Press.

Pidduck, J (2012) Exile Media, Global News Flows and Democratization: The role of Democratic Voice of Burma in Burma's 2010 elections. *Media, Culture and Society, 34*, 5, pp. 537–553.

Pirrie, A (2001) Evidence-based Practice in Education: The best medicine? *British Journal of Educational Studies, 49*, 2, pp. 124–136.

Platt, J (1981a) Evidence and Proof in Documentary Research: 1. Some specific problems of documentary research. *Sociological Review, 29*, 1, pp. 31–52.

Platt, J (1981b) Evidence and Proof in Documentary Research: 2. Some shared problems of documentary research. *Sociological Review, 29*, 1, pp. 53–66.

Plummer, K (2001) *Documents of Life 2: An invitation to a critical humanism*. London, Sage.

Poldner, E, van der Schaaf, M, Simons, P, van Tartwijk, J, and Wijngaards, G (2014) Assessing Student Teachers' Reflective Writing through Quantitative Content Analysis. *European Journal of Teacher Education, 37*, 3, pp. 348–373.

Pooley, C (1999) From Londonderry to London: Identity and sense of place for a protestant Northern Irish woman in the 1930s. *Immigrants and Minorities, 18*, 2–3, pp. 189–213.

Power, S, and Gewirtz, S (2001) Reading Education Action Zones. *Journal of Education Policy*, 16, 1, pp. 39–51.

Prior, L (2003) *Using Documents in Social Research*. London, Sage.

Proksch, S-O, Slapin, J, and Thies, M (2011) Party System Dynamics in Post-war Japan: A quantitative content analysis of electoral pledges. *Electoral Studies*, 30, pp. 114–124.

Prøitz, T (2015) Learning Outcomes as a Key Concept in Policy Documents through Policy Change. *Scandinavian Journal of Educational Research*, 59, 3, pp. 275–296.

Punch, K (2005) *Introduction to Social Research: Quantitative and qualitative approaches*. London, Sage, second edition.

Purvis, J (1992) Using Primary Sources when Researching Women's History from a Feminist Perspective. *Women's History Review*, 1, 2, pp. 273–306.

Rassool, C (2010) Rethinking Documentary History and South African Political Biography. *South African Review of Sociology*, 41, 1, pp. 28–55.

Reyneke, R (2017) Apples and Pears: Engaging social work students in social dialogue. *Research on Social Work Practice*, 27, 2, pp. 239–247.

Richards, I (2017) 'Good and Evil' Narratives in Islamic State Media and Western Government Statements. *Critical Studies on Terrorism*, 10, 3, pp. 404–428.

Richards, K, and Seedhouse, P (eds) (2005) *Applying Conversation Analysis*. Basingstoke, Palgrave Macmillan.

Rickinson, M, de Bruin, K, Walsh, L, and Hall, M (2017) What can Evidence-use in Practice learn from Evidence-use in Policy? *Educational Research*, 59, 2, pp. 173–189.

Rigby, J, Milligan, C, and Payne, S (2014) Improving Inpatient Hospice Environments for Older People in England: A documentary analysis. *Progress in Palliative Care*, 22, 4, pp. 187–194.

Riley, E, Harris, P, Kent, J, Sainsbury, P, Lane, A, and Baum, F (2018) Including Health in Environmental Assessments of Major Transport Infrastructure Projects: A documentary analysis. *International Health Policy and Management*, 7, 2, pp. 144–153.

Robert, E, and Ridde, V (2013) Global Health Actors no Longer in Favour of User Fees: A documentary study. *Globalization and Health*, 9, 29, 16pp.

Robert, M, Séguin, M, and O'Connor, K (2010) The Evolution of the Study of Life Trajectories in Social Sciences over the past Five Years: A state of the art review. *Advances in Mental Health*, 9, 2, pp. 190–205.

Roessger, K (2017) From Theory to Practice: A quantitative content analysis of adult education's language on meaning making. *Adult Education Quarterly*, 67, 3, pp. 209–227.

Rogers, R (2004) *An Introduction to Critical Discourse Analysis in Education*. New York, Routledge.

Rooks, D, and Munoz, C (2015) Brilliant, Bored or Badly Behaved? Media coverage of the Charter School debate in the United States. *Teachers College Record*, 17, pp. 1–48.

Rose, C, and Flynn, C (2018) Animating Social Work Research Findings: A case study of research dissemination to benefit marginalized young people. *Visual Communication*, 17, 1, pp. 25–46.

Rourke, L, and Anderson, T (2004) Validity in Quantitative Content Analysis. *Educational Technology Research and Development, 52*, 1, pp. 5–18.

Rowlands, I (1999) Patterns of Scholarly Communication in Information Policy: A bibliometric study. *Libri, 49*, pp. 59–70.

Ruggiero, D, and Green, L (2017) Problem Solving through Digital Game Design: A quantitative content analysis. *Computers in Human Behavior, 73*, pp. 28–37.

Ryan, G, and Bernard, R (2003) Techniques to Identify Themes. *Field Methods, 15*, 1, pp. 85–109.

Rycroft, S, and Jenness, R (2012) J B Priestley: Bradford and a provincial narrative of England, 1913–1933. *Social and Cultural Geography, 13*, 8, pp. 957–976.

Rytterstrom, P, Arman, M, and Unosson, N (2013) Aspects of Care Culture in Municipal Care for Elderly People: A hermeneutic documentary analysis of reports of abuse. *Scandinavian Journal of Caring Sciences, 27*, pp. 354–362.

Salmons, J (2016) *Doing Qualitative Research Online*. London, Sage, second edition.

Sanders, P, and Woodward, S (2014) Veracity of the Archive: A research approach to the collection and verification of urban morphological records using qualitative data analysis software. *Journal of Map and Geography Libraries, 10*, 2, pp. 173–203.

Saunders, M, and Sin, S (2015) Middle Managers' Experience of Policy Implementation and Mediation in the Context of the Scottish Quality Enhancement Framework. *Assessment and Evaluation in Higher Education, 40*, 1, pp. 135–150.

Savage, M (2008) Changing Social Class Identities in Post-War Britain: Perspectives from mass-observation. *Historical Social Research, 33*, 3, pp. 46–67.

Schwippert, K (2002) Forty-Six Years of *IRE*: A statistical and documentary survey. *International Review of Education, 48*, 1–2, pp. 111–129.

Scollon, R (2008) *Analyzing Public Discourse: Discourse analysis in the making of public policy*. London, Routledge.

Scott, D (2007) Resolving the Quantitative–Qualitative Dilemma: A critical realist approach. *International Journal of Research and Method in Education, 30*, 1, pp. 3–17.

Scott, J (1990) *A Matter of Record: Documentary source in social research*. Cambridge, Polity Press.

Seale, C (2018) Secondary Analysis and Official Statistics. pp. 387–402 in Seale, C (ed.) *Researching Society and Culture*. London, Sage, fourth edition.

Seale, C, and Tonkiss, F (2018) Content and Text Analysis. pp. 403–428 in Seale, C (ed.) *Researching Society and Culture*. London, Sage, fourth edition.

Shaw, S, Elston, J, and Abbott, S (2004) Comparative Analysis of Health Policy Implementation: The use of documentary analysis. *Policy Studies, 25*, 4, pp. 259–266.

Shea, P, Hayes, S, Smith, S, Vickers, J, Bidjerano, T, Gozza-Cohen, M, Jian, S-B, Pickett, A, Wilde, J, and Tseng, C-H (2013) Online Learner Self-regulation: Learning presence viewed through quantitative content and social network analysis. *International Review of Research in Open and Distance Learning, 14*, 3, pp. 427–461.

Shephard, K (2005) *Presenting at Conferences, Seminars and Meetings*. London, Sage.

Sidnell, J (2010) *Conversation Analysis: An introduction*. Chichester, Wiley-Blackwell.

Silvia, P (2014) *Write It Up: Practical strategies for writing and publishing journal articles*. Washington, DC, American Psychological Association.

Sim, L (2015) Theorising the Everyday. *Australian Feminist Studies*, 30, 84, pp. 109–127.

Simien, E, and McGuire, D (2014) A Tribute to the Women: Rewriting history, retelling herstory in civil rights. *Politics and Gender*, 10, pp. 413–431.

Sink, A, and Mastro, D (2017) Depictions of Gender on Primetime Television: A quantitative content analysis. *Mass Communication and Society*, 20, 1, pp. 3–22.

Sixsmith, J, and Murray, C (2001) Ethical Issues in the Documentary Data Analysis of Internet Posts and Archives. *Qualitative Health Research*, 11, 13, pp. 423–432.

Sjøvaag, H and Stavelin, E (2012) Web Media and the Quantitative Content Analysis: Methodological challenges in measuring online news content. *Convergence*, 18, 2, pp. 215–229.

Smiraglia, R (2005) Content Metadata: An analysis of Etruscan artefacts in a museum of archeology. *Cataloging and Classification Quarterly*, 40, 3–4, pp. 135–151.

Smith, M (2010) Victim Narratives of Historical Abuse in Residential Child Care: Do we really know what we think we know? *Qualitative Social Work*, 9, 3, pp. 303–320.

Smith, R (2013) Documenting Essex Boy as a Local Gendered Regime. *International Journal of Gender and Entrepreneurship*, 5, 2, pp. 174–197.

Smith, S (2005) Women's Admission to Guilds in Early-Modern England: The case of the York Merchant Taylors' Company, 1693–1776. *Gender and History*, 17, 1, pp. 99–126.

Spitzer, A, and Perrenoud, B (2007) Reforming the Swiss Nurse Education System: A policy review. *International Journal of Nursing Studies*, 44, pp. 624–634.

Starck, N (2004) *Writes of Passage: A comparative study of newspaper obituary practice in Australia, Britain and the United States*. PhD thesis, Flinders University of South Australia.

Starck, N (2006) *Life after Death: The art of the obituary*. Melbourne, Melbourne University Press.

Steedman, C (2001) *Dust*. Manchester, Manchester University Press.

Stewart, D (1984) *Secondary Research: Information sources and methods*. Beverly Hills, CA, Sage.

Stone-Johnson, C (2014) Responsible Leadership. *Educational Administration Quarterly*, 50, 4, pp. 645–674.

Sullivan, J (2013) Electronic Resources in the Study of Elite Political Behaviour in Taiwan. *The China Quarterly*, 213, pp. 172–188.

Suri, H, and Clarke, D (2009) Advancements in Research Synthesis Methods: From a methodologically inclusive perspective. *Review of Educational Research*, 79, 1, pp. 395–430.

Sweeney, J (2005) Historical Research: Examining documentary sources. *Nurse Researcher*, 12, 3, pp. 61–73.

Takeshita, C (2017) Countering Technocracy: 'Natural' birth in *The Business of Being Born* and *Call the Midwife*. *Feminist Media Studies*, 17, 3, pp. 332–346.

Tartz, R, and Krippner, S (2008) Cognitive Differences in Dream Content between Argentinian Males and Females using Quantitative Content Analysis. *Dreaming, 18,* 4, pp. 217–235.

Tartz, R, and Krippner, S (2017) Cognitive Differences in Dream Content between Japanese Males and Females using Quantitative Content Analysis. *Dreaming, 27,* 3, pp. 193–205.

Tashakkori, A, and Teddlie, C (1998) *Mixed Methodology: Combining qualitative and quantitative approaches.* Thousand Oaks, CA, Sage.

Tashakkori, A, and Teddlie, C (eds) (2010) *Sage Handbook of Mixed Methods in Social and Behavioral Research.* Thousand Oaks, CA, Sage, second edition.

Teh, L, Hotte, N, and Sumaila, U (2017) Having it All: Can fisheries buybacks achieve capacity, economic, ecological and social objectives? *Maritime Studies, 16,* 1, pp. 1–18.

Thomas, G, and Pring, R (eds) (2004) *Evidence-based Practice in Education.* Maidenhead, Open University Press.

Thomas, H, and Qiu, T (2013) Continuing Professional Development: Accountability, autonomy, efficiency and equity in five professions. *British Journal of Educational Studies, 61,* 2, pp. 161–186.

Thomas, S, and Gilson, L (2004) Actor Management in the Development of Health Financing Reform: Health insurance in South Africa, 1994–1999. *Health Policy and Planning, 19,* 5, pp. 279–291.

Thomson, A (1996) *Critical Reasoning: A practical introduction.* London, Routledge.

Tickell, S (2010) The Prevention of Shoplifting in Eighteenth-Century London. *Journal of Historical Research in Marketing, 2,* 3, pp. 300–313.

Tight, M (2009) The Structure of Academic Research: What can citation studies tell us? In Brew, A and Lucas, L (eds) *Academic Research and Researchers.* Maidenhead, Open University Press, pp. 54–65.

Tight, M (2017) *Understanding Case Study Research: Small-scale research with meaning.* London, Sage.

Tight, M (2018) *Higher Education Research: The developing field.* London, Bloomsbury.

Tillery, A, and Chresfield, M (2012) Model Blacks or 'Ras the Exhorter': A quantitative content analysis of Black newspapers' coverage of the first wave of Afro-Caribbean immigration to the United States. *Journal of Black Studies, 43,* 5, pp. 545–570.

Tonkiss, F (2018) Discourse Analysis. pp. 477–492 in Seale, C (ed.) *Researching Society and Culture.* London, Sage, fourth edition.

Torgerson, C (2003) *Systematic Reviews.* London, Continuum.

Tosh, J (2015) *The Pursuit of History: Aims, methods and new directions in the study of history.* London, Routledge, sixth edition.

Trachtenberg, M (2006) *The Craft of International History: A guide to method.* Princeton, NJ, Princeton University Press.

Trowler, P (2003) *Education Policy.* London, Routledge, second edition.

Turner, D (2012a) Oral Documents in Concept and *in situ*, Part I: Grounding an exploration of orality and information behaviour. *Journal of Documentation, 68*, 6, pp. 852–863.

Turner, D (2012b) Oral Documents in Concept and *in situ*, Part II: Managerial decrees. *Journal of Documentation, 68*, 6, pp. 864–881.

Urbano, A, and Keeton, W (2017) Carbon Dynamics and Structural Development in Recovering Secondary Forests of the Northeastern US. *Forest Ecology and Management, 392*, pp. 21–35.

Van Bommel, K (2014) Towards a Legitimate Compromise? An exploration of integrated reporting in the Netherlands. *Accounting, Auditing and Accountability Journal, 27*, 7, pp. 1157–1189.

Van Leeuwen, T (2008) *Discourse and Practice: New tools for critical discourse analysis*. Oxford, Oxford University Press.

Van Leuven, S, Heinrich, A, and Deprez, A (2015) Foreign Reporting and Sourcing Practices in the Network Sphere: A quantitative content analysis of the Arab Spring in Belgian news media. *New Media and Society, 17*, 4, pp. 573–591.

Vieira, N, and Brito, C (2017) Brazilian Manatees (Re)discovered: Early modern accounts reflecting the overexploitation of aquatic resources and the emergence of conservation concerns. *International Journal of Maritime History, 29*, 3, pp. 513–528.

Viswambharan, A, and Priya, K (2016) Documentary Analysis as a Qualitative Methodology to Explore Disaster Mental Health. *Qualitative Research, 16*, 1, pp. 43–59.

Waldschmidt, A (2009) Disability Policy of the European Union: The supranational level. *ALTER, 3*, pp. 8–23.

Wallace, D, and Stuchell, L (2011) Understanding the 9/11 Commission Archive: Control, access and the politics of manipulation. *Archival Science, 11*, pp. 125–168.

Ward, S, Bagley, C, Lumby, J, Hamilton, T, Woods, P, and Roberts, A (2016) What is 'Policy' and what is 'Policy Response'? An illustrative study of the implementation of the leadership standards for social justice in Scotland. *Educational Management, Administration and Leadership, 44*, 1, pp. 43–56.

Weber, W, and Rall, H-M (2017) Authenticity in Comics Journalism: Visual strategies for reporting facts. *Journal of Graphic Novels and Comics, 8*, 4, pp. 376–397.

Webster, L, and Mertova, P (2007) *Using Narrative Inquiry as a Research Method: An introduction to using critical event narrative analysis in research on learning and teaching*. London, Routledge.

Weller, W, and Malheiros da Silva, C (2011) Documentary Method and Participatory Research: Some interfaces. *International Journal of Action Research, 7*, 3, pp. 294–318.

Wellfelt, E (2009) Returning to Alor: Retrospective documentation of the Cora du Bois collection at the Museum of World Culture, Gothenburg, Sweden. *Indonesia and the Malay World, 37*, 108, pp. 183–202.

Wertz, F, Charmaz, K, McMullen, L, Josselson, R, Anderson, R, and McSpadden, E (2011) *Five Ways of Doing Qualitative Analysis: Phenomenological psychology, grounded theory, discourse analysis, narrative research, and intuitive inquiry*. New York, Guilford Press.

Wheeler, D, and Garcia-Herrera, R (2008) Ships Logbooks in Climatological Research: Reflections and prospects. *Trends and Directions in Climate Research*, 1146, pp. 1–15.

Whittle, A, and Wilson, J (2015) Ethnomethodology and the Production of History: Studying 'history-in-action'. *Business History*, 57, 1, pp. 41–63.

Widdowson, H (2007) *Discourse Analysis*. Oxford, Oxford University Press.

Williams, S (2015) The Incursion of 'Big Food' in Middle-income Countries: A qualitative documentary case study analysis of the soft drinks industry in China and India. *Critical Public Health*, 25, 4, pp. 455–473.

Williams, T, and Shepherd, D (2017) Mixed Method Social Network Analysis: Combining inductive concept development, content analysis and secondary data for quantitative analysis. *Organizational Research Methods*, 20, 2, pp. 268–298.

Willy, M (1963) *English Diarists: Evelyn and Pepys*. London, Longmans, Green.

Winder, G (2010) London's Global Reach? Reuters News and Network, 1865, 1881 and 1914. *Journal of World History*, 21, 2, pp. 271–296.

Wodak, R, and Meyer, M (eds) (2016) *Methods of Critical Discourse Analysis*. London, Sage, third edition.

Wong, S, Kwan, J, Hodson, D, and Yung, B (2009) Turning Crisis into Opportunity: Nature of science and scientific inquiry as illustrated in the scientific research on Severe Acute Respiratory Syndrome. *Science and Education*, 18, pp. 95–118.

Wooffitt, R (2005) *Conversation Analysis and Discourse Analysis: A comparative and critical introduction*. London, Sage.

Wright, D, and Sharpley, R (2018) The Photograph: Tourist responses to a visual representation of a disaster. *Tourism Recreation Research*, 43, 2, pp. 161–174.

Zhang, Y-a, and Du, Y (2016) Lessons in Ambivalence: The Shanghai Municipal Council's opium policies, 1906–1917. *International Journal of Drug Policy*, 37, pp. 136–142.

INDEX

access issues, 22–24
analysis,
   of audio-visual texts, 139–142
   of written texts, 136–138
anthropology, 40–42
archival research, 62, 64–65, 110–119
   definition, 110–111
   examples, 115–118
   types, 11–115

business/management, 42–43

conferences, 185–186
content analysis,
   examples, 149–151, 162–163
   qualitative, 160–163
   quantitative, 148–153
conversation analysis, 167–169
   examples, 169
criticality, 33–34

discourse analysis, 163–167
   examples, 166–167
documents,
   accessing, 22–24
   analysis, 136–143
   definition, 8–10
   reading, 32–34
   varieties, 10–13

documentary research, 4–5, 22
   advantages of, 13–15
   combined with other methods,
      15–17, 66–71
   definition, 18
   ethics, 24–26
   issues, 29–32
   purpose of, 18
   research design, 62–67
   social sciences, 38–55

economics, 43–44
education, 44–46
ethical issues, 24–26
evaluating your research, 184–185
examples, 11–12, 15–17, 28–29, 69–70, 81–82,
      90–93, 102–104, 116–117, 126–129,
      141–142, 149–151, 159–160, 162–163,
      166–167, 169, 171–172, 179

geography, 46–47

healthcare/medicine, 55
historical research, 62, 64–65, 110–119
   definition, 110–111
   examples, 115–118
   types, 11–115
history,
   social, 55–56

information science, 47–48

law, 48
literature reviews, 62–63, 73–83
   definition, 74–76
   examples, 81–82
   function, 76–78
   processes involved in, 80–81
   types, 78–79

media studies, 48–49
meta-analysis, 62–63, 86, 91–94
   definition, 91–92
   examples, 92–94
mixed methods approaches, 176–180
   examples, 179

narrative analysis, 169–172
   examples, 171–172

policy research, 62, 65, 122–131
   definition, 122–124
   examples, 126–130
   types, 125–126
political science, 49–51
psychology, 51–52
publishing, 186–188

qualitative approaches, 67–68, 158–173
   content analysis, 160–163
   conversation analysis, 167–169
   discourse analysis, 163–167
   narrative analysis, 169–172
   thematic analysis, 158–160
quantitative approaches,
   67–68, 146–155
   content analysis, 148–153

record keeping, 34–35

sampling and selection, 27–29
search engines, 24
secondary data research, 62, 64, 96–108
   advantages and disadvantages, 98–100
   definition, 96–98
   examples, 102–105
   sources of, 105–108
   types, 100–101
seminars, 185–186
social work, 52–53
social sciences, 38–55
sociology, 54–55
systematic review, 62–63, 86–91
   definition, 87–88
   examples, 90–91
   processes involved in, 89

thematic analysis, 158–160
   examples, 159–160
triangulation, 176–177

writing up, 186–188